1

ILLINOIS CENTRAL

W9-BYV-190

Revolving Gridlock

10/06

WITHDRAWN
I.C.C. LIBRARY

TRANSFORMING AMERICAN POLITICS

Lawrence C. Dodd, Series Editor

Dramatic changes in political institutions and behavior over the past three decades have underscored the dynamic nature of American politics, confronting political scientists with a new and pressing intellectual agenda. The pioneering work of early postwar scholars, while laying a firm empirical foundation for contemporary scholarship, failed to consider how American politics might change or recognize the forces that would make fundamental change inevitable. In reassessing the static interpretations fostered by these classic studies, political scientists are now examining the underlying dynamics that generate transformational change.

Transforming American Politics brings together texts and monographs that address four closely related aspects of change. A first concern is documenting and explaining recent changes in American politics—in institutions, processes, behavior, and policymaking. A second is reinterpreting classic studies and theories to provide a more accurate perspective on postwar politics. The series looks at historical change to identify recurring patterns of political transformation within and across the distinctive eras of American politics. Last and perhaps most important, the series presents new theories and interpretations that explain the dynamic processes at work and thus clarify the direction of contemporary politics. All of the books focus on the central theme of transformation—transformation in both the conduct of American politics and in the way we study and understand its many aspects.

BOOKS IN THIS SERIES

I.C.C. LIBRARY

Revolving Gridlock

POLITICS AND POLICY FROM JIMMY CARTER TO GEORGE W. BUSH

SECOND EDITION

I.C.C. LIBRARY

David W. Brady
Stanford University

Craig Volden
The Ohio State University

A Member of the Perseus Books Group

JK
421
.B73
2006

All rights reserved. Printed in the United States of America. No part of this publication may be reproduced or transmitted in any form or by any means, electronic or mechanical, including photocopy, recording, or any information storage and retrieval system, without permission in writing from the publisher.

Copyright © 2006 by Westview Press, A Member of the Perseus Books Group

Published in the United States of America by Westview Press, 5500 Central Avenue, Boulder, Colorado 80301-2877, and in the United Kingdom by Westview Press, 12 Hid's Copse Road, Cumnor Hill, Oxford OX2 9JJ.

Find us on the world wide web at www.westviewpress.com

Westview Press books are available at special discounts for bulk purchases in the United States by corporations, institutions, and other organizations. For more information, please contact the Special Markets Department at the Perseus Books Group, 11 Cambridge Center, Cambridge, MA 02142, or call (617) 252-5298 or (800) 255-1514 or email special.markets@perseusbooks.com.

Library of Congress Cataloging-in-Publication Data

Brady, David W.
    Revolving gridlock : politics and policy from Jimmy Carter to George W. Bush / David W. Brady.— 2nd ed.
        p.   cm. — (Transforming American politics)
    Includes bibliographical references (p.   ) and index.
    ISBN-13: 978-0-8133-4320-4 (pbk. : alk. paper)
    ISBN-10: 0-8133-4320-8 (alk. paper)
    1. United States—Politics and government—1993–2001. 2. Coalition governments—United States. 3. United States. Congress House. I. Volden, Craig. II. Title. III. Series.
JK421.B73 2005
320.973'09'049—dc22

                                                                                        2005014147

The paper used in this publication meets the requirements of the American National Standard for Permanence of Paper for Printed Library Materials Z39.48–1984.

9/06 B&T 20.00

Contents

Tables and Figures

Tables

Figures

Preface to the
Second Edition and Acknowledgments

We wrote the first edition of this book midway through the Clinton presidency. We had seen how the unified Democrats came to office in 1993 excited about their prospects for governance, and how many went home in defeat two years later. We had also seen the Republicans enter Congress jubilantly in 1995 only to be outmaneuvered on the budget and other issues by the Democratic minority and President Clinton. What we had not seen in quite some time, however, were substantial government surpluses, unified Republican government, a major attack on American soil, and a strong wartime president.

In writing this second edition, then, we were interested in applying the ideas of our first edition to such changing circumstances. Those ideas were centered around the concept that policy change is tough to come by in Congress. It takes an alignment of preferences among large majorities in the House and Senate, sufficient to end a filibuster and overcome a potential presidential veto. It takes compromise, which is difficult under any circumstances, but particularly challenging when the government is running large deficits. And it therefore takes patience, with one proposal's defeat giving way to a new idea with somewhat greater support time and again until broad coalitions for policy change can be achieved. Those lacking the patience to work through this process risk legislative failure and electoral defeat.

The changes of the past eight years convinced us that we were on the right track in our description of policymaking in Congress. And this second edition gives us a chance to illustrate how the revolving gridlock theory holds under a broad set of circumstances. We now are in a position to analyze divided government with both Republican and Democratic presidents, as well as unified Democratic and unified Republican control of Congress and the presidency. Moreover, we can see how and why coalitions formed around issues of terrorism and foreign policy after 9/11, only to return to the familiar gridlock of previous decades. Issues and political parties continue to revolve in and out of favor, but gridlock remains a mainstay of American politics.

In this edition, we have taken numerous opportunities to update and strengthen our analysis. Chapter 2, once again, contains the theoretical heart of the book, updated in time and expanded to discuss how gridlock may be overcome and how policymakers cope with gridlock when it persists. Chapter 3 now stands alone as a characterization of how the federal budget process impacts policy change and policy gridlock. It is no longer tied to an analysis of the Reagan administration. Rather, this chapter now captures how the budget process has changed over the past thirty years, and how those changes have affected policy gridlock.

Chapters 4, 5, and 6 test the theory presented in the earlier chapters in a chronological fashion. Chapter 4 examines the coalitions formed under Democratic control of the House during the Republican presidencies of Ronald Reagan and George H. Bush. Of particular interest is showing how the time period of 1980–1992 ushered in the rise of tough budgetary politics that contributed to polarized debates in Congress, to more media attention on the budget, to less time for other congressional activities, and, ultimately, to policy gridlock. Chapter 5 is broken largely into two parts, the first characterizing unified Democratic governance, and the second pitting a Republican Congress against President Clinton. Both show in detail how the lack of broad coalitions led to the defeat and diminution of expansive policy initiatives. Finally, Chapter 6 brings the book up to date, first exploring what could be accomplished under unified Republican governance and how particular budget-forming mechanisms interacted with the preferences of moderates to determine the parameters of policy change. Then that chapter shows how things changed and yet remained the same when the country's focus turned toward the previously dismissed policy area of international terrorism.

As with the first edition, we are left with many debts. Students at Stanford University, the University of Chicago, Claremont Graduate University, and the Ohio State University all helped us focus our views over the past decade (and more). Each fall the students change but their collective intelligence and their questions have pushed us to look for better explanations for why Congress passes prescription drug coverage for Medicare but not universal health care, or why Congress gives enormous authority to the president in times of crisis. Their intelligence and interest has been and continues to be an inspiration. Three students made special contributions and thus should be thanked—Sara Anderson, Shawn Chen, and Brigitte Zimmerman.

A second debt is owed to our colleagues who study legislatures specifically and political economy more generally. We have gained immensely from the insight of those too numerous to list, but are particularly thankful for our interactions with Jim Alt, Martin Anderson, David Baron, Paul Beck, Jon Bendor, Ted Brader, Kara Buckley, Greg Caldeira, Brandice Canes-Wrone, Cliff Carrubba, Joseph Cooper, Larry Dodd, David Epstein, John Ferejohn, Tom Gilligan, Rick Hall, Hahrie Han, Mark Hansen, Sunshine Hillygus, Will Howell, Gary Jacobson, Rod Kiewiet, Keith Krehbiel, David Lawrence, Sandy Maisel, David Mayhew, Mat McCubbins, Terry Moe, Mike Neblo, Roger Noll, Sharyn O'Halloran, Carl Pinkele, Keith Poole, Nelson Polsby, Randall Ripley, Doug Rivers, Howard Rosenthal, Ken Shepsle, Gary Segura, Barry Weingast, Alan Wiseman, and Jack Wright. They all deserve more gratitude than we could offer here. We owe special thanks to John Cogan for sharing his immense knowledge of the federal budgetary process and the politics thereof, and to John Raisian, Director of the Hoover Institution, for providing us with the time and resources to finish the book. Despite the guidance of so many great scholars, we have much left to learn. Of course, we take full responsibility for all errors.

We are most indebted to our spouses and children, and thus the book is dedicated to Carolyn, Emily, Beth, and Anna on the Brady side, and to Andrea on the Volden side.

David W. Brady
Craig Volden

1

The Origins of
Revolving Gridlock

When the American people voted in 2004, they made a surprisingly rare choice, re-electing a President and a Congress controlled by the same party. President Clinton had been reelected in 1996, facing a Republican Congress. Presidents Reagan, Nixon, and Eisenhower's reelections were all accompanied by Democratic control of the House of Representatives. But George W. Bush would continue to preside over a unified Republican government and had won an outright majority of the popular vote, something no President had done since his father's election in 1988. Despite the closeness of the election in key battleground states, President Bush saw his victory as a mandate and quickly vowed to spend his hard-won political capital. By the 2005 State of the Union Address, the President had asserted Social Security reform as his top domestic policy goal, and personal accounts would be the cornerstone of that reform.

Democrats in Congress responded immediately, denouncing the risky nature of privatizing Social Security, and raising two key points. First, the Democratic leadership proclaimed that they had a coalition of more than forty Senators who would stand against the President's proposal. That key number of forty-plus-one was important to all who were familiar with Senate rules. With the support of forty-one Senators, a successful filibuster could be mounted. Without a supermajority—sixty votes—the majority party would be unable to stop such a tactic. And, second, the Democrats linked Social Security reform to the budget deficit. Adding personal accounts to the Social Security system would cost two trillion dollars or more by some estimates. As large surpluses had already turned to deficits on Bush's watch, framing the debate in terms of the budget and fiscal responsibility might not only defeat the proposal, but also give Democrats a leg up in the next rounds of elections.

The long-term fate of Social Security is far from resolved, and the need to reform other entitlement programs (like Medicare) will remain pressing long into the future. Yet, the goal of political science is not to wait and provide descriptions, but instead to offer predictions and explanations. Having observed actions of Congress and the President for decades, we have seen patterns emerging that can

1

be explained in a fairly straightforward manner, by examining members of Congress in terms of their preferences and the institutions in which they make decisions. We have seen the importance of House–Senate differences and of large coalitions needed to overcome filibusters and presidential vetoes. And we have also seen the growing importance of budgetary matters before Congress.

While the reelection of a President with majority party control of the Congress is a relatively rare event, the politics of 2005 are not new. They were evident in the 1980s when President Reagan secured major tax reforms only to have to confront major budget deficits for the rest of his term. They were evident in the 1990s when President Clinton promised major reforms under a unified Democratic government. We began work on the first version of this project in 1993 and 1994, as a paper on the first two years of the Clinton administration. The press had just begun to shift from positively appraising the President's job thus far to questioning how far he would get with health care, campaign finance reform, welfare, crime, and the rest of the agenda. Our view was that the quick passage of the family leave act and the motor voter act were not indicative of how successful the President ultimately would be, given the Congress that was elected in 1992 and the possibilities of conservative filibusters in the Senate. Subsequent events showed that unified government was not able to break policy "gridlock." The election of the first Republican Congress in forty years in 1994 and the new majority's subsequent attempt to shift policy to the right, combined with President Clinton's use of the veto to shift policy back toward the center, led us to expand the paper into a book.

In the process of expanding the work to cover the 104th Congress, we came to better understand what caused gridlock and what could end it. In order to understand the causes of gridlock, we were forced to recognize the dominance of budget politics and policy in the Congress, and we became convinced of the importance of elections in determining where policy stands and in what direction it will evolve. Reading new accounts of the Reagan 1981 budget battle, the Bush 1990 budget debacle, and the standoff in 1995 between the Republican Congress and President Clinton clearly leaves one with the feeling that little has changed in American politics over the past quarter century. Because the first part of this period was characterized by Republican Presidents and Democratic Congresses, it is easy to see why so many people believed that electing a unified government would break policy gridlock, and why many were surprised when the election of a Democratic President in 1992 did not actually do so.

Political science demands that we draw lessons from these earlier events, treating them as data to test theories of how political processes work. And that is our goal in this book. In the following chapters we shall attempt to define gridlock and to explain why gridlock has been so prevalent over the past thirty years, despite the changing cast of characters in the White House and on Capitol Hill. Over this time period, we have seen a Republican President with a Republican Congress, a Republican President with a Democratic Congress, a Democratic President with a Republican Congress, and a Democratic President and Congress. We are seeking to advance a theory that explains congressional politics through all these sets of circumstances. Our explanation, however, will not focus on the role of political parties, nor of special interests, nor of the media, and it does not rely heavily on presidential leadership. This is not to say that these variables don't play a role in making public policy—clearly they do. Nevertheless, our explanation for gridlock focuses on two primary factors: (1) the preferences of members of Congress regarding particular policies, and (2) supermajority institutions—the Senate filibuster and the presidential veto. We will use a simple median voter model both to define gridlock as a concept and to explain broad policy results during the 1980 to 2005 period.

The idea is really quite straightforward. When considering the U.S. Congress, instead of thinking of which party is in control, think of the members as arrayed from left to right—liberal to conservative.[1] The further left a member is positioned, the more that member favors increased government activity on health care, the environment, education, and so on. The further right one moves, the more the members favor less government activity on health care, the environment, and education; these members thus favor lower taxes. Given this ordering of preferences, what does it take to achieve a policy change?

Those who claimed that divided government caused gridlock would argue that the coupling of Republican Presidents with Democratic Congresses or vice versa was the culprit. It would then follow that Clinton's election, securing the first unified government since 1980, should have ended gridlock. But by 1994 no one was any longer making that claim. Our view is that the answer to what it takes to effectively change policy (and end gridlock) hangs on knowing the policy preferences of those members of both houses of Congress near the median (at or about the 218th member in the House and at or about the 50th member in the Senate) and on determining how close present policy (the status quo) is to these crucial members' preferences. Gridlock can be overcome only when the status quo is further from crucial members' preferences than are the alternative policies proposed by the President or others. In short, if current Social Security policy is agreeable to the 218th House voter or the 50th Senate voter, then attempts at dramatic change, such as partial privatization through personal accounts, will fail—and gridlock will result.

Because in some legislation a minority of members can block a majority, the gridlock region (the range of status quo policies that is nearly impossible to change) can be sizable. Consider the filibuster as allowed by Rule XXII in the Senate. That rule, roughly, allows forty-one determined Senators to dominate floor activity so as to prohibit a bare majority from enacting its legislation. Such supermajoritarian institutions are common in state legislatures and in many foreign legislatures. The idea is that in some matters 50 percent is not enough to make fundamental changes, so rules requiring a supermajority are used. In the next chapter we will draw out this point in some detail. It is sufficient here to argue that in some issues more than a majority is required to change policy.

By narrowly focusing on preferences, supermajority institutions, and the status quo of present policies, we will leave unexplored much of the role of the parties, leadership, committee decisions, the press, and special interests in the day-to-day maneuvering that makes up the U.S. policy process. What do we hope to gain by focusing on this narrow set of explanatory variables? Our goal is to explain the broad parameters of U.S. public policy over the past three decades, and the concept of gridlock is after all not a specific matter but a general one involving deadlock in government. Moreover, one supposed culprit in gridlock—divided government—is again a rather broad concept. The narrow focus on preferences, supermajority institutions, and status quo policies is particularly informative with regard to budgetary policy, which we regard as a further cause of policy gridlock over the past quarter century. Given the recent dominance of budget issues, especially when the public takes notice of deficit spending, members of Congress and the President are faced with hard choices regarding programs and funding. Under such conditions, increasing spending on one program often means cutting another program, not creating a new program, or raising taxes; thus in a sense funding decisions are interrelated. Programs then are no longer viewed separately; rather, they are viewed in terms of tradeoffs with one another—boosting one program at the expense of another, or else maintaining both at constant levels. In short, deficit politics creates winners and losers and thus exacerbates the already contentious nature of policymaking.

Our argument is that, as of the late 1970s, congressional policymaking has shifted from a policy regime in which new programs—entitlements and others— were added and existing programs were expanded to a policy regime in which budgetary policy (when focused on the deficit) encompasses and constrains all congressional policymaking. The New Deal of Franklin Roosevelt began and greatly expanded the American welfare state. Presidents after Roosevelt (with the possible exception of Eisenhower) had offered new programs or packages of policies extending the welfare state. Truman's Fair Deal, Kennedy's New Frontier, Johnson's Great Society, and Nixon's New Federalism (in his first term) all testify to this phenomenon. Funding these programs took place under a budget process (aptly described by Wildavsky 1988 and Fenno 1973) in which taxes rose slowly and expenditures rose roughly within the limits of increased revenues.

By the Nixon presidency, there was little room for maneuver in fiscal policy. The first two years of the Carter presidency saw the end of the old regime. By 1979 there was a tax revolt among the citizenry, the Social Security Trust Fund was nearly broke, entitlement spending from program creation and expansion in the Johnson and Nixon presidencies was rising rapidly, and the Soviet invasion of Afghanistan forced President Carter to raise military expenditures, thus canceling Congress's plan to exchange cuts in military expenditures for increased domestic spending. The new policy regime would be characterized by tight, real budget constraints and omnibus reconciliation budgets. Politicians who raised individual income taxes or who sought cuts in entitlements would suffer in the polls. We focus on legislator preferences and use median voter and supermajority institutional analyses to show where gridlock comes from, given this new budget-centered policy regime.

A key reason to focus on preferences and supermajority institutions, rather than on special interests, parties, the media, and so on, is that in an important sense these latter variables are subsumed in the election results and the winning members' preferences. In every district and every state there are special local interests as well as national issues that play a role in the nomination and election of candidates. In Montana, wheat farmers, environmentalists, the National Rifle Association (NRA), mining and smelting interests, and labor union interests make their presence known early in the electoral process. Each interest will decide which candidates they prefer and will choose a level of support. By the time of the general election, the interests and political parties will be aligned for and against the final House and Senate candidates, and the winning candidates will go to Washington with a set of established policy preferences.

Elections are in an important sense a final if temporal judgment (made every other year), based on party affiliation and personal interest, by voters determining which set of candidates will decide where public policy will be headed. In the United States, party positions on issues will vary across the country, as will the strength of interest groups. The Democratic Party in Texas, Montana, and Idaho will differ from the Democratic Party in New York and Illinois on gun control. Likewise there will be differences among local and state parties across all fifty states and 435 congressional districts on civil rights, environmentalism, tax policy, foreign policy, and any number of other issues. The congressional Democratic and Republican Parties (those members actually in Congress) will therefore be characterized by both inter- and intraparty differences. Some Democrats will be conservatives on tax policy, gun control, and environmental issues whereas some Republicans will be liberal on the same set of issues. In general, we will find that Republicans are more conservative than Democrats across a broad set of issues; however, despite the polarization in preferences today, there remains enough variation in intraparty preferences to prohibit strict party control of policy. As a result, just because Republicans control the House and Senate does not guarantee that a Republican President will always get his way in Congress. Indeed, it is precisely the intraparty variance in preferences that leads to the use of a median voter model in predicting policy outcomes. Members of Congress who please their constituencies get reelected, even though they may vote against their party.

One important reason that members of the same party vary in their preferences over policy is the fact that interest groups' influence varies from district to district and region to region. Environmentalists are more numerous in the West than in the Midwest and East. The NRA is stronger in the South and the West than it is elsewhere. The National Organization for Women (NOW) has more members in the North than in the South. The National Farmers Union (NFU) has more members in the Dakotas and Minnesota than the American Farm Bureau Federation (AFBF), which is stronger, in contrast, in the lower Midwest—Illinois and Iowa. More NRA members are Republican than Democrat; AFBF members tend to be Republican; but more environmentalists, NFU, and NOW members are Democrats. Thus across districts, states, and regions interests are sorted differently and influence varies accordingly. In addition to interests and interest groups, individual voters' views matter; for example, about 70 percent of Californians are pro-choice across both parties, putting pro-life candidates at a disadvantage when running for statewide office. Traditional California Republicans like former Senator and former Governor Pete Wilson are pro-choice even though the Republican national party's official position is pro-life. One cannot simply take the Congress members' party affiliations to predict abortion policy. When Ronald Reagan was President (and pro-life) and the Senate was Republican, pro-life supporters could not pass a bill or an amendment repealing the *Roe v. Wade* Supreme Court decision. Our analysis focusing on the preferences of members of Congress should be viewed as summarizing the thousands of decisions made by voters, candidates, and interest groups, which yield an electoral result in the Congress. We simply take that end result and assume that the preferences of the members are exogenous; and we try to understand policy given these preferences that are in some large part the result of a complicated nomination and election process.

Given this assumption it should be clear that, in our view, the main impetus for policy change is electoral change. In general, we propose that if the same members are elected time after time, the status quo policy will prevail. If over 90 percent of incumbent House members run for reelection and 95 percent of them win, then their combined preferences over major policies will not change.[2] This is especially true of budget issues, which have always been prominent and more recently have been dominant. Major debates on levels of taxation and expenditure have been raised in 1981, 1982, 1984, 1986, 1990, 1993, 1995, 1997, 2001, 2003, and beyond; and any members of Congress surviving all these changes can be said to have accurately gauged their choice and fitted it to being reelected. If one goes by party affiliation, conservative Republicans will not vote for individual income tax increases whereas liberal Democrats will not support cuts in entitlements and welfare spending. Congressional preferences since the end of the Carter presidency have shifted dramatically to the right twice—in 1980 and 1994; and once moderately left—in 1986. This does not mean that elections in other years were not important—they were—only that the 1980, 1994, and 1986 elections represented more dramatic shifts.

Calling an election a "dramatic shift" sounds impressive but what does it mean? It need not indicate a new majority party throughout Congress because only 1994 yielded a new House majority. Essentially, a "dramatic shift" indicates that the new median Representative (the 218th) or Senator (the 50th) is significantly more conservative or liberal than in the previous Congress. In the case of the 104th House (1995–1996) and the 97th Senate (1981–1982), this meant that the new median member was in all likelihood a Republican rather than a moderate Democrat, as was the case in the 103rd House (1993–1994). In the case of the 97th House, although the majority was still Democratic, the median voter was now a very conservative southern Democrat rather than a moderate Democrat.

Note that for the purposes of this analysis, it does not matter whether the 50th voter in the Senate is a Democrat or a Republican. What matters is that member of

Congress's policy preference and where on the spectrum that preference lies relative to the status quo and the proposed alternative policy. This is important because since at least the time of V. O. Key (1964), political scientists have pointed to differences in the parties' compositions. Key argued that each party had a presidential and a congressional branch, such that when the party controlled the presidency the presidential branch dominated, whereas without the presidency the congressional branch dominated. James M. Burns, in *The Deadlock of Democracy* (1963), argued that "the deadlock" was due to differences between the southern and northern wings of the Democratic Party, and between the northeastern (Rockefeller) and midwestern wings of the Republican Party. Southern Democrats and midwestern Republicans often voted together as a conservative coalition to block liberal policies. The point is that such "splits" or "differences" within the parties have long occurred. Moreover, when "deadlock" or "gridlock" has been broken, it is largely because an election has dramatically shifted the distribution of preferences in Congress.

Our argument here differs from previous works in the assumption that each congressional member's individual preference over a policy is the determining factor in whether that policy will find support, rather than the more general ascriptive characteristic of, for example, southern Democratic support for a Republican President. Moreover, using member preference as the fundamental building block, one can more precisely locate those groups of House and Senate members who are crucial to understanding why Congress does what it does. Granted, preferences are correlated with party affiliation—liberals are more likely to be Democrats and conservatives are more likely to be Republicans. However, what matters most are the preferences of pivotal members of Congress, such as the 218th House voter and the 50th Senate voter when majorities are required, and not whether the policy result is the work of a so-called "conservative Democrat" or "moderate Republican." The circumstance of a unified government means very little here because a conservative Democrat would not have voted for the Clinton or Kennedy health care bills in 1994 when the status quo policy was closer to that member's preference. Hence a Democratic President elected with a Congress that was essentially the same as the Congress the previous Republican President faced (in terms of the distribution of preferences) should *not* have been expected to enact major policy changes. Just as there was divided-government gridlock under George H. Bush in 1992, there was unified-government gridlock under Clinton in 1993,

In essence, we maintain that the policy preferences of members of Congress at or near the median are among the crucial determinants of policy outcomes. The distribution of preferences over the members in conjunction with how many voters are needed to move the policy—one-half (a simple majority), three-fifths (to break a filibuster), or two-thirds (to override a veto)—determines policy. Thus if the preferences of key members of Congress remain similar from one administration to the next, the party of the President won't tell us much about policy results. In addition to the distribution of preferences, supermajority institutional rules, specifically the Senate filibuster and the presidential veto (or threat to veto), also affect policy in that these political instruments change who the crucial deci-sionmakers are—from the 50th to the 60th member of the Senate in the case of the filibuster. Given these variables of preferences and supermajority rules, all that needs to be determined are the relative positions of the present policy and the pro-posed policy.

This simple theory of the median voter has been circulating for some time in political science, starting with Duncan Black (1958), and has been used to explain the policy decisions of school boards, city councils, and other legislative bodies for which majority rule determines decisions. A major criticism of median voter models is that, although they work in one dimension, shifting to a second dimen-sion makes it "impossible" to determine who the median is and thus where the policy will be located. A simple example might be useful. Suppose three legislators are deciding how much to spend on defense. Legislator A prefers $100, B $40, and C prefers not to spend anything. It is obvious with a minimal amount of compu-tation that the legislators will agree to spend $40 on defense. If we add a second dimension to the policy space, say a social budget over which A prefers to spend $10, B $40, and C $100, it can be shown that in two dimensions there is no stable solution. There will always be some other policy in these two dimensions pre-ferred by two members over any present policy. Even the median position (B) in each dimension of spending $40 for each program could be defeated if A and C get together to increase spending for both programs. For example, if A proposes spending $50 each on defense and social programs, C will vote with A, defeating B. In turn, B could propose a point appealing to either A or C, and so on. Given that this is true in such a simple case, how could we apply such a model to any-thing as complex as the U.S. Congress with its thousands of programs spending well over two trillion dollars annually? This problem has discouraged scholars from applying the model to real legislatures as extensively as they might.

It is our view that, even when multiple policy dimensions are present, the more central members of the dimension of primary concern will be determinative of the outcome, because they will be easier to entice into a coalition and are thus considered pivotal. Consider a bill where member B is undecided how to vote or is mildly for or against the bill, whereas A is strongly against and C is strongly in favor. It will be easier for C (or A) to convince B to vote yes (or no) than it would be to get A (or C) to vote differently. Thus, even if B gets something in return on a different dimension—a federal building or a presidential appearance in the home district—voter B is pivotal to the issue of primary concern. In short, because B determines whether the bill will pass or not, then that legislator can largely deter-mine the final appearance of the bill. In either case—one or two dimensions—our strategy is to focus on the pivotal voters in the relevant dimension. Where two members are needed to change policy, the median member B is pivotal. If all three are needed for a supermajority (unanimity), the member most resistant to change (closest in preference to the present policy) is pivotal.

Moving away from the three-person example it can be argued that, even though there are often relevant off-dimension policies, it is still the pivotal (and often centrist) representatives with respect to the primary policy dimension who determine policy results. For example, in trade issues there are pro–free trade representatives and pro–protectionist representatives, and in between these two positions are a smaller set of members who could vote either way. These members near the median are relatively indifferent about voting for or against a trade bill like the North American Free Trade Agreement (NAFTA). Their votes can be swayed relatively easily by appealing to them with concessions in other policy dimensions, whereas it would be prohibitively costly to sway the vote of a legislator with a strong view on NAFTA through concessions in other dimensions. In short, the votes that can be most easily swayed for purposes of gaining a majority or a supermajority are precisely those of the voters who are most indifferent about the specific issue under consideration. If the vote is on the budget, which involves programs in many dimensions and determines the rates of taxation and spending, then who determines the outcome? Those on the left who favor more spending and taxing and those on the right who favor cuts in taxes and programs will not determine the result. Rather, those members at or near the median—those favoring fewer cuts than the right and less spending than the left—will determine the final makeup of the budget. New policies can be adopted only by altering significantly who these pivotal members are or what they will support. The normal mechanism to provide such a shift in American government is an election.

In addition to the above reasons to focus on the main policy dimension despite the possibility of multiple dimensions, there is strong empirical support for the existence of a main policy dimension for a number of issues. Poole and Rosenthal (1997) address the history of roll call voting in the Congress and find that preferences along a single dimension can account for about three-fourths of the votes of members of Congress on a wide range of issues. Although member preferences may vary from issue to issue, it is preferences along the *main* policy dimension of any particular piece of legislation that will determine which policy proposals can be adopted and which will lead to continued gridlock.

In the next chapter we will present an explanation of the revolving gridlock model, using the case of minimum wage for explanatory purposes. Our intent is to bring some precision to the definition of gridlock, to show how gridlock can be explained in terms of preferences and institutions, and to determine conditions under which gridlock might end.

In Chapter 3 we tackle the role of the federal budget in explaining policy gridlock. We trace the collapse of consensus budgeting in the 1970s to a series of conditions, from the rising entitlements coming out of the 1960s through public pressures to hold down taxes through the continued threats of the Cold War. The 1980 elections shifted the preferences of the Congress decidedly to the right, resulting in the passage of a tax policy that was significantly more conservative than the status quo policy of the time. The new tax policy eliminated "bracket creep," resulting in a constraint on spending and, with the downturn in the economy, a dramatic increase in the deficit. This legislation resulted in a new gridlock region that frustrated both the liberal tax-and-spend representatives and the tax-less, spend-less conservatives. Although modified throughout the mid–1980s, tax policy had solidified by 1986. Throughout the 1980s and 1990s, no firm coalition could be found to support major increases or decreases in either taxation or spending. Deficit-reduction legislation such as Gramm-Rudman-Hollings in 1985 or Pay-As-You-Go (PAYGO) in 1990 linked budget and program decisions together so that increases in one area would cause decreases in another. Combined with the need for super-majorities, this constraint caused gridlock for more than a decade. Budget surpluses surprised pundits and politicians in the late 1990s and allowed a conservative coalition in 2001 and 2003 to cut taxes dramatically. Coupled with an economic downturn, stock market slump, and increased spending in the wake of 9/11, these changes led back to familiar deficits, resulting in tough budget decisions once again.

After laying out the theory with regard to preferences, institutions, and budget politics, in the latter chapters we assess the evidence for and against the theory by examining political coalitions and proposals for policy change over the past quarter century. In Chapter 4 we examine legislation between 1981 and 1992, focusing on the budgetary and policy gridlock that characterized the Reagan and (George H.) Bush years. Here it becomes clear that without major changes in the preferences and positions of members of Congress, little can be done to modify policy.

In Chapter 5 we argue that this gridlock continued throughout the Clinton administration, both under unified Democratic control and then following Republican control of Congress won in the 1994 elections. Although legislation previously vetoed by Republican Presidents was signed by Clinton in 1993, little was actually accomplished by what was touted as a gridlock-breaking unified government. The constraints of filibusters in the Senate and the individual preferences of members of Congress guaranteed that the Democratic Party would not act as a unified force to implement the policies set forth in its party platform. Major policy actions such as NAFTA and the 1993 budget act can best be seen as a continuation of congressional policies first developed during the George H. Bush administration rather than as a change in direction due to unified government. We then argue that the 1994 election moved congressional preferences to the right and made Congress the agenda setter. President Clinton's major weapon in the policy disputes was the veto, which he used to shift policy toward the left, away from the Republican Congress's preferences. Without the ability to garner the votes of two-thirds of the Senators, the Republicans found that their Contract with America had been reduced to a wish list, left unfulfilled due to gridlock.

Chapter 6 brings us up to date, exploring Congress and policymaking during the presidency of George W. Bush. We begin again with the budget, noting how the rise of surpluses allowed a coalition for major budgetary change to be established once again. Yet, rather than seeking broad consensus on the budget, conservatives pushed for a set of sizable tax cuts opposed by many of the more liberal members of Congress. This continued the pattern dating back to the 1970s and 1980s of identifying budget winners and losers. While budget issues were important, the defining moment of the Bush presidency has been the terrorist attacks of September 11, 2001. Politicians of all stripes realized that our current status quo policies had been far out of line with the country's needs. Democrats and Republicans united for major changes in American domestic and foreign policy. Yet even a crisis of this magnitude could not put an end to policy gridlock. As the crisis atmosphere faded and attention turned to other issues, fundamental differences in politicians' preferences combined with time-honored institutions to lead the country back to gridlock once again.

Notes

1. Thinking about individuals and minority groups in government is far from a new idea. In some sense, our argumentation is consistent with that raised by Madison in *Federalist Papers* 10 and 51, that there are no natural majorities but only natural minorities, in that majorities are fleeting and exiting from them is easy.

2. The incumbency effect that allows vast numbers of members of Congress to hold their seats has been noted in political science literature for decades. See, in particular, Erikson (1976), Jacobson (1981), King and Gelman (1991), Fiorina and Prinz (1992), and Alford and Brady (1993).

2

Theoretical Foundations

Presidential candidate George H. Bush was hitting his stride.[1] *The postconvention boost in the polls had subsided and he still had a lead of five to eight points. Picking the conservative Dan Quayle had ensured support from the right, leaving Bush room to cater to the political center. With two months to go before the 1988 presidential elections, the Bush–Quayle team was looking for issues from which Bush could benefit by taking a stand as a political moderate. Abortion was out. There was no solid middle ground there. Defense was out. Testing the waters with an endorsement of "partial deployment" of the "star wars" Strategic Defense Initiative (SDI) system had found too many conservative sharks. The position was now "full deployment." Crime was out. How better to defeat Michael Dukakis than with a tough stand on crime, set against the Dukakis "policy" of granting furloughs to hardened criminals?*

So the Bush–Quayle team turned its sights to current legislation before Congress. They found two bills of potential interest. The first was the family leave bill. It appeared that legislation to provide unpaid leave from the workplace to family members with newborns or ailing relatives had the support of majorities in both the House and the Senate. This issue also raised sympathy among the American people. The second issue was the minimum wage. The last increase in the minimum wage had been passed during Carter's first year in office in 1977. Due to a decade of low to moderate inflation, that wage seemed paltry to laborers and politicians alike. A wage increase also appealed to middle-class voters, whose children often worked minimum wage jobs. As such, there was broad support in Congress for a minimum wage hike, perhaps even enough support to override a Reagan or Bush veto.

The campaign team decided to support the latter legislation and oppose the former. The family leave bill would hurt small businesses and upset conservatives. Bush could stop the legislation with a veto if he were elected, enabling him to wield the power of a veto threat on other issues. The minimum wage legislation, however, had such wide support that undoubtedly something would be passed in the next Congress. If Bush opposed it, Democrats in Congress would water down the bill enough to override a veto, giving the President an early defeat. If he supported an increase, perhaps he could be involved in determining the size of the increase. It could turn into a legislative victory and make him look moderate during the campaign. A winning issue.

This chapter, describing the theory upon which our book is based, is divided into six sections. First, we describe how personal preferences and congressional institutions put constraints on policy formation. Second, we address the uncertainty faced by legislators in making policy choices. Third, we look at exogenous factors affecting legislator preferences and policy positioning. Fourth, we take a closer look at the role of the President in the legislative process. Fifth, we explore how politicians may overcome or cope with the gridlock presented here. Finally, we compare the revolving gridlock theory to two others that have been advanced and widely accepted as explanations of executive–legislative policy formation.

To help clarify the theory and put it in the context of the period we are studying, we will use as an example minimum wage policy throughout the 1980s and 1990s. In 1977, with the Democrats in control of Congress and the presidency, President Carter called for an increase in the minimum wage and Congress exceeded his expectations. Congress passed legislation raising the minimum wage over a four-year period from $2.30 an hour to $3.35 an hour. As the 1980 election neared, President Carter asked Congress to postpone the January 1980 increase, fearing that it would add to high inflation and unemployment. The argument is that artificially high wages lead to inflated prices. Additionally, employers who could not pay the higher wages would cut back on the number of employees on their payrolls. Despite Carter's request, Congress did not delay the scheduled wage increase. When Reagan was elected in 1980 along with a more conservative Congress, the new leaders chose to leave minimum wage policy alone. There were still enough liberal Senators to filibuster any decrease in the minimum wage, but definitely too few to override the certain Reagan veto of an additional increase. Due to inflation, the 1981 minimum wage of $3.35 commanded less and less purchasing power as the 1980s progressed.

By the 1988 presidential campaign, Democrats in Congress were arguing that a minimum wage increase to $4.50 an hour would be necessary to make up for the lost purchasing power that had accumulated throughout the Reagan years. Bills that even exceeded this proposed raise were drafted in committees in both the House and the Senate. But legislators facing uncertain prospects in the upcoming elections were wary of upsetting either the labor unions or the combined forces of the national Chamber of Commerce and the National Federation of Independent Business. As such, neither chamber held a vote to pass the minimum wage hike. Conservative Senators filibustered action on the Senate committee's bill until the Democratic leadership dropped the issue for another year. The House bill was also tabled. The issue would be faced again early in the Bush presidency, only to be addressed once more during the Clinton administration.

This case study raises many interesting questions. How often are legislative changes made? What determines the legislative outcome when changes *are* made? What impact does unified or divided government have on these outcomes? The answers to these questions lead to a better understanding of what is known as policy gridlock.

Preferences and Institutions

John Chafee was being approached from all sides. When the Democratic leadership heard that George Bush was attempting to neutralize minimum wage as a campaign issue for 1988, they knew what had to be done. Majority Leader Robert Byrd called up S837, the bill supporting a $1.20 increase in the minimum wage. Byrd and Ted Kennedy, chief sponsor of the bill, were quite certain the bill would be filibustered by Republicans or vetoed by Reagan. If the bill made it to the White House and Bush did not use his influence as Vice President to gain Reagan's signature, the Democrats could claim that Bush was already breaking campaign promises. If the bill were filibustered, a weaker case could be made. As such, the cloture vote to end the conservative filibuster of S837 was a crucial one. And John Chafee, Republican Senator from Rhode Island, knew it.

Chafee was also aware that his seat was still considered "vulnerable" in the upcoming elections. In 1982, he had squeaked out a victory with 52 percent of the vote. This year his challenger in the largely Democratic state had a name that meant something to Chafee: Licht. In 1968, Frank Licht ousted Chafee from the governorship. Two decades later, his nephew Richard Licht was looking to do the same in the United States Senate. Chafee knew that the people of Rhode Island generally supported the minimum wage increase, which would have typically made his decision easy. But politics during an election year is seldom easy.

Republicans Bob Dole of Kansas and Orrin Hatch of Utah made the case in support of the filibuster. They were opposed to the minimum wage increase, claiming it was unnecessary and would hurt the economy. They were opposed to the Democratic tactic of trying to pass a bill that Reagan would veto and that would never become law. And they saw a political opportunity of their own. The last twenty-five Reagan nominees to lifetime federal judgeships were still awaiting consideration by the Senate. Perhaps there was room for a political compromise here. They would not let minimum wage go through to be vetoed until the judicial appointments had been dealt with. If the Democrats wanted to win a political point, it would be a costly one. But to pull off the compromise, they needed support and couldn't afford to lose many like Chafee to the other side.

The pressures on Chafee from home and from his party were increased by the prospects of interest group involvement. If he opposed the minimum wage hike, labor groups might throw more support to Licht. If he favored the increase, however, his support from Republican business groups might be diminished. Also, considering Licht's claims that Chafee was only responsive to his constituents during election years, Chafee couldn't be certain of getting credit for supporting a wage increase even if he did so.

On September 22, Chafee voted to end the filibuster, against the wishes of his party's leaders. Fifty-two Senators voted with him, seven shy of the sixty needed for cloture. The following day, Chafee felt more confident voting the same way on a second attempt to end the filibuster. Licht had no new issue to seize. John Chafee's decisions on this and other issues would lead him to an eight-point victory in November.

Legislators have preferences about policy decisions. These preferences are based on their partisan slant on the issues, on the degree to which they wish to be representative of their constituents' desires, on their responsiveness to organized interests, and on their personal views about politics and good government. On any particular issue, politicians will take a wide variety of positions, based on preferences ranging from very liberal to very conservative.[2] Looking at an issue, we often find the current (status quo) policy somewhere near the middle of these preferences, not as liberal as many Democrats would like it, and not as conservative as many Republicans would wish. This much is obvious, and results largely from legislative compromise.

Much more can be said about when bills will be passed and what the outcomes will be on a liberal–conservative scale.[3] The "revolving gridlock theory" is based on a one-dimensional spatial model.[4] We claim that, on any particular issue, legislators can be assigned positions from the most liberal to the most conservative. As a practical matter, preferences may be revealed through interest groups' ratings or other measures of legislators' positions on a variety of issues.[5] We explore these practical issues in greater detail in Chapter 4 with regard to the 1980 electoral shift, in the Appendix with regard to preferences over time, in Chapter 5 with regard to interest group ratings, and in Chapter 7 with an example of one particular representative.

In addition to the positions of individual legislators, the position of the status quo policy on each given issue likewise can be discerned. Based on the position of that status quo point relative to the positions of the members of Congress, we can speculate with some accuracy where a bill will need to be positioned to pass successfully through the institutional structure of lawmaking. The Senate filibuster and the presidential veto provide the institutional constraints on policymaking according to the revolving gridlock theory. If a bill is to become law, it must gain a majority in both houses and must not be killed by a filibuster or a veto. We argue that these constraints caused by legislators' positions and supermajority institutions are the reason policy gridlock is prevalent in the American legislative arena today.

The first institutional feature of note is the filibuster. The Senate has always been known for its slow and deliberate consideration of issues. In particular, a Senator, once given the floor, can continue to speak for extended periods of time. When a Senator's right to hold the floor indefinitely is utilized to slow or stop the advancement of a bill, the action is commonly referred to as a filibuster. The filibuster gained particular notoriety during the passage of civil rights bills in the 1950s and 1960s. In one instance, Strom Thurmond of South Carolina, speaking out against civil rights legislation, held the floor for twenty-four hours and eighteen minutes. Obviously, filibusters could keep the Senate from acting on important legislation. As a result, the Senate has, over time, adopted rules limiting the use of the filibuster. Of great significance is Senate Rule XXII, allowing for a cloture vote to end debate. To invoke cloture, sixty Senators must agree that the issue has been sufficiently discussed and that the Senate should continue on with its business, often leading to a vote on the bill being filibustered. The cloture rule thus limits the power of any small group of Senators who wish to talk an issue to death.

But it still allows a minority to have significant power over an issue. If forty-one Senators wish to kill a bill through a filibuster, they can do so by voting against cloture. This institutional feature thus can have a great impact on policy outcomes.[6]

Figure 2.1 helps illustrate this point. The range from F_L to F_R represents the central twenty members of the Senate, with M being the median member. The forty-one Senators to the left of and including F_L could successfully filibuster a bill. Likewise, F_R and the forty Senators to the right could successfully filibuster. The Senators are placed along this line based on their positions on the issue at hand. For example, if we are looking at minimum wage legislation, legislators could be lined up based on what dollar level they feel is appropriate for a minimum wage.[7] If the status quo (Q) on a particular issue is between F_L and F_R, we argue that no policy movement can occur. That is, if the central twenty Senators believe that the minimum wage should be between $4.00 and $5.00, and the current minimum wage is $4.25, that wage cannot be changed. Looking again at Figure 2.1, if the majority to the right of Q attempts to enact legislation moving policy to the right, F_L and the 40 Senators to the left will filibuster to prevent any legislative movement. This does not mean that the minority on the left can dictate policy, however. Indeed, if they attempt to move policy any further to the left, F_R and the forty Senators to the *right* will filibuster to prevent *that* movement. Thus policy Q cannot be changed by the Senate. This analysis holds true for any status quo policy in the range between F_L and F_R. Because, in this example, a majority would like to enact a more conservative policy but no change is possible, the institutional feature of the filibuster alone is enough to lead to cries of "gridlock."

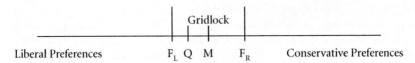

Liberal Preferences F_L Q M F_R Conservative Preferences

FIGURE 2.1   Policy Constraints Caused by Filibusters

This "gridlock region" within which no policy change can occur is actually even larger than described above. The reason for this is found in a second institutional feature: the presidential veto. If the President adopts a conservative position on an issue, the region of inaction is extended further to the right. The logic here is much the same as with the filibuster. If the status quo policy is fairly conservative and Congress acts to make the policy more moderate, the President can veto that legislation. Instead of needing the forty-one conservative Senators required to maintain a filibuster, the President only needs thirty-four conservatives to sustain a veto. Because a cloture vote requires three-fifths of the Senate and a veto override requires two-thirds, the veto provides a greater constraint on policy action. When the President is conservative and the Senators are ranked along the main policy dimension, this region of inaction, or gridlock, stretches from the forty-first Senator to the sixty-seventh. With a liberal President holding veto power, this region stretches more to the left, from the thirty-fourth Senator to the sixtieth. If previous policy has positioned the status quo in this region, then Congress can successfully undertake no further policy action. Movement to the left or the right will be halted by successful filibusters or vetoes, as indicated by points F_L and V in Figure 2.2.

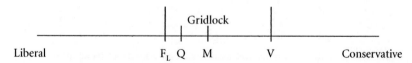

FIGURE 2.2   The Full Gridlock Region

In these diagrams, we are defining the edge of the gridlock region nearest the President to be determined by the number of legislators, based on their preferences, necessary to override a veto. However, if a President is in a position more centrist than this veto-pivotal member (denoted as "V" in the figure), the constraint will then be the President and not this member of Congress. As such, compromises will have to appeal to the President for the sake of avoiding a veto, rather than appealing to enough members of Congress to override the veto. Thus the gridlock region could stretch from the filibuster point to the veto point or to the President's ideal policy point. For extremely centrist Presidents, the veto is of little concern and the gridlock region is defined only by the filibusters, as in Figure 2.1.

After Congress passed the minimum wage increase in 1977, the new wage was securely in the region between the thirty-fourth and the sixtieth Senator. A movement to increase or decrease the wage could be stopped through either a filibuster or a veto. Indeed, even when President Carter asked his own party to delay the minimum wage increase, there was not enough support for congressional action. From 1977 to 1989, policy gridlock reigned on the minimum wage, even as inflation caused its real purchasing power to steadily fall. Very liberal Congressmen again saw the wage slip out of line with their own preferences, and they noted that they could not change policy. They were frustrated with what they called partisan gridlock. Very conservative members, on the other hand, saw the declining value of the minimum wage as more in line with their policy preferences. They had no reason to complain about policy inaction. Eventually, however, inflation and other economic conditions caused the value of the $3.35 wage to fall so far behind that it again became out of line with the preferences of the majority of Congress. At that point, gridlock was brought to an end under a Republican President.

The assumption that the extensive use of filibusters and vetoes is favored by Senators and Presidents is questionable. Is it actually in the interest of a President or of a group of Senators to repeatedly veto or filibuster legislation? Would the political costs associated with being labeled an "obstructionist" not outweigh the policy benefits? George H. Bush's repeated vetoes perhaps even helped lead to his electoral defeat in 1992.[8] But his defeat was not the necessary outcome of his vetoes. With an aggressive campaign, he could have used the vetoes to argue that he was fighting against the liberals in Congress. Indeed, this was precisely what he argued at the end of his campaign. As it turned out, the press had already characterized him as a do-nothing-at-home President. And, come election time, the public had bought this story.[9] And as for the conservatives filibustering early Clinton policies in the Senate, they typically represented constituents who were pleased to hear that liberal policies were being defeated. Although conservative Senators may have preferred legislative action on many issues, stopping action that would have been against their constituents' interests was considered good work. It should be no surprise, then, to hear repeated filibuster threats from Senate Democrats against George W. Bush's proposals on Social Security and other matters more recently. Nevertheless, it is important to be aware of how filibusters and vetoes are perceived and whether this affects how often they are used.[10]

The gridlock region described above is important with regard to policy *action* as well as policy inaction. Figure 2.3 shows the policy region for the Senate with a conservative President, stretching from the filibuster point (F) to the veto point (V). The Senator at point F plays a pivotal role in policy formation. If the status quo policy is to the right, that Senator joins the forty liberals to the left in filibustering any further movement to the right. If policy is to the left, then the pivotal Senator allows a shift to the right just so far as is in that Senator's interest. The pivotal Senator will join the forty colleagues to the left to filibuster bills that go too far. We refer to this Senator as the *filibuster pivot*, as this lawmaker plays a pivotal role in deciding which bills are satisfactory and which should be filibustered.[11] The Senator at point V holds similar powers concerning policy shifts to the left, and is referred to as the *veto pivot*. The thirty-three Senators to the right can be joined by the veto pivot to sustain a presidential veto. Likewise, the sixty-six Senators to the left can be joined to override a veto. Thus this Senator's position is pivotal in deciding whether a bill is conservative enough to pass the Senate, even with a veto threat. We call the region between the filibuster pivot and the veto pivot the *gridlock region*. Policies in this region are maintained, whereas those outside are moved inside.

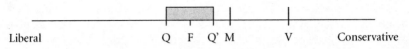

Liberal   Q   F   Q' M   V   Conservative

FIGURE 2.3   Possible Outcomes with a Filibuster Threat

Looking again at Figure 2.3, the point Q represents a status quo that is outside of the gridlock region. The Senate can thus take successful action in this policy area; but this action is again constrained by the threat of a filibuster. If the Senate proposes a bill that would shift policy to the right of Q', the bill would certainly be filibustered. The Senator at F and the forty Senators to the left all would be disadvantaged by a bill to the right of Q' because such a bill is further from their ideal policy than was Q. If a bill is proposed that would move policy to Q', the Senator at F is indifferent about whether to let the bill go through or to filibuster to stop it. Because of the possibility of a filibuster, the only policies that can be adopted are those in the shaded region between Q and Q'. In actuality, the predicted outcome is somewhere between F and Q'.[12] All movements from Q toward F are advantageous to the Senator at F. Only as a proposal becomes more conservative than Senator F's ideal policy does this Senator consider a filibuster to halt bill movement toward the right. The policy will end up between F and Q'; the exact position of the bill in this region is subject to agenda setting and political bargaining.[13] The conservative President and a majority of Senators prefer the point Q', but the filibustering group, often less impatient than the majority to get something passed, prefers point F. The minority might filibuster until a compromise is made, or a few Senators might find their position unpopular back home, causing the filibuster to break and the majority on the right to benefit.[14]

A diagram similar to Figure 2.3 can be drawn with regard to minimum wage legislation in 1989.[15] In Figure 2.4, the status quo policy has the minimum wage at $3.35 an hour, as it was when Bush took office. The veto pivot is positioned at $4.00 an hour.[16] The region between $3.35 and $4.65 is shaded, showing policy outcomes that would be advantageous to the legislator at the veto pivot. As legislation allows the minimum wage to rise toward the $4.00 mark, the legislator preferring the $4.00 wage will vote for it over the status quo wage. That legislator would even prefer a wage at $4.50 to one at $3.35. But when the proposed minimum wage reaches $4.65, the veto pivot legislator becomes indifferent; a wage that is 65 cents too low (i.e., the status quo) and one that is 65 cents too high (i.e., the proposed new wage) are equally unpalatable. If the proposed wage is above $4.65, the legislator at the veto pivot ($4.00) and those who are more conservative will oppose the change. The bill will be vetoed by the President and that veto will be sustained.

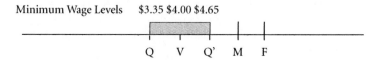

Minimum Wage Levels $3.35 $4.00 $4.65

Q   V   Q'   M   F

FIGURE 2.4   Possible Outcomes on Minimum Wage Policy (1989)

It should be clear that the outcome of this legislative process will be a minimum wage set between $4.00 and $4.65. The vast majority, including the veto pivot, prefer a raise to at least $4.00. And the veto pivot is indifferent to a choice between the status quo wage and a $4.65 wage. Liberal and moderate members of Congress would attempt to get as close to the $4.65 wage as possible, whereas conservatives would try to keep the wage increase as small as they could. At this point there is a standoff.

The initial Democratic proposal in 1989 was a minimum wage of $4.65. Bush needed to establish a counter-position. If he picked a position that increased the wage too much, his position would be frowned upon by his party and his electoral constituency. If he picked too low a wage, his coalition on the right could be broken by a compromise proposal. Some of the legislators he was counting on to sustain a veto could be won over by the majority with the argument that Bush was appearing too conservative and too much a proponent of gridlock. Bush knew that *some sort* of a wage increase would pass. The size of the increase would depend on the President's position and on the political bargaining game.

In short, the revolving gridlock theory predicts that status quo policies inside the gridlock region will be maintained, and policies outside the region will be brought inside, usually through minor policy adjustments. With very little resulting policy change, even where a majority approves change, this model starts to explain what is referred to as policy gridlock. When this gridlock occurs under unified party control of government, we call it *unified gridlock*. Unified gridlock resulted under the 103rd Congress during the first two years of the Clinton administration. Unified gridlock explains the limits on major policy change in the 109th Congress today.

It should not be assumed that this model rests on the *observance* of filibusters and vetoes. The mere *threat* of a veto or a filibuster is often enough to kill a bill or to force it to be altered so as to override a veto or to gain sufficient votes for cloture. Successful vetoes and filibusters might actually be quite rare. Because time and effort are scarce commodities in Congress, it would be easier for the majority and the leadership to abandon a bill early on than to lose it to a filibuster or veto. However, in some circumstances politicians may wish to go down swinging.[17] Opponents can raise the issue of repeated sustained vetoes, such as those in the George H. Bush presidency, as an example of the President and his party causing gridlock. And Democrats could claim that the repeated filibusters by Bob Dole and other conservatives in the 103rd Congress were "obstructionist." Of course, on the other side of the coin, during the 1994 elections Republicans effectively claimed that the Democrats were poor at policymaking, unable to pass major legislation even with control of Congress and the presidency. Fear of a similar label may have contributed to George W. Bush's reluctance to veto any legislation through his entire first term in office.

The above discussion has concentrated mainly on the Senate. There similarly exists a gridlock region for the House. As filibusters are not allowed in the House, this region only stretches from the House median to the House veto pivot. With a conservative President, status quo policies in this region cannot be shifted to the right because a majority would not vote for such a shift, and policies cannot be moved to the left because such a shift would be vetoed and the veto sustained. Because this region is smaller than in the Senate, it is often less of a constraint on policy.[18] However, the need for a supermajority to override a veto is a serious constraint in both the House and the Senate.

Figure 2.5 shows the bicameral situation as we perceive it today, with a fairly conservative House and Senate and a Republican President. The gridlock region in our bicameral system is determined on the left by the filibuster in the Senate, and on the right by the need for a two-thirds supermajority in both the House and the Senate to overcome any presidential veto. Veto threats will thus constrain any proposed movements to the left. Filibusters will limit the size and success of conservative proposals to move policies to the right. For example, unless at least a handful of conservative Senate Democrats join with Republicans to support Bush's proposals, they will go nowhere.

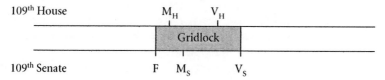

FIGURE 2.5   Gridlock Region in the Bicameral 109th Congress

The position of the President and his veto threat determines which side of the gridlock region will be stretched out to the veto pivot. With the election of Bill Clinton in 1992, the previous extension of the gridlock region to the veto pivot on the right was altered such that the filibuster pivot was on the right and the veto pivot was on the left. Policies that were held in place by Bush vetoes were released for action by Congress. But they were still constrained by the filibuster pivot in the Senate. Unless President Clinton's proposals were made suitably conservative, the Senator at the filibuster pivot and colleagues to the right would have voted to stop the legislation with a filibuster, voting down cloture attempts until the bill died or a compromise was reached. This was the fate of many Clinton proposals in 1993, including the national service legislation and the jobs stimulus package. Following their electoral victories in 1994, Republicans' proposals also were constrained, this time from the left, with a Clinton veto sustained in the House and Senate.

George W. Bush's election in 2000 returned the veto pivot to the right side of the gridlock region. Policy movements to the right were still limited by politicians on the left. Now, however, opponents needed to secure 41 votes in the Senate to successfully filibuster rightward movement, rather than the one-third of House or Senate members to sustain a Clinton veto. This need for a larger blocking minority meant that some policy proposals from the Republican Revolution in 1994 could finally be successfully adopted.

Uncertainty

"It's Friday. Some people are confused," Bob Dole explained. The Friday in question was September 23, 1988, and the Minority Leader had just lost five more Republican votes in his attempt to keep the minimum wage filibuster going. The cloture vote had still failed, as nine Senators had not been present to vote. But Dole was concerned about the apparent weakening of his coalition. This issue was a bit complex, as they

were voting on a procedural issue, not on whether to actually pass a higher minimum wage. But wasn't it a straightforward procedural vote? Maybe not.

The actual impact of an increase in the minimum wage was uncertain. Earlier in the summer, the San Francisco Federal Reserve reported that a minimum wage increase could boost inflation by a noticeable amount. Since then, several studies were released claiming that the proposed minimum wage hike could cause the loss of up to a million jobs. Such news raised questions among the Senators voting on that late September day. How soon would these effects on the economy take place? Would the voting public be able to trace the blame to those who voted for an increase in the minimum wage? Would these hardships counterbalance the benefits that constituents would perceive from increased wages for those with low incomes?

The actions of interest groups raised more questions in the minds of legislators. Even if no economic hardships materialized before the elections, would the varied interested parties influence the elections depending on my vote? If I vote for a wage increase, will my support from small businesses diminish? If I vote against an increase, will organized labor raise more support for my opponent? Even Dole was frustrated with the involvement of some of these interest groups. "How many Labor Committee bills from organized labor do we need before we go home?" he asked.

But Dole had not taken steps to make the issue clearer for his colleagues in the Senate. In fact, he muddied the waters further, by tying action on minimum wage to the approval of Reagan's nominees to federal judgeships. "I am advised by members on my side to bring this place to a halt until we get some action" on the judicial appointments, Dole said. This led to even more questions. If a Senator supported the filibuster, would he then be perceived as being involved in a type of blackmail to get conservative judgeships?

With the issue so complicated and the uncertain prospects of elections so close on the horizon, Dole should not have been surprised to see some flip-flops in voting. Over the weekend he would make sure that he would not lose the next cloture vote, leaving the Democratic leadership with the lose-lose proposition of either prolonging the stalemate or dropping the bill. By Monday it was clear that the conservative filibuster could continue indefinitely, so the Democratic leadership dropped the bill.

In forming policy, legislators face uncertainty on a number of levels. Of concern to the theory here are two types of uncertainty: uncertainty over the actual policy results of passing a bill, and uncertainty over constituent reactions to voting for or against a bill.[19] Although members of Congress are forced to live with some level of uncertainty, they take many steps to minimize that uncertainty.[20] They listen carefully to constituents, paying attention to surveys and polls. They take advice from experts, whether committee members who have specialized in a policy area or authorities who give testimony in hearings.[21] Still, the remaining uncertainty leads to mistakes.

First, there is uncertainty over the actual policy results of passing a bill. In the above section, we assumed that the status quo policy and the alternative proposed by the bill were known and were easily placed on a one-dimensional line. Legislators then simply pick whichever policy is closer to their preferred outcome. In reality, policymaking is an uncertain activity. Budget estimates made over a five-year period are undoubtedly going to lose accuracy over time. Members of Congress cannot accurately predict which interpretations and actions government agencies and bureaus will take. Policymakers and policy analysts are unsure of just how many people will qualify for programs, find loopholes, or be indirectly affected by a policy change. And in foreign affairs, strategic behavior by other countries raises a host of uncertainties. Legislators try to find out as much as they can about the policy consequences of various actions, and then they must take a risk and vote.

The uncertainty of policy outcomes could have a beneficial or adverse effect on the chances of a bill's passage, depending on perceptions of the status quo. When the public seems pleased with present policies, it may be difficult to pass new legislation. Although the proposed policy could actually improve the status quo, legislators feel no pressure to take chances. Such was the case with minimum wage legislation in 1988. Pollsters predicted that incumbents would fare quite well in that year's elections. The economy was fairly strong, and it appeared that George H. Bush would be elected President. Congress felt that tinkering with the minimum wage while otherwise in such a strong position so close to the elections raised too much uncertainty. The San Francisco Federal Reserve reported that a minimum wage increase could boost inflation by a noticeable amount.[22] Analysts released a variety of studies claiming that a minimum wage hike could cause a loss of up to a million low-wage jobs. This potential job loss combined with the grassroots lobbying campaign by business groups led the House leadership to avoid votes on the bills proposed out of committee.[23] Although Congress did consider the issue, there was no outrage over legislative inaction, and if Congress had acted there was a great risk of making economic and political conditions worse.

In contrast to this case of uncertainty leading to inaction, at times politicians embrace an uncertain outcome. When the current policy is considered poor, the public perceives that things cannot get any worse. This paves the way for a string of new, uncertain policy proposals. Had economic conditions been different in 1988, perhaps members of Congress would have supported a minimum wage increase. For example, if there were an outcry about large numbers of working Americans living below the poverty line, legislators could address the issue through a minimum wage hike just before the election. The public would think that Congress was being responsive, and the inflation and job loss would not be felt before the election. Whereas typically members of Congress are looking to avoid uncertain options, under these conditions they may embrace a major change.

Thus uncertainty over policy outcomes can either add to or relieve policy gridlock. When legislators are uncertain about the consequences of their actions, they may either take small steps or make no changes to current policy. But when there is demand for immediate action, uncertainty could trigger a major policy change that would have been unacceptable to legislators had they been perfectly aware of the outcome. As the uncertainties are resolved over time, members of Congress can better judge what they have done. If the results are found to be in the "gridlock region," no further policy changes are made. Such was the case with minimum wage policy under President Carter. When he realized that the wage increase he had called for was hurting the economy, Carter asked Congress to delay its implementation.[24] However, so many members of Congress agreed with the wage increase that it went forward as planned. Even though the policy outcome was more dramatic than expected, the results were still in the gridlock region. If the uncertainty is resolved with the discovery that the policy enacted did not move into the gridlock region at all, or even that it overshot the region, modifications to the policy will be made. For example, when the 1981 tax cuts in concert with the economic downturn yielded large budget deficits, President Reagan supported minor tax increases over the next few years. And when the catastrophic health care measure passed by the 100th Congress was found to be catastrophic itself, it was quickly repealed.

In addition to being uncertain about where the policy outcome of a bill will lie, members of Congress face a second uncertainty: how their constituents will react to how they vote. In the above section, we argued that members of Congress are aligned from liberal to conservative. Their positions on various issues can be determined by observing how they vote over time. When they vote, members of Congress seeking reelection must be aware of how their constituencies view their votes on the issue at hand. And yet these members are uncertain as to what the reaction will be back home. Many policy votes will simply be ignored by constituents; others will be observed but play little or no role in swaying voters; and still others will become major campaign issues. Furthermore, the uncertain reaction of constituents is compounded by the uncertain policy outcomes. Even though they may have the best of intentions, legislators will be blamed for the unforeseen results of their actions (or inaction).

Because legislators are trying to maintain their popularity among constituents, they must try to resolve the uncertainties concerning voters' perceptions of the issues. In particular, members of Congress attempt to reduce uncertainty by judging the salience of an issue to the public and the leanings of the public either for or against a bill. Legislators pay attention to surveys and polls as well as to calls and letters from constituents. Over time, they settle on a position with which they are comfortable, whether they derive benefit from their party, from their constituents, from campaign contributors, or from a sense of doing what is right for the American people.[25] Throughout 1988 and early 1989, lawmakers were deciding on their positions regarding minimum wage increases. They were careful in 1988 not to upset the labor movement on one side of the issue or business groups on the other.[26] Either side could have helped finance challengers against incumbents who weren't carefully positioned.

As the legislators themselves are converging on their final positions on a particular issue, the bill being produced is also changing. Support for a legislative change in policy early in the formulation of a bill does not necessarily mean that anything will be done in the end. It certainly does not mean that the President or the majority party is free to push through its bill of choice. As uncertainties are resolved about where the status quo, the various new bills, and the legislators' own positions lie, we can fairly accurately predict the policy outcome. If the status quo is found to be in the gridlock region with a large number of legislators on each side of it, policy change can be stopped through filibusters and vetoes.[27] If the status quo is found to be outside the region, as was shown in Figure 2.3, it will be brought inside the region, but seldom as far as those promoting change had wished.

On many issues Congress deals with, most of the major uncertainty can be resolved before action is taken. In such cases, the revolving gridlock theory should be expected to hold without exception. Additionally, we can accurately predict when uncertainty will play a large role. Uncertainty influences policy when legislators face two constraints: complexity and time. When dealing with a multiyear budget and an uncertain constituent reaction, or with health care bills involving a major portion of the American economy, or in making foreign policy decisions in the face of international crises, legislators can make mistakes. The issues are so complex that all of the uncertainty cannot be removed. Also, when dealing with the time constraint of enacting a policy just before elections, uncertainties cannot be removed from the legislative process because all the variables cannot properly be addressed. Although members of Congress wish to campaign on the strength of a new program they have just passed, they do so at the risk of finding that they have made a mistake when they return to Congress the next year. We claim that the revolving gridlock theory will hold true generally, even where uncertainty surrounding legislative decisions makes the process more complex.

Elections and Exogenous Shocks

"I can't tell you what a very significant departure this is from what we've had over the past eight years." Democratic Senator Ted Kennedy was obviously pleased that minimum wage was again being discussed in March 1989. He had seen the wage shrink in terms of purchasing power for years, and had been a strong supporter of an increase. To raise the minimum wage to $4.60 an hour would only restore the purchasing power it enjoyed in 1981, Kennedy argued. It would not make up for the years of decline that people living on minimum wage had endured.

Now was the time to do something about the minimum wage. The newly elected President had issued a campaign promise to raise the minimum wage. And he had not brought in many conservative members of Congress on his coattails who would oppose a wage hike. As such, a large majority in both houses of Congress supported an increase.

Although President Bush had only supported an increase to $4.25 an hour, Kennedy believed that a greater increase would have enough support to override a veto. But would Bush be foolish enough to veto the increase? About 80 percent of the public favored an increase in the minimum wage. If Bush vetoed the bill passed by Congress, he would lose credit for any increase whatsoever, and would hopefully lose a veto fight as well. Kennedy therefore wanted to propose an increase that would restore much of the purchasing power of former wages, and one that would also be an embarrassment *to Bush if he vetoed it. On March 23, the Senate decided on a wage of $4.55, just three thin dimes more than Bush's proposal. With the approval of the House, the ball would soon be back in the President's court.*

In previous pages we defined the gridlock region and argued that policies in that region could not be changed, due to the diverse preferences of members of Congress and to the institutional structure involving the use of filibusters and vetoes. Status quo policies outside the gridlock region are brought just inside it. Because of uncertainty, policies are sometimes formulated that are outside the gridlock region. We claim that when these outlying policies are discovered, they are brought back inside the gridlock region. If all of this is true, it would seem that over time Congress would get around to dealing with every policy area, bringing each policy outcome into the gridlock region where it is then held in place. We argue that this would be the case if there were no shocks to the system. But in the constantly changing world of politics and policy, a number of exogenous factors impact upon the theory. The exogenous factors of greatest concern to us are threefold: the election of new politicians, the changing preferences of constituents, and the shifting of policy realizations over time.

Because the band of policy possibilities that we call the gridlock region is defined by the preferences of legislators in the House and Senate, a change in these members or in their preferences could alter the size and placement of the region. If such a change leads to a state in which some current policies are no longer within the region, then those policy areas are released for legislative action. The most straightforward way to change the placement of the gridlock region is to change the members who define its position. For example, if the Republicans gain a number of seats in a given election, the region is likely to shift to the right. This may result in no policy change, if there were no fairly liberal status quo policies just inside the gridlock region. Or it could result in across-the-board changes, if a large number of status quo policies are released from the gridlock region.

Thus policy gridlock depends on both the *size* and the *shifting* of the gridlock region. The size of the region is determined by the difference in preferences between the pivotal members on both edges of the region. If the preferences of the forty-first (filibuster pivot) and sixty-seventh (veto pivot) members are quite similar (as with a large number of centrists), little gridlock will occur. However, if the preferences of these members are quite different, policy changes over a vast range of policies will be unachievable. This is perhaps why commentators worry about the "lack of a political center" in today's Congress. In the Appendix, we show the distribution of preferences in the House of Representatives over the past thirty years. Note that, given these polarized preferences, the gridlock region has been sizable in recent years. However, not only the size of the gridlock region but also its *movement* matters. Even if the gridlock region had about the same size after the 1980 elections as before, the dramatic shift to the right released a number of policies that were formerly in the gridlock region and that could now move to better reflect the preferences of Congress and President Reagan.

However, most elections do not bring about sweeping changes.[28] The vast majority of incumbents are reelected.[29] Additionally, changes at the margins often do not affect the position of the gridlock region to any great extent. If ten liberal members and ten conservative members all lose their seats and are replaced by new members on the opposite sides, the region may not be changed at all. The moderate legislators at the endpoints of the gridlock region may remain the same, whereas the legislators on the wings change dramatically. Furthermore, voters may take into account the preferences of the other members of Congress and of the President in order to strike some sort of balance or include checks on other politicians.[30] Although we are indeed interested in the link between policies and elections, our main focus is on what happens when politicians are already in the government, emphasizing that it takes major electoral shifts to move policy left or right.

If the gridlock region *does* move noticeably in one direction, this is often the result of the "coattails" effect that, until recently, had been frequently found in presidential elections.[31] If the party of the President changes from Democrat to Republican and a number of conservative Senators and Representatives are brought in with the new President, liberal status quo policies become vulnerable to change. The President will certainly wish to enact change in all of those policy areas before the typical loss of seats during the midterm elections.[32] This explains the phenomenon known as the "honeymoon," in which a new President is able to quickly bring about policy change on a number of issues.[33] (Often within the first few months of a presidency, most of the policies with low uncertainty are brought back into the new gridlock region.) Because policy movement is still restricted by the possibility of a filibuster in the Senate, the President often will not get all that he wants during his honeymoon. The more extreme a President's position, the more he will appear to be losing in the compromises he is forced to make. Because the policy outcomes illustrated by the above figures were not dependent on how extreme the President's position was, a President often appears more powerful by asking for what he knows can be passed rather than by asking for what he wants and then having to abandon the policy or cave in to the opposition.[34]

This is an important point in our understanding of presidential requests. It is possible that President Bush, in 1989, wanted the minimum wage to stay where it was. But this was an unpopular position in Congress, where a raise to at least $4.00 was inevitable. By taking a position supporting a raise to $4.25, Bush appeared to be moderate while also challenging those who wanted an increase beyond $4.25. Had he positioned his proposal any lower, he may have appeared too conservative, risking the breakdown of his coalition. Had he requested a higher wage, Bush would have been giving away more than he had to, perhaps hurting the economy as an outcome. Had he ignored the issue entirely and left Congress to pass increases that he would veto, Bush would eventually have had to give in to a small increase or risk having his veto overridden and the steam taken out of his presidency early in his first term. Bush's proposal turned a losing issue into an early victory.

After the honeymoon, the President is left to deal with those policy areas containing the greatest uncertainty, those policies that cannot easily be adjusted back into the gridlock region. This is when the legislative challenge really begins. President Reagan was able to use the uncertainty surrounding supply-side economics to his advantage. President Clinton, on the other hand, lost popularity in his first year by trying to enact his own ideal policies only to end up giving concessions to conservative Senators. In 1994, when facing the uncertainties of health care reform, members of Congress tried to distance themselves from Clinton's unpopularity.

The gridlock region can be changed not only through legislator turnover but also through a shift in the preferences of legislators. As described above, legislators' preferences are complex; they depend on party strength, on public opinion of their constituencies, on the influence of interest groups, on the amount of available information, and on the legislators' own personal preferences independent of outside forces. When any of these factors shifts dramatically, a legislator's preferences will follow.

If the President is enormously popular and has agreed to campaign for members of his party who support him, those legislators are able to vote with the President even if they lose some support from interest groups or constituents. Any such loss of support can be won back in a grand fashion if the President campaigns on behalf of the legislator. But a President without such popularity will see members of his own party distancing themselves from him. Likewise, if public opinion is shifted through advertising campaigns, such as the "Harry and Louise" ads against the Clinton health care plan, legislators may alter their voting preferences in order to please their constituents. And if interest groups join in on an issue at the last minute, or provide new information to Congress, a shift in legislator preferences is again likely.

When these shifts are dramatic, members of Congress may change their preferences to the extent that policies previously in the gridlock region are now to the left or right of it. In such cases, Congress will pass bills to bring policies back in line with the preferences of its members. Of note here is a beneficial side effect of gridlock. Because of the lack of policy movement in the gridlock region, members of Congress do not spend all of their time chasing small shifts in public opinion. If it weren't for the threat of filibusters and vetoes, legislation could be raised and passed with the slightest change in legislator preferences. These institutional constraints sometimes mean that the majority's proposals can be stopped by a minority, but they also encourage Congress to act only when significant action is needed.

The first two exogenous shocks to the revolving gridlock model—a change of legislators and a change of legislators' preferences—affected the positioning of members of Congress, and thus of the gridlock region. A third exogenous factor involves the position of the status quo policy relative to the gridlock region. As was discussed above, there is often uncertainty with regard to the actual outcome of legislation adopted by Congress. Although some laws have been unchanged on the books for decades, others are changed all the time. Congress is unable to specify a budget for more than a year or two into the future. Minimum wage, Medicare, and Medicaid benefits are constantly being adjusted. With an increase in crime, a crisis overseas, a natural disaster, a dramatic increase in the cost of health care, a newly discovered disease, an economic recession or depression, or any of a number of other unforeseen events, new issues constantly arise for Congress to deal with.

When new issues arise, or old issues take on a new significance, members of Congress face a high level of uncertainty as to what should be done. Congress devotes most of its attention to dealing with these unpredictable issues when they arise, then returning to the normal business of adjusting policies that have drifted outside of the gridlock region. With the economic difficulties of the late 1970s and early 1980s, Congress dealt with the problem through an attempt at supply-side economics. When this reaction led to growing budget deficits, Congress became seriously restricted in its ability to initiate new programs and was forced to raise taxes and limit spending just to avoid a crisis.

In response to the terrorist attacks of September 11, 2001, Congress needed to act to prevent similar attacks in the future. Over the next weeks and months, Republicans and Democrats came together on this issue, realizing that the United States had an unacceptable status quo policy on terrorism. Congress passed the Patriot Act with wide margins and authorized President George W. Bush to launch military operations in Afghanistan. As time moved on, uncertainties were resolved and political wrangling returned, even on issues of national security. The establishment of a Department of Homeland Security was caught up in political discussions about civil service protections for its employees; the restructuring of the nation's intelligence community was slowed by tensions over military and civilian intelligence needs and the chain of command. And Congress deferred to the President regarding the war in Iraq, partly because of the uncertainty associated with the evidence of weapons of mass destruction and links between Iraq and terrorist groups. Rather than acting forcefully to declare war against Iraq, such that they may face blame in the future, members of Congress ceded a large amount of control to the President, with some preparing to blame him if the military operations and reconstruction went poorly.

Many other issues are also characterized by exogenous shocks, although on a much smaller scale. Shocks to minimum wage policy were slower in coming and more predictable than terrorist attacks, for example. Inflation during the 1980s caused wages to lose about one quarter of their purchasing power. When the minimum wage had thus dropped to levels unacceptable to legislators, they called for a wage hike. This was not the result of a liberal shift in the preferences of members of Congress, nor in divided or unified government. Outside factors had caused the minimum wage to become skewed away from the preferences of lawmakers, who therefore changed the policy.[35]

Most of the significant action taken by Congress has occurred as a reaction to exogenous shocks to the legislative system. When new legislators are elected and there is a major shift to the left or right, new legislative action is likely. When public opinion solidifies behind an issue, such as during the Great Depression, the world wars, the space race, or 9/11, the preferences of legislators are altered enough to bring about significant change. And when unforeseen policy shocks arise, legislative action is again possible. Often these shocks occur under extraordinary circumstances. The revolving gridlock theory is significant in its ability to explain the results of these occurrences as well as to address the day-to-day legislation passing through Congress. When lawmakers fail to respond to exogenous shocks, they put their seats at risk. The inability of Republicans to react to the events of the Great Depression led to enormous Democratic victories. When the Democrats failed to respond to cries for tax relief throughout the 1970s, Republicans gained control of the Senate and presidency and found enough support to enact huge tax cuts in 1981.

In the absence of major electoral and policy shocks, the government falls into periods of legislative gridlock during which either no policy is passed or only incremental changes around the edges of the gridlock region are made. It is our contention that the election of Bill Clinton in 1992 with only 42 percent of the vote and few coattail victories did not represent a major shock to the American political system. As such, although the 103rd Congress and the presidency were controlled by the same political party, the government was in a period of continuous policy gridlock, with abandoned policy proposals and incremental changes. It was a unified government with unified gridlock. Just as continuous policy inaction during a public outcry for change can lead to electoral turnover, so too can there be electoral repercussions from forcing policy action. As will be shown in later chapters, the party-based pressure on some conservative Democrats to support Clinton proposals (including the 1993 budget act) led many members to vote against their constituents' preferences; this, in turn, led their constituents to vote *against them* in 1994, bringing about significant Republican gains.

In a similar manner, George W. Bush's reelection in 2004 with a majority of the popular vote (unseen since the 1980s) and a gain in seats for House and Senate Republicans seems to lay the groundwork for an impressive mandate. Yet, absent the support of moderates, including some Senate Democrats needed to overcome a filibuster, conservative proposals will find no traction in Congress. Moreover, if the unified Republicans in the 109th Congress were to follow the model of the unified Democrats from 1993, passing a budget outside of the mainstream with no support of the other party, Republicans from moderate districts would similarly have trouble holding on to their seats in the next election. And yet, absent some tough budget decisions, the public is likely to blame the unified Republicans for budget deficits once they start having a noticeable negative impact on voters' pocketbooks.

These few examples of electoral reactions to policy change (or lack of change) show the dynamic nature of elections and policymaking. Exogenous shocks to policies or preferences may lead to inaction or to new policy outcomes. Such legislative action (or inaction) has electoral implications. And these elections in turn act as even further shocks to the system. It is a constant struggle for politicians to please the electorate while attempting to make compromises to break gridlock. We are describing *revolving gridlock*. Although legislators' preferences and institutional constraints always lead to a certain amount of gridlock, politicians and the electorate are always attempting new and different tactics to bring about what they perceive as good policy. Politicians are either caught in gridlock or making dramatic compromises in the attempt to overcome it. The public, when dissatisfied with congressional and presidential activities, can do little but vote them out of office.[36] Throughout the 1980s, America had Republican Presidents, a Democratic House, and much talk of gridlock. Unified government was thus attempted in 1992, and Republican control of Congress in 1994. With unified Republican government recently, all configurations have been tried. And yet, due to the reasons discussed here, this revolving of politicians has not brought an end to policy gridlock.

The Role of the President

Members of the Bush White House were pleased with their cleverness. Democratic leaders had held off sending the minimum wage bill to the White House. Congress cleared HR2 on May 17, 1989, but the Democrats wanted their new House leadership in place before engaging in a confrontation with the President. On June 13, that leadership was in place, George H. Bush was out west on a two-day trip, and the Democrats felt that it was time. They sent the bill to the White House, and scheduled a press conference for 3 p.m. There, they would make arguments intended to give the President great discomfort if he actually vetoed the bill, which raised the minimum wage above his $4.25 target.

But Bush was ready for them. His staff had made certain that he carried his veto message with him to Wyoming. At 1:39 p.m. the President was informed aboard Air Force One that the bill had reached the White House. He immediately vetoed it, having members of his team in Washington finish the paperwork to send the bill back to Capitol Hill half an hour before the Democrats' press conference. "This may be the first faxed veto in history," White House chief of staff John Sununu joked.

The President was confident about his veto, knowing that neither the House nor the Senate had passed the bill by the two-thirds needed to override it. Additionally, he had a promise from more than thirty-four Senators that they would sustain his veto. Now if only the American people would realize that he was committed to a wage increase, but not the bloated one that had passed through the Congress. . . . By undermining the efforts of the Democratic leadership to get the first punch in, Bush had taken a large step toward his objectives.

In previous sections we explain how the theory of revolving gridlock is based on the preferences of members of Congress and on congressional institutions, without much mention of the role of the President. Indeed, we feel that the President's role in domestic policymaking is less significant than he is often given credit (or blame) for in the press and in the minds of the voters. Nevertheless, the President does play an important role in the legislative process, a role that can be brought to light through the revolving gridlock theory. He affects lawmaking in at least four areas: setting the legislative agenda, influencing the preferences of legislators, vetoing legislation, and compromising with pivotal legislators.

The first significant role of the President in the theory of legislative policymaking is in bringing an issue to the attention of the public and of Congress.[37]

Congress often has a number of issues on its plate at the same time. When a President emphasizes an issue during a campaign, a press conference, or the State of the Union Address, he is looking to bolster public awareness and encourage legislative action. Where there is a large degree of uncertainty surrounding a policy area, Congress may be hesitant to act without a push from the President. It is possible that the health care debate raised in 1994 would not have occurred without all of the publicity generated by Bill and Hillary Clinton. Likewise, George W. Bush set off the discussion of Social Security reform with his actions and speeches in 2005. Whereas the revolving gridlock theory argues that legislator preferences and institutions affect *where* policy will end up, the President can help decide *which* issues will be addressed. From this view, the President becomes more an agenda setter than a force influencing policy outcomes. This is not to say that once Congress starts dealing with an issue the President can back off. If he does, the bill could easily die before it ever reaches the floor. Rather, the President must keep the issue in the public eye and help to resolve uncertainty about the issue through task forces and the advice of experts and executive agencies.

In a second role, the President and his party can influence the preferences of members of Congress.[38] A popular President can help members of his party through fund-raisers, media publicity, and campaign activism. In close votes, the President and party leadership can offer side benefits to legislators in exchange for their votes, when they are indifferent to the issue at hand.[39] These benefits could come in the form of pork or of campaign financing and publicity. Additionally, a popular President can provide cover for members of Congress who are nervous about policy votes. By taking a public stand, the President provides the opportunity for legislators to say that they are voting with the President on the issue at hand rather than having to explain their position in greater detail and thus upsetting a segment of their constituency.

The most formal involvement of the President in the legislative process comes through the use of the presidential veto. As described and illustrated above, the possibility of a veto stretches the gridlock region in the direction of the President's position. This means that policies close to the President's position often cannot be made more moderate even if a majority in Congress would prefer such a change. Furthermore, with a change in the party of the President, the direction of the gridlock region's expansion changes, often releasing policy areas that had been left alone because of veto threats by a President of the other party. In addressing these newly released policy areas, the President has a chance to gain popularity and appear active. When a newly elected President replaces a President of his own party, the gridlock region does not change (the veto pivot is still on the same side of the median). As such, not as many policies are found outside the gridlock region for the new President to act upon. This situation undoubtedly added to the impression that George H. Bush, who replaced a President of his own party, was ineffective in the legislative arena. And the same logic explains why Presidents entering their second terms in office are not typically able to achieve as many early successes as new Presidents do.

The effect of the veto is evident in our minimum wage example. When the minimum wage was raised in 1977, the constraint on this increase was the possibility of a filibuster in the Senate. Had a conservative President been in office, the constraint on policy change would have been the more-restrictive veto threat. Had Gerald Ford been elected in 1976, the minimum wage hike would have been smaller than the $1.05 increase that President Carter secured. Likewise, had Michael Dukakis been elected in 1988, the ninety-cent increase allowed by President Bush would have been surpassed. As the theory suggests, institutional conditions and the preferences of members of Congress always constrain the size and substance of a policy change. The greater these constraints (veto threats rather than filibuster threats), the greater the cries of gridlock. In minimum wage policy, we may see a difference of a few dimes in wage increases because of the position of the President. In dealing with the defense budget and entitlements, the difference may be billions of dollars.

The final role of the President in the revolving gridlock theory relates to policy compromises made with the pivotal legislators in the model. Recall from Figure 2.4 that the policy shift from the status quo to a point inside the gridlock region could result in raising the minimum wage to any amount between $4.00 and $4.65 an hour. In this case, $4.00 was the ideal policy point for the veto pivot and $4.65 was the position that made the veto pivot indifferent to selecting between the old policy and the new. Depending on the compromise made with the veto-sustaining minority, any new minimum wage between $4.00 and $4.65 could be passed. By appearing ready to veto wage increases beyond his request of $4.25 an hour, President Bush could pull the outcome closer to $4.00, making a better deal for himself.[40] But if the President had taken the unpopular position of opposing any increase, he may not have been able to gain the votes necessary to sustain a veto. Indeed, he may have been forced to give in to a policy outcome nearer the opposing legislators' position than his own. This would have led to the appearance of caving in and thus to a drop in his popularity. Even when a President is able to influence the policy outcome, however, he seldom gains as extreme an outcome as he might want. Based on the model, Bush was faced with a policy outcome of between $4.65 and $4.00, whereas his ideal minimum wage was probably less than $4.00 an hour. A President is always forced to accept policy results within the narrow band of the gridlock region. By taking a position of $4.25 and vetoing any increase beyond that point, President Bush won the bargaining game with the congressional leadership. In the end, the Democratic leadership was more interested in passing the increase that Bush proposed than in risking a second loss to the President on another sustained veto.

Coping with Gridlock and Overcoming Gridlock

When President Clinton took office in 1993, increasing the minimum wage was not his top priority. Reforming health care and addressing the budget deficit would come first. Besides, there would always be time and a lot of Democratic support for a wage hike beyond the limited increase under the Bush administration. Wouldn't there?

Less than two years later, minority leader Newt Gingrich orchestrated the Republican Revolution, putting his party in control of the House, with himself as its Speaker. Suddenly Clinton was dismissed from his role as agenda setter. A minimum wage increase would be portrayed as a "job killer" and an "unfunded mandate" on businesses. With a Republican House and a Republican Senate, what hope was there for another wage bill?

And yet, by 1996, inflation had diminished the value of the $4.25 wage, and there was no Republican veto to hold it in place. Opinion polls showed up to 85% of Americans in favor of an increase, and it was an election year. Senate majority leader Bob Dole was the front runner for the Republican nomination for President. And clever Senate Democrats like Ted Kennedy and John Kerry thought they could undermine his authority with the minimum wage issue.

On the same day that Dole secured his party's nomination, Kerry and Kennedy found an opportunity, introducing a minimum wage amendment to a controversial federal parks bill. The amendment could be removed, but it would take the 60 Senators needed for a cloture vote. Finding only 55 votes, Dole reluctantly pulled the parks bill from the floor. But the same thing happened three weeks later on an immigration bill. Dole was being framed as an ineffective leader in the Senate and as out of touch with the wishes of most Americans.

In the House, Gingrich was faring little better. He held a closed-door party meeting to discuss possible strategies to stop a wage increase. He was surprised when about 70 Republicans expressed support for the increase. Concerned about reelection, a bloc of moderate northeastern Republicans from urban areas was ready to break from the party on this issue. Without the votes to stop the wage increase, and with popular sentiment against them, the best the Republican leaders could hope for was a compromise. A limited defeat on this issue would be better than a major defeat at the polls in November.

By mid-summer, Congress increased the minimum wage to $5.15, but coupled it with a $4.25 training wage for teenage workers and a small tax cut for businesses. Clinton held a triumphant signing ceremony, and Gingrich was left to proclaim, "I would say to my friends, the Democratic Party, you won a great victory. Some of us swallowed more than we wanted to, yet it was clearly the American people's will."

We have shown how legislator preferences coupled with supermajority institutions can lead to policy gridlock. This gridlock may be *exacerbated* by the uncertainty surrounding issues and by the positions taken by a President. Yet politicians have also found clever ways to overcome gridlock or to cope with its effects.

We described above how the President can help set the legislative agenda by going public on an issue he deems important. Not only does a public pronouncement increase the likelihood that an issue will be addressed, but it can also influence the positions of pivotal legislators. A President can try to gain the support of members of Congress by having voters contact their representatives to advocate the President's position. Others with access to the public may make their cases as well. Where policies were in the gridlock region only because Senators and Representatives were not responsive to the wishes of the electorate, such appeals would help overcome gridlock.

More often, however, gridlock is maintained through members from diverse districts who are very responsive to the electorate and thus at odds with their fellow legislators. In these cases, gridlock can be overcome only through legislative compromise, and only when status quo policies are outside the gridlock region. When a policy advocate suggests a change so major that supermajorities are difficult to achieve, the change will be stopped by a filibuster or veto. To build the needed coalition for cloture or a veto override, compromises will need to be struck, often taking one of two forms. First, the policy itself could be watered down. This was the main way that President Clinton overcame Republican filibusters in 1993 on issues like the job stimulus package, voter registration, and family and medical leave. A smaller change was more acceptable to moderate Senators.

A second possible compromise with these pivotal members needed to build a supermajority involves concessions not on the ideological position of the bill at hand, but on other issues. Often these include distributive budgetary items, like roads, bridges, research labs, and targeted tax cuts. Riders attached to budget bills add these benefits needed to smooth out compromises on earlier bills. Quite clearly, to the extent that budget concessions are needed to build coalitions on all sorts of issues, gridlock is more likely when Congress is confronting deficits than when it is ignoring them or facing surpluses.

When status quo policies are in the gridlock region and concessions are not forthcoming, Congress explores other options for overcoming gridlock. On a narrow yet important set of issues, the Senate has been willing to set aside the possibility of a filibuster, making policy change easier. One of these issues is the federal budget. As described in the next chapter, Congress adopted a budget reconciliation procedure in the early 1970s that requires only a majority in the House and Senate for passage. The procedure is complex, however; it places a number of limits on policy change, and has not been used regularly. The Senate also sets aside the filibuster on some foreign trade bills operating under "fast track" provisions (also known as "trade promotion authority"). To make it more likely for the President to successfully negotiate trade agreements, Congress will often agree in advance to vote them up-or-down by majority votes. Again, this is a way to overcome gridlock on important issues before Congress. But, as in any policy area, Senators desire change not for its own sake but only when policy can be moved in a favorable direction. Thus, when the President seems unlikely to advance proposals in their interests, Senators are reluctant to extend him fast track authority.

Occasionally, the steps needed to overcome gridlock involve not rule changes in the Senate, but rather the empowerment of actors outside the legislative branch. For example, unable to agree on which military bases to close at the end of the Cold War, Congress developed a bipartisan Base Realignment and Closing Commission to recommend a package of closings. Because it was politically balanced and perceived as making recommendations on legitimate grounds, the Commission's proposal was difficult to oppose in Congress. Congress has also relied upon outside commissions to make recommendations on politically charged or complex and uncertain policies like Social Security reform.

Such delegation of legislative powers to others is not new. Congress has long relied on executive and independent agencies to make rules and regulations. Especially when faced with uncertainty, legislators may wish to rely on the expertise of bureaucrats.[41] Formulating general guidelines for pharmaceutical approval, Congress relies on the Food and Drug Administration (FDA) to develop and implement the details. Many complexities of environmental policies are left to the Environmental Protection Agency (EPA). And so on across the alphabet soup of the federal bureaucracy. When these agencies are filled with experts wishing to carry out the will of Congress, this process runs fairly smoothly.

When Congress and the agencies are at odds, however, and especially when major policies are in the gridlock region, discretion to bureaucracies may be problematic for legislators. For example, Terry Moe and William Howell (1999) argue that, when Congress cannot act, the President will.[42] Through executive orders and administrative actions, the President may unilaterally set policy that Congress cannot change without a sufficient supermajority to override a presidential veto.[43] Of course, the President and agencies are limited by the level of legislative discretion, and Congress can influence agencies through budgets, oversight, and the like. But the point is a good one. Lack of policy action by Congress does not mean lack of policy change at all. Bureaucrats, Presidents, courts, state governments, and other policy players may step in to overcome or cope with the congressional gridlock.

Unilateral action by Presidents and delegation of legislative powers are limited in domestic policies by a fairly vigilant and active Congress. In foreign policy, however, congressional uncertainty, indecision, and gridlock is often resolved by ceding extensive policy control to the President. Aaron Wildavsky (1966) labeled this phenomenon "the two presidencies." Presidents exert much more control over foreign policy than over domestic policy. Nevertheless, the revolving gridlock theory remains relevant in both foreign and domestic policy areas. Foreign policies are often more uncertain and are subject to more presidential influence. But when presidential actions or exogenous shocks cause foreign affairs to be out of line with the preferences of supermajorities in the Senate and House, we will expect strong congressional action. Anticipating this, Presidents are constrained in their foreign policy activities.

Ultimately, public policy is shaped by many actors. Compromises may be struck to overcome gridlock. Procedures may be modified. And Congress may rely on others for help. But whether or not we see policy change through these various mechanisms always depends on the same factors. Which policies do members of Congress prefer? And do they have enough votes to bring about policy change? Absent strong support in Congress, gridlock remains.

Opposing Theories

To further clarify the theory we are setting forth, we have found it useful to contrast the revolving gridlock theory with two others that have been circulating in the media and academia for more than a decade. These theories have been used as assumptions in many works, but have not been fully addressed in any one work. The first is the "strong party theory," in which the control of Congress and the presidency by one party is expected to result in policy outcomes reflecting that party's ideal platform, whereas control of these two branches of government by opposing parties leads to gridlock. The second is the "compromise between branches theory," in which the Congress and the President strike a compromise between their ideal policy outcomes. According to this theory, a liberal Congress and a conservative President might agree on moderate policies, whereas a liberal President and a liberal Congress will certainly come to a (liberal) political compromise.

Those who argue that political parties play a strong role in Congress present different mechanisms through which parties might act. For example, Cox and McCubbins (1993) suggest that parties serve as legislative "cartels," advancing a common agenda and keeping members in line through rewards and sanctions. Aldrich (1995) and Rohde (1991) argue that parties are powerful only when certain conditions are met, such as when there are aligned preferences among members within each party and divergent preferences across parties. Legislative scholars have spent the past decade debating exactly when and why parties may be strong.[44]

The assumptions of the strong party theory underlie many arguments about divided and unified government. Either explicitly or implicitly, those who write about divided government believe that control of the executive and legislative branches by different parties has policy consequences.[45] Political scientists (Fiorina 1996; Jacobson 1990; Cox and Kernell 1991) have tended to be explicit on the causes of divided government and to be less explicit about the consequences. Broadly speaking, however, the consequences can be sorted into two kinds of claims: (1) divided government makes an already unwieldy constitutional system of government unworkable; and (2) divided government obscures responsibility.

Those who focus on the claim that divided government makes the system of governance unworkable are essentially arguing that divided government yields policy gridlock. Sundquist compares divided government unfavorably with a unified model of government that assumes an active President supported by cohesive legislative majorities. Essentially, divided government gives each branch of government incentives to undermine the actions of the other branch (Sundquist 1988, 629–630). Ginsburg and Shefter (1990) make a similar argument, claiming that in divided government, governing becomes posturing and decisions satisfy no one. Although scholars who fit into the gridlock mold tend to be general rather than specific about policy consequences, some have claimed specific effects. Lloyd Cutler, for example, claims: "In modern times high deficits have occurred only with divided government. . . . The correlation between unacceptably high deficits and divided government is much too exact to be a coincidence" (Cutler 1989, 391). McCubbins (1991, 83–111) corroborates this analysis, arguing that the high deficits between 1981 and 1987 were the result of party preferences and divided control of government. Alt and Lowry (1994) look for a connection between divided government and budget deficits in the states. McKenzie and Thornton

(1996, 157) agree with the general thrust of these arguments, claiming that divided government exacerbates the problems of dealing with deficits.

Those who claim that divided government diminishes electoral accountability argue that under divided control citizens cannot tell who is to blame; thus the meaning of electoral outcomes is rendered confusing (Fiorina 1996). This line of reasoning is so enmeshed in the normative argument about responsiveness and responsibility that sorting it out depends upon one's values. Thus we deal here only with the gridlock argument.

The major case against those who believe that divided government has policy consequences is made by David Mayhew in *Divided We Govern* (1991). In this work Mayhew argues that there is no relation between divided government and significant policy results; he further argues that there is no relation between divided government and congressional investigations of the executive branch.[46] Mayhew concludes by arguing among other things that divided government does not mean less coherence in individual laws, and that there is no evidence that those initially less well off are made worse off by divided government (Mayhew 1991, chap. 7). Mayhew's findings contradict those scholars who assume that, without a strong President and cohesive congressional majorities, policy gridlock ensues.[47] Mayhew, however, never describes the underlying model of government that would allow the passage of significant legislation even under Republican Presidents and Democratic legislatures.

Looking at the strong party theory in conjunction with the institutional constraints of the filibuster and veto in the revolving gridlock model yields a surprising result. Instead of bringing about an end to gridlock, strong parties actually *expand* the region in which gridlock occurs.[48] Imagine the Democratic and Republican Parties deciding what policy outcomes they would like. One would be rather liberal, the other rather conservative. If the status quo policy falls somewhere in between, a movement to the right would be halted by a Democratic filibuster (or a sustained veto from a Democratic President). A movement to the left would likewise be successfully filibustered by the Republicans. With each party having more than forty seats in the Senate, the strong party assumption not only expands the gridlock region, but it also predicts the *same* region regardless of the party of the President. The gridlock region for strong parties stretches from one party's ideal policy point to the other's. Thus if we observe gridlock under George H. Bush, we should expect the same gridlock under Bill Clinton and George W. Bush.[49]

In 1992, the media and the Clinton campaign's rhetoric led the public to believe that Democratic control of the Congress and the presidency would end the policy gridlock of twelve years of Republican rule. Similar thoughts are entertained about unified Republican control today. There are two main problems with such an argument. The first is that this strong party model ignores the institutional constraints of the filibuster and the veto. When these constraints are included, the gridlock region actually expands out to the party ideal policies (and not just to the ideal policies of party moderates), leading to the likelihood of even more gridlock than under the weak party assumption that we have used. (Such an argument leads many Republicans to the further belief that they need sixty Republicans in the Senate to overcome Democratic filibusters.)

But the second problem with this theory is more dramatic: political parties in the United States are not necessarily strong.[50] Members often defect from their parties when it is in their interest to do so. Republican filibusters are broken when the policy under debate is made conservative enough to make vote switching favorable for the most liberal Republicans. Indeed, in the minimum wage example, Senator Chafee abandoned the Republican filibuster attempt in 1988. Presidents are often forced to look for votes from the other party, as Reagan did with southern Democrats, as Bush did with the 1990 budget deal, and as Clinton did with the North American Free Trade Agreement (NAFTA). When the House sustained President Bush's veto of the minimum wage increase, the President lost twenty of the most liberal Republicans, but gained twenty-eight Democrats, twenty-five of them southerners. It is our contention that much of the appearance of party strength comes in the alignment of preferences: conservatives are typically Republicans and liberals are typically Democrats. Only where party interests are in conflict with personal preferences would we expect to see a break with the party; such breaks, however, are commonplace. Those who follow their party instead of constituent preferences will find themselves out of step with their districts and out of office soon thereafter.[51] The revolving gridlock theory relies on legislators' preferences and constraining institutions to explain policy gridlock and the positioning of bills that do pass.[52] The strong party theory is much less explicit about the role of institutions, and has been brought into question by Mayhew and others.

Having discussed the strong party theory, we turn to a comparison of the revolving gridlock theory with the compromise between branches theory. This theory is also implicit in many works, but explicit in few; it supposes that policy-making power rests with both the President and Congress. The policy outcome will therefore be somewhere between the ideal policy of the President and the ideal policy of Congress; where in this region it will fall depends on the relative strengths of Congress and the President during the period in which policy is being formulated. If a President is strong and popular, the theory argues, he can publicize his ideal policy and gain concessions from Congress. If weak, he will be forced to the sidelines, as Congress works through the details. This theory of compromise between the branches of government is applied regardless of the party affiliations of the President and the majority in Congress, thus differentiating it from the strong party theory.

The theory's limitations are to be found in the question of where this presidential power arises in the legislative arena. As noted above, a number of claims have been put forth in the literature. Some scholars claim that presidential power is the power to persuade (Neustadt 1960). According to this argument, the President can try to lead members of Congress to his point of view. When legislators are reluctant to come around to his line of thinking, the President can "go public" on the issue, hoping that constituents will persuade legislators that it is in their best interest to go along with the President (Kernell 1993). Other authors argue that presidential power originates in veto power (Rohde 1991, Cameron 2000). In essence, a President can claim that he will veto any bill that does not meet his requirements, as Clinton did with universal coverage for health care. But this argument ignores credibility concerns; if Clinton had received a health care bill covering *most* Americans, would he have vetoed it, settling for no bill over a bill that came close to what he wanted? Or, should Congress take a veto threat by George W. Bush seriously after years without vetoing anything? Still other scholars synthesize these presidential powers. Jones (1994), for example, emphasizes a President's strategic position as it relates to public popularity, electoral mandates, and the lawmaking sequence.

The revolving gridlock theory gives the President the power to influence legislators' preferences by persuasion or by going public. It also gives the President the crucial veto power. But it does not assume that he will act in any way other than in his own interest. When a bill that has passed through Congress is closer to the President's preference than the status quo policy, he will generally sign it; when it is further, he will veto it. The result of the revolving gridlock theory presented in this chapter is not simply a compromise between Congress and the President, but a constrained policy within the Congress, with the President doing what he can to influence policy around the edges. Often, due to institutional constraints, a policy outcome is more conservative (or more liberal) than both the median member of Congress and the President would prefer; but it is the best outcome they can get, so they agree to it.

The revolving gridlock theory is a significant advancement over these prior theories, explaining executive–legislative relations in a system of relatively weak parties in a way that is unique and compelling. The theory assumes that legislators in the House and Senate will attempt to move policy toward their preferred outcomes. They are constrained in doing so by supermajority institutions. Particular members of Congress in key positions at the edges of the gridlock region enforce these constraints through support of filibusters and vetoes. Status quo policies in this region cannot be changed. Actions taken under uncertain conditions as well as exogenous shocks to the legislative system can knock policies out of the gridlock region. Congress will be able to bring these policies back inside the region only so far as is possible to keep the pivotal members from voting down cloture or sustaining a veto. Attempts to make more extreme policy shifts will be killed by filibusters and vetoes. This theory is an improvement on previous work in the field. It looks at legislators' preferences rather than simply at their partisan affiliations. It takes into account the constraining institutions ignored by the strong party theory. And it more clearly defines the nature of the compromise between members of Congress and the President.

The theory explains minimum wage policy formation quite capably. Throughout the 1980s, the minimum wage was losing purchasing power, causing the $3.35 level to fall out of line with the preferences of most members of Congress. This is an example of an *exogenous shock* (here, inflation) pushing a status quo policy outside the gridlock region. When the issue was raised in 1988, it was first used more as a political tool than as a target for policy change. The Democrats used policy proposals to call Bush's "bluff" on minimum wage policy, whereas the Republicans used the issue as an attempt to secure federal judicial positions. No bill was passed in 1988 because the situation was *uncertain* so close to the election. When would the economic downside to a wage hike come into effect? Would interest groups play a large role in the elections as a result of this issue? Would one side or the other be in a better position in the next session due to the election results? Congress abandoned the issue. In 1989 the federal government addressed the minimum wage once again, this time with less uncertainty. Bush proposed a wage of $4.25 an hour, and the Democratic leadership countered with $4.55. Either wage level was preferred by the vast majority to the current $3.35 wage. But the President was able to use the veto and his influence to win a victory for his minimum wage plan. As such, he appeared strong in his veto power and secured nearly the lowest wage politically possible. The revolving gridlock theory is clear as to why this policy outcome occurred. The constraint was the veto pivot to which Bush appealed with his veto of the higher wage. By issuing an alternative policy favorable to the veto-sustaining minority, the President was able to win his showdown with the Congress, securing the $4.25 wage in late 1989.

In 1996, President Clinton took his opportunity to raise the minimum wage further. The constraint on his wage hike was the filibuster in the Senate instead of the more constraining veto pivot of conservative Presidents. Despite Republican control of the House and Senate, an increase to $5.15 passed. Moderate Republicans, fearing electoral repercussions, voted with Democrats for this move in a liberal direction. Here, once again, a focus on individual preferences, electoral pressures, and supermajority institutions helps explain policy change.

Since the unified Democratic control of the early 1990s, journalists and academics have taken greater notice of the policy implications of the supermajority institutions of the filibuster and the veto. For example, in the conclusion of their article about partisanship in Congress, Cooper and Young (1997, 269) note:

> In the House a veto requires not merely 218 votes to overcome (if all members vote) but 291, and in the Senate 67 votes are required (if all members vote) not merely 51. These are very difficult levels to obtain in partisan Congresses unless majority margins are extremely high. Moreover, in the Senate, practice with respect to the filibuster has changed so that the 60 votes required to impose cloture are also required to win any major policy battle. As a result, the passage of major legislation still requires forms of behavior and negotiation that are coalitional, but in a context in which the character of party divisions provides poor incentives for such behavior. The public's disgust with paralysis may spur action when elections approach, but such a response is only the flip side of the political maneuvering to gain electoral advantage that dominates policy making and usually stymies action.

The revolving gridlock theory expands upon and clarifies this argument, noting specifics of how these supermajority institutions, along with elections, budget constraints, and members' policy preferences, led to specific policy outcomes or gridlock over the last quarter century.

In the next chapters we will take a broader policy view, attempting to explain many of the legislative outcomes of the periods of divided and unified government from Reagan's first term, through unified Democratic government following Clinton's election, through the 1994 capture of Congress by the Republicans, through recent unified Republican governance, all using the revolving gridlock theory. In Chapter 3, we will take an extensive look at the budget process and how budget policies have changed since 1980. The conservative members of Congress who came in with Reagan in 1981 acted as an exogenous shock, allowing previously entrenched policies to be changed. Even still, the policies enacted were determined by those near the middle of the political spectrum. As such, Reagan needed to gain the support of conservative Democrats. He used this support to enact a huge tax break and to peg tax rates to inflation. Politics of the 1980s and 1990s then revolved around the need to rein in budget deficits. These pressures resulted in divisive coalitions of winners and losers, making gridlock even harder to overcome. After a short period of surpluses at the end of the century, we have returned to deficit politics, lowering the prospects of overcoming gridlock in the future.

As we will highlight in the next chapter, dramatic budget deficits combine with supermajoritarian institutions to further policy gridlock in four ways. First, as mentioned above, pivotal members of Congress must vote with the majority to secure policy change. These votes are typically gained either through adjusting the policy at hand toward these legislators' preferred outcomes or by guaranteeing support for these members on other bills, typically by providing them with pork in budget bills. With the budget wells running dry with the significant deficits of recent years, however, those seeking policy change found the latter option for gaining the pivotal members' support to be no longer available. As such, compromises that could be forged only through budgetary concessions now fell apart. Second, deficits led Congress to link together most budgetary decisions. Increases in one program area needed to be offset by decreases elsewhere or by increases in taxes. As can be imagined, this had a further impact in terms of policy gridlock. Once a supermajority coalition was established in support of a legislative proposal with budgetary implications, bill proponents had to convince coalition members to support tax increases or program cuts elsewhere. This was a significant enough constraint to lead to inaction on issues in which a majority or supermajority agreed that change was necessary. Third, the increasing difficulty and importance of budgetary decisions gave members of Congress even less time to deal with nonbudgetary issues. Without the necessary time to secure supermajorities or to resolve uncertainties, other issues fell into gridlock as well. Finally, the complexity of budget legislation in an era of omnibus budget bills and huge reconciliation packages led to further confusion, frustration, and gridlock.

Clearly the budget constraints on Congress combined with electoral and institutional constraints to bring about further policy gridlock. It is to these budgetary issues that we turn next.

Notes

1. The comments, quotations, and details presented in the italicized sections throughout this chapter are drawn from various public sources.

2. While our work emphasizes the preferences of members of Congress and the President, it does not emphasize the *intensity* of these preferences. This is largely due to our focus on voting institutions within Congress that give everyone equal say. However, as Hall (1996) points out, members of Congress feel more strongly about some issues than others, leading them to different degrees of participation in committees, subcommittees, and in the brokering of deals over final legislative decisions. As we note below, the intensity of a legislator's preferences may play a role in whether others may try to influence that legislator's vote, as well as in what final bargain may be reached among the House, Senate, and the President within the limited range of possible outcomes.

3. Much of the theory presented in this chapter is introduced and analyzed formally in Keith Krehbiel's "Institutional and Partisan Sources of Gridlock: A Theory of Divided and Unified Government" (1996). Krehbiel's *Pivotal Politics: A Theory of U.S. Lawmaking* (1998) includes a relatively nontechnical overview of the "pivotal politics theory" and subjects the theory to a wide range of empirical tests on legislative action that occurred throughout the postwar period. As a general matter, we regard his studies and ours to be complementary with respect to the tests, analyses, and interpretations. Indeed, these works have a common ancestor in Brady, Krehbiel, and Volden (1994). Throughout this chapter we note differences between Krehbiel's formal analysis and our portrayal with regard to uncertainty, exogenous shocks, and bargaining between the President and Congress over final outcomes. In this work we use the term "revolving gridlock theory," but we also find Krehbiel's tag, "pivotal politics theory," accurate and appropriate.

4. Political scientists have used spatial models widely since Anthony Downs's *An Economic Theory of Democracy* (1957) and Duncan Black's *The Theory of Committees and Elections* (1958). Single-dimensional voting with a majority rule was found to lead to median voter outcomes. However, without such a limitation to a single dimension, even imposing a particular voting rule often led to indeterminate outcomes (see Arrow 1951; Black and Newing 1951; Plott 1967). The chaos result formalized by McKelvey (1976) indicated that in all but a few special cases a series of proposals could be developed to lead from any given policy status quo to any other policy in the choice space. This result troubled formal theorists more than it troubled most political scientists who, without empirical support for this "policy cycling" result, discounted the value of such spatial models. The response to this "anything can happen" view was the reassurance that there are political structures in place that keep such ludicrous results from happening. Kenneth Shepsle's "Institutional Arrangements and Equilibrium in Multi-dimensional Voting Models" (1979) led to an argument about which structures or institutions are relevant in leading to various outcomes. In particular, do legislative committees with their proposal powers lead to agendas that provide them with beneficial outcomes? This article set off a debate on the power of committees, as well as on

which institutions lead to the so-called "structure-induced equilibria." Major ground-work for further study of politics through spatial models was made by Romer and Rosenthal (1978) with regard to the control of legislative agendas, by Baron and Fere-john (1989) with regard to the sequencing of proposals leading to political bargains, and by Gilligan and Krehbiel (1987, 1990) with regard to the role of information in leg-islative decisions. For an excellent review of these advancements through the 1980s, see Krehbiel (1988). Our view is that, in the modification of spatial models in political sci-ence over the past few decades, some simple advancements and applications have been overlooked. In particular, even restricting the model to a single dimension, much can be gained by looking at the institutional structures that require supermajorities to pass legislation. See Krehbiel (1998, chaps. 7, 8) for an excellent analysis of how the single-dimensional pivotal politics theory works in the face of empirical findings regarding agenda setting, partisanship, uncertainty, and presidential influence.

5. Poole and Rosenthal (1991a, 1997) provide an excellent compilation of voting in Congress and thus legislator preferences.

6. Binder and Smith (1996) provide the most comprehensive analysis of fili-busters to date. For more information on the rise of the filibuster and other changes leading to a more individualistic and competitive Senate, see Davidson (1985) and Sinclair (1989).

7. Krehbiel and Rivers (1988) use such an alignment in their analysis of commit-tee positions and proposals with regard to minimum wage. Volden (1998) also relies on this alignment to establish the role of sophisticated voting in the face of presiden-tial vetoes.

8. Groseclose and McCarty (2001) illustrate how Presidents may face public blame for vetoing popular measures. Cameron's (2000) analysis thoroughly examines the costs and benefits of the President's veto bargaining powers.

9. For a similar argument of how the press portrayed the economy in 1992 and how it led to Bush's defeat, see Hetherington (1996).

10. Some theories would suggest that members of both houses err on the side of willingness to use blocking tactics in order to avoid blame, on the assumption that avoiding blame is more important than taking credit. See, for example, Weaver (1986) and Arnold (1990). We raise some of these concerns below in our discussion of uncertainty.

11. What is important to us here is the near indifference of this pivotal legislator to the proposed policy change. This indifference may make this pivotal individual the tar-get of persuasion to either cement the deal or sabotage it. Although we do not explore the matter of legislator preference intensity here, in a similar fashion, legislators who have a low intensity of preferences (for whom the issue at hand is not very salient) might also be easily persuaded to vote for or against the legislation. For more on legis-lator preference intensity and the resultant participation decisions, see Hall (1996).

12. Note that policies in the region between Q and F are outside the gridlock re-gion, and thus would be adjusted further by the Senate.

13. This result is different from that derived by Krehbiel (1996). Krehbiel limits the interaction to a single veto and override attempt (and likewise a single filibustering

effort). In actuality, legislation that is vetoed may be attempted again in a revised form. We do not derive results from a formal game of this nature here, but simply note that the ensuing action is a form of bargaining in which the resultant outcome is in the range between the main actors' ideal points and is dependent on their bargaining strengths. Additionally, if the President or congressional committee makes a proposal in this range under a closed rule, it will be accepted by the pivotal members who prefer the proposal to the status quo; while under an open rule, the median member and concurring majority will push policy toward the median (although the policy is still constrained by Q'). As such, our finding is not inconsistent with the seminal agenda-setting work of Romer and Rosenthal (1978).

14. The intensity of preferences may play a role in influencing the patience of the actors who participate in the bargaining (Hall 1996) and what final outcome is reached.

15. The minimum wage increases from left to right on the diagram. Therefore the figure does not fit the traditional left-to-right spectrum, in which conservatives are positioned on the right and liberals on the left. Here, the position of Bush and the conservatives is on the left, favoring a lower minimum wage. We hope that this arrangement is less confusing than the inverse, with dollar amounts decreasing from left to right.

16. This assumption is justifiable in hindsight, based on voting behavior, but may have been a bit trickier to judge at the time. Nevertheless, Democratic leaders had proposed a $4.65 minimum wage, claiming that they could collect enough votes to override a veto. This would be the case with a veto pivot at $4.00, where that legislator would be indifferent to whether the minimum wage were 65 cents higher or 65 cents lower. Volden (1998) explores the positions of legislators (and the possibility of their voting strategically) with regard to the 1989 minimum wage vote, corroborating the values set forth in this chapter as quite accurate in representing legislator preferences.

17. Gilmour (1995) notes conditions under which Congress might provoke vetoes or otherwise promote stalemate through strategic actions.

18. On legislation that cannot be filibustered in the Senate, the gridlock region in the Senate becomes like that in the House, stretching from the median to the veto pivot. Such legislation includes budget reconciliation as well as trade bills set on the "fast track." This smaller gridlock region acts as less of a constraint to policy change, thus allowing for more policy action and limiting the power of a minority to stop legislation. While the lack of a filibuster threat on such legislation affects the size and shape of the gridlock region, it does not affect the overall theory with regard to this region. Status quo policies in the gridlock region cannot be changed. Those outside of the region will be brought in, with limitations similar to those seen in Figure 2.3. The theory surrounding this smaller gridlock region will be clarified further in the next chapter, which attempts to explain the major budget changes that have passed Congress since 1980.

19. Note that Krehbiel's work (1996) does not contain uncertainty. Nor do we introduce uncertainty in a formal modeling sense here. Our point is that uncertainty and the complexity of forming legislation may lead to further policy gridlock under certain conditions. This thesis is explored in greater detail in later chapters.

20. Where this uncertainty cannot be suitably resolved, legislators might try blame-avoidance tactics. See Weaver (1986, 1988), and Arnold (1990).

21. For an analysis of the information provided by committees and the surrounding incentives to gaining expertise, see Krehbiel (1991).

22. Reported in the *New York Times*, July 6, 1988.

23. For more on the pressures surrounding this decision, see the 1988 *Congressional Quarterly Almanac*, 255.

24. Reported in the *New York Times*, December 8, 1978.

25. These decisions are part of the strategic choice process followed by politicians with regard to elections. See Jacobson and Kernell (1982); Jacobson (1983) and (1989); and Rosenstone and Hansen (1993).

26. As reported in the *New York Times*, September 19, 1988, members of Congress were being very careful about their positions on minimum wage.

27. Stopping policy change does not necessarily mean that no bill will be passed. For political reasons, legislators could pass a "hollow" bill, one that does not change policy to any great degree.

28. See Brady (1988).

29. See Erikson (1976); Fiorina (1991b); Jacobson (1991); Ansolabehere, Brady, and Fiorina (1992); and Alford and Brady (1993).

30. Our view is not inconsistent with that held by Alesina and Rosenthal (1989, 1995) who argue that voters at the margins will choose liberal Democrats to counter conservative Republicans. Fiorina (1991a, 1996) presents the case that voters may want to elect politicians who will provide a "check" on other politicians. As a baseline against which voters might decide to temper policy outcomes, voters often perceive particular politicians as espousing particular issues or viewpoints. Jacobson (1990) and Petrocik (1991) present a form of "issue ownership" argument. Jacobson argues for the public perception that Democrats might better address local problems and Republicans national issues. Petrocik argues that each of the parties owns a set of issues, with Republicans seen as preserving low taxes and pursuing prosperity and Democrats seen as espousing kindness through social spending.

31. The "coattails" effect refers to the election of other members of the President's party to their respective offices due to a surge of presidential supporters going to the polls. See Ferejohn and Calvert (1984).

32. See Erikson (1988), but also note that the decline in coattails and the success of the President's party in midterm elections recently may suggest less dramatic shifts in the gridlock region in the future.

33. See Brody (1991) for views on the role of the "honeymoon" in assessing a President.

34. Rivers and Rose (1985) discuss how the size of a President's program affects its likelihood of success.

35. Weaver (1988) attempts to explain conditions under which Congress indexes programs to inflation, leading to "automatic government" without the need to continually deal with the exogenous shocks of inflation.

36. Hibbing and Theiss-Morse (1995) explore this public dissatisfaction with Congress, finding that the actions and activities of politicians disgust the public equally regardless of the political party. Politicians of both parties are seen as being identical in

the types of actions they take, regardless of the distinctions they attempt to make on particular policy issues. This is consistent with our belief that politicians act on their own preferences, using the institutions of government to their best advantage. Often such behavior is to the best advantage of their constituents as well, and, when this is perceived by the public, the politicians are reelected.

37. Important theoretical and empirical work on this issue has been advanced by Samuel Kernell (1993) and by Brandice Canes-Wrone (2001).

38. Neustadt (1960) has long argued that the president's main power in the legislative arena is the "power to persuade."

39. The effectiveness of using presidential popularity to aid members of Congress is brought into question by Collier and Sullivan (1995).

40. Volden (1998) argues that this bargaining process is complex, often leading to members of Congress voting against their immediate preferences in what is referred to as a "sophisticated vote."

41. See Epstein and O'Halloran (1999) for an excellent theoretical and empirical treatment of congressional delegation to bureaucracies. Volden (2002) examines discretion decisions in light of the executive veto.

42. Howell (2003) extends this argument in a more complete treatment.

43. Such an argument is consistent with Deering and Maltzman's (1999) conception of executive orders.

44. Some of the more interesting twists and turns in this debate include articles by Krehbiel (1999); Snyder and Groseclose (2000); and McCarty, Poole, and Rosenthal (2001). Chiou and Rothenberg (2003) argue that party and leadership roles explain legislative choices better than do pivotal politics gridlock models. Volden and Bergman (2005) tie the party strength debate to the revolving gridlock theory presented here.

45. See Fiorina (1996) for an excellent summary of the literature pertaining to divided government.

46. Mayhew's study was greeted with much skepticism and controversy. For major contributions to this debate, see Coleman (1999); Edwards, Barrett, and Peake (1997); and Howell et al. (2000).

47. James Pfiffner (in Thurber 1991) argues that unified governance with strong parties is necessary for directional coherence of legislation.

48. For further details and a formal proof of this finding, see Krehbiel (1996).

49. Some views of the strong party assumption consider only a strong majority party. This would still lead to an expansion of the gridlock region when compared to our weak party assumption of individual preferences mattering more than the party preferences.

50. It is not our intention here to become enmeshed in the debate about how strong or weak political parties are. It is clear to us that, as Cox and McCubbins (1993) suggest, parties can use various powers to gain mutually beneficial compromises. We also recognize, as Krehbiel (1993) does, that parties are limited in their abilities and that a strict test of party strength is a difficult endeavor. Our view of political parties in the United States today is that party leaders and the President can influence the preferences of members of Congress, but cannot dictate how they will vote. Party members also

have other interests, mainly reelection. We believe that parties are weaker than they once were (for a view on parties at a time when they were stronger, see Brady and Epstein 1997). We also see a strong link between preferences and party, with conservatives tending to be Republicans and liberals tending to be Democrats. (In Krehbiel's view this is exactly what parties are—aggregated preferences.) In some ways our view is not unlike that found in the political science literature of the 1960s and 1970s. Following E. E. Schattschneider's responsible party thesis (1942, APSA 1950), David Truman's work (1959) reversed the strong party notion by focusing on congressional parties as blocs of voters with party leaders near the party's center. We speak of preferences where Truman, as well as Burns (1963), focused on blocs or wings, but their view of parties as aggregates of different views is not unlike our own.

51. See Canes-Wrone, Brady, and Cogan (2002) for an empirical test of this argument, and Canes-Wrone, Rabinovich, and Volden (2005) for an examination of individual members' responsiveness to electoral and party pressures over time.

52. In this way, our work complements that of John Gilmour (1995), who argues that the need to satisfy constituents (preferences) often leads to pursuit and avoidance of ideas and proposals, with politicians provoking vetoes (supermajority institutions) and taking positions that cause greater difficulty in the negotiations necessary to reach compromise (gridlock).

3

Revolving Gridlock
and Budgetary Politics

Making public policy in the United States is obviously a complex business. The opinions of voters and interest groups, institutions like the separation of powers and federalism, and changing economic and world events shape the making of public policy. In this book we simplify this elaborate, complicated process by proposing that one can identify the basic location of public policy if one knows the preferences of members of Congress, the location of the status quo policy, supermajority institutional conditions, and the position of the newly proposed policy (often the President's proposal). One of our major goals is to explain why a unified government such as Bill Clinton's or George W. Bush's doesn't end gridlock. We define "gridlock" as a situation in which the status quo cannot be changed despite majority support in the country or the Congress for a specific policy change. If the status quo policy point is not far out of line with the preferences of moderate members of Congress, then we predict that, regardless of unified or divided government, policy will not shift dramatically. Presidents who propose policies to the left or right of the "gridlock region" will see their policies either fail or be modified to accommodate the preferences of moderate Representatives and Senators. In our view the major factors that account for policy shifts are mainly electoral. In other words, if an election results in a shift of member preferences to the right or left, then policy may shift right or left accordingly.

Elections are complex events in which voters choose between candidates who normally differ in personal characteristics, party identification, and policy preferences. Voters' choices are affected by domestic and global events, and in turn electoral results change policy. Thus in the early 1960s, when African Americans campaigned for equal justice and Lyndon Johnson buried Barry Goldwater in the 1964 election, policy on civil rights began to change. Likewise during the late 1970s, when income, property, and state taxes increased dramatically, voters signaled a desire to reduce taxation; in the early 1980s, major changes in tax policy resulted. Each of these changes in policy brings about both a new policy status quo and a new set of problems. The civil rights movement raised the issue of compensatory justice and gave rise to affirmative action policies; affirmative action has led to a new set of policy concerns.[1] Likewise tax cuts in the 1980s generated economic effects that led to new problems and solutions for the 1990s.

In an important sense, current policy (the status quo) is normally within the gridlock region and, as the civil rights and tax examples indicate, those regions can shift left or right or remain stable depending upon the preferences of members of Congress. Given the importance of the federal budget in national politics today, we believe that gridlock regions and congressional coalitions cannot be explained without an adequate understanding of the history of budgetary politics. This is essentially a story of increases in entitlement spending, shifts in the tax burden, and largely defense-related external events that have occurred since the end of World War II. Because these factors are important to our argument, we devote this chapter to tracing budget policy and politics over the past half century. Postwar policies explain subsequent politics; those politics explain the next wave of policies; and so on. Without an understanding of the budget policies and processes of the 1970s, one cannot adequately explain policy gridlock in the 1980s. Without understanding the role of deficits in the 1980s and 1990s, today's politics and policy choices would remain a mystery.

In this chapter we explain the role of budget politics in the revolving gridlock theory. We begin by presenting an overview of the federal budget, noting how broad categories of spending and taxing have changed over time. We then discuss the budget process that led to these outcomes. We trace budget politics from classic consensus budgeting through the inflation of the 1970s, from the deficit politics in the 1980s and 1990s through the subsequent swings of surpluses and deficits that lead us ultimately to an assessment of the future. By the end of this journey, a clear picture will emerge of the ties between the new budgetary politics and the revolving gridlock theory presented in the previous chapter.

Taxing and Spending in Historical Context

The taxing and spending decisions of today are not made in a vacuum. They are influenced by past policies, by preferences, and by institutions. Some of the most important restrictions on budgetary changes today have their origins in these conditions as faced by Congress and the President in the early 1980s and in their decisions to, among other things, cut income taxes and peg them to inflation. Just as decisions today do not occur in a political vacuum, so too is it necessary to place the decisions made in the 1980s and afterward in their proper context.

To understand the constraints that the budget places on congressional politics and policymaking, we need to examine how large categories of the federal budget have changed over time.[2] Table 3.1 highlights spending changes for the period from 1958 to 2003. And Table 3.2 shows the taxation side of the equation.

Throughout this entire period, overall national spending ranged between about 19 and 21 percent of the country's overall economic output, measured by the gross domestic product (GDP). This steadiness masks dramatic changes across budget

TABLE 3.1 Budget Expenditures 1958–2003 (as percentage of GDP)

Major Categories	1958	1968	1978	1988	1998	2003
National Defense	10.2%	9.4%	4.7%	5.8%	3.1%	3.7%
Human Resources	4.8	6.8	10.9	10.6	12.0	13.1
Net Interest on Debt	1.2	1.3	1.6	3.0	2.8	1.4
Other	2.5	3.0	3.5	1.8	1.3	1.7
Total	18.7	20.5	20.7	21.2	19.2	19.9

Sources: U.S. Government Printing Office, 2004; Congressional Budget Office, 2005.

TABLE 3.2 Budget Revenues 1963–2003 (as percentage of GDP)

Major Categories	1963	1968	1978	1988	1998	2003
Individual Income	7.9%	7.9%	8.2%	8.0%	9.6%	7.3%
Corporate Income	3.6	3.3	2.7	1.9	2.2	1.2
Social Insurance	3.3	3.9	5.5	6.7	6.6	6.6
Other	3.0	2.5	1.6	1.5	1.6	1.3
Total	17.8	17.6	18.0	18.1	20.0	16.4

Sources: Congressional Budget Office, 2005.

categories. In 1958, with the end of World War II giving way to the Cold War, national defense accounted for 10.2 percent of GDP. This was more than half of the federal budget, dwarfing other major categories like human resources (4.8 percent of GDP), and net interest on the debt (1.2 percent of GDP). Two decades later, this situation had largely reversed, with defense spending under 5 percent of GDP and human resources accounting for over 10 percent. Defense spending rose in the 1980s, before the country enjoyed the "peace dividend" that came with the end of the Cold War. Growth in human resources spending was slowed to about that of the country's economic growth rate throughout the 1980s, but then continued its rise once more.

Overall national taxation also remained fairly steady, with the federal government taking in more than 16 and less than 20 percent of GDP. Here again, variance occurs in the subcategories. Individual income taxes make up about half of the federal government's revenue. They usually amount to about 8 percent of GDP, although they rose to 9.3 percent in 1981 and to 10.3 percent in 2000, only to be cut back through popular proposals by Republican Presidents.[3] Corporate income taxes as a percent of GDP have fallen fairly steadily over the past forty years. Payroll taxes for social insurance purposes doubled as a percentage of GDP between 1963 and 1988 before leveling off at 6.6 percent.

Four broad points are crucial to understanding the numbers and how they relate to budgetary politics. First, deficits are the rule in national budgeting, rather than the exception. The national government, on average, spends about 20 percent of GDP while taking in about 18 percent. Such a two-percent gap would be the equivalent of an over $200 billion yearly budget deficit in today's $11 trillion economy. Over the past forty years, the national government has been in surplus only a handful of times—in 1969 and in 1998–2001.

Second, the rise in expenditures for human resources since 1958 was largely the result of Social Security and the entitlement programs enacted in the 1965–1968 and 1969–1975 periods. The 1958 figure for human resources (4.8 percent of GDP) mainly represented programs enacted during Franklin Roosevelt's New Deal. The last New Deal entitlements were enacted in 1935 (unemployment compensation, Aid to Families with Dependent Children, and Social Security). The only entitlement program enacted from 1935 through 1964 was the Social Security Disability Insurance Act of 1956. Thus in 1961, John Kennedy's first year as President, less than 6 percent of GDP was spent on human resources (about 30 percent of the federal budget).

Beginning with Johnson's Great Society and proceeding through the Nixon years, a spate of entitlement programs was passed. Table 3.3 gives a list of these programs. We divide the programs into two eras mainly for political reasons. The Great Society programs were passed largely by a Democratic majority, whereas the 1969–1975 programs were passed by a bipartisan majority both in Congress and across institutions—specifically, a Republican President and a Democratic Congress. In terms of cost, the two major programs are Medicare and Medicaid. These programs grow as the population ages and the number of eligible recipients increases. In 1970, for example, five years after Medicare was originated, the federal government spent $13.8 billion on the program (all figures in terms of real 2005 dollars). By 1981, Ronald Reagan's first year as President, Medicare expenditures had grown to $84.7 billion and they were estimated to rise to $181.2 billion by 1990. The increase from 1970 to 1980 was by a factor of greater than five. It is easy to see how the growth of these entitlements increased the proportion of the budget and the GDP devoted to human resources, which accounted for 25 percent of the budget and 4.8 percent of GDP in 1946, but 53 percent of the budget and 10.9 percent of GDP in 1978. This context is especially important beginning in the next chapter, when we explore revolving gridlock at the start of the Reagan administration.

Third, as entitlement spending rose, national defense spending declined. It is perhaps surprising to see how dramatically defense spending as a percentage of GDP declined during the 1970s, especially given the continuance of the Cold War. This should be seen in the context, however, of spending on the Korean War in the 1950s and the Vietnam War in the 1960s and early 1970s. Nevertheless, cuts in defense expenditures, coupled with continued concern about the Soviet Union, led to public outcry for a return to a stronger foreign policy posture. Arguing that President Carter was not adequately heeding that call, Ronald Reagan campaigned successfully on building a stronger defense.

Defense spending was increased to about 6 percent of GDP early in Reagan's first term, and it remained near that level until the collapse of the Soviet Union. Following the end of the Cold War, the defense budget was cut in half as a percentage of

TABLE 3.3   Major New Entitlements (1964–1975)[1]

Program	Year	Public Law
Food Stamps[2]	1964	PL88-525
Medicare	1965	PL89-97
Medicaid	1965	PL89-97
Guaranteed Student Loans	1965	PL89-329
Child Nutrition Programs[3]	1966	PL89-642
Social Services Block Grant[4]	1967	
Black Lung Benefits	1969	PL91-173
General Revenue Sharing	1972	PL92-512
Supplemental Security Income[5]	1972	PL92-603
Pension Benefits Guarantee	1974	PL93-406
Child Support Enforcement	1975	PL93-647
Earned Income Tax Credit	1975	PL94-164

[1]*Source:* Cogan (1997).

[2]Prior to 1964, the program operated under an Executive Order issued by President Kennedy in 1961.

[3]The main nutrition program, the National School Lunch program, was created in 1946. The 1966 law authorized an open-ended appropriations and transformed the program into a mandatory program.

[4]In 1956, state social services expenditures for welfare recipients became eligible for federal matching funds. In 1967, states were required to establish a single organizational unit for administering social services, and the federal social services program was formally separated from the cash assistance welfare program. In 1975, the Social Services Block Grant program was formally established by the enactment of Title XX.

[5]The SSI program replaced the Federal Grants to States for old-age assistance and for the permanently disabled.

GDP before rising again following the terrorist attacks in 2001. This peace dividend was sizable enough to offset human resources spending growth, putting a balanced budget in sight by the end of the 1990s.

Fourth and finally, it is important to note that, just like the budget constraints evident in defense and entitlement spending, there are limits to what policies are deemed acceptable for taxation. Here again, broad historical context is important. In the 1930s individual income taxes were about 1 percent of GDP and corporate taxes averaged about 1.5 percent of GDP. The need to finance World War II drove income taxes up to over 8 percent of GDP and corporate taxes to over 7 percent, and, in spite of the resumption of a peacetime budget in 1945, income taxes never fell back below 5.9 percent of GDP. After the Korean War income taxes were fairly stable, at about 8 percent of GDP until the late 1970s. This overall stability in the rate of income taxes masks important changes, however.

In the 1950s and 1960s, state and local taxes grew; and payroll taxes for Social Security and Medicare continued to rise through the 1960s and 1970s. These increases were somewhat offset by declining revenues elsewhere in the federal budget. Excise taxes went down as a percentage of GDP largely due to two factors: the tax act of 1965, which cut excise taxes, and inflation, which caused them to erode. Corporate income taxes also fell during this time period; corporate profits as a percentage of GDP fell and taxes fell correspondingly, and rates for deductible interest rose.

The changes in the *mix* of taxation rather than the level is what is important for understanding the "tax revolt" of the late 1970s. During the years following World War II, "excluded income" (such as mortgage interest payments and employer contributions to health and pension plans) grew. Itemized deductions on tax forms also increased during this period, from about 4 percent to over 9 percent of gross income. By far, however, the most dramatic change was not the increase in exclusions but rather the decline of the personal exemption. In combination, these factors brought about great changes in *who* was taxed. In 1948, in all taxpayer filing categories, 46.8 percent of all income was exempt from taxation. In 1981, prior to the Reagan cuts, taxpayers with four dependents were only able to exclude 13.3 percent of their income. Increases such as these, plus Social Security tax increases, meant that by the mid–1970s the working poor and middle-class families were paying higher rates.

Appealing to these groups, Reagan was able to forge a coalition of Republicans and southern Democrats who would cut income taxes across the board. Income taxes were kept low (although still above historic standards as a percentage of GDP) through Reagan veto threats in the 1980s. But when the public turned its attention away from taxes to the growing budget deficits, the Democrats in Congress joined with President George H. Bush and then President Clinton in raising rates once again.

While the burden of income taxes in 2000 was no longer nearly as onerous on the working poor as it had been in 1980, income taxes at 10.3 percent of GDP were politically unacceptable, especially in the face of budget surpluses. President George W. Bush thus found a receptive Republican Congress to support his proposed tax cuts.

Taken together, these four factors provide the parameters for the exercise of budget politics in Congress. Defense spending has been cut about as much as is politically possible. Entitlement spending will continue to rise on its own, unless checked by Congress (which seems unlikely, given the 2003 Medicare Reform Act). Pressure to cut income taxes seems to arise whenever they exceed about eight percent of GDP. Thus deficit spending becomes an attractive alternative, at least until the public pressures Congress to address that problem as well.

Overview of Budget Politics

Having seen the results of the budget process in terms of the broad categories of taxing and spending, it is now possible to take a closer look at how Congress develops these policies on a yearly basis. In the last chapter, we discussed how policymaking generally depends on the preferences of members of Congress and on institutional constraints. Budget decisions are no exception. When most members are aligned behind a particular policy, it has a good chance of success. When their preferences diverge, however, politics becomes much harder and gridlock ensues. Over the past thirty years, such a breakdown has occurred in Congress over budget decisions. Consensus budgeting has become contentious budgeting. Winners and losers have emerged. And the inability to build broad coalitions on the budget undermines attempts to build the supermajority coalitions needed to overcome gridlock in other policy areas as well.

Classical Budgeting

The classical period of budget politics, according to Wildavsky (1988), occurred from 1946 to 1973. There is some debate about when the classical period ended—1967, 1969, or later—but this is not of primary importance. During the classical period the appropriations process was dominated by the President and the Appropriations Committees in the House and Senate. Fenno's work (1973) shows that the Appropriations Committees were successful (by winning on the floor) when they reached a consensus in the committee and reported out a "committee bill" that all members—liberal and conservative, Republican and Democrat, northern and southern—could support. Fenno's analysis further shows that during the classical period the Appropriations Committees were able, with few exceptions, to achieve a consensus. The consensus was maintained in large part because the members agreed on a few basic principles. Wildavsky (1988) identifies these principles as follows: (1) long-term deficits are bad; (2) spending helps those in need but must be paid for; and (3) taxes are necessary but they must be constructed so as to avoid strong public opposition.

In applying these principles, members of the Appropriations Committees faced a dilemma—how do we retain power yet maintain the support of our colleagues who want programs funded? Power originated from the ability to cut presidential and agency requests; yet cutting spending too much would cause members in the House and Senate to limit the Committee's power.[4] This dilemma was resolved by cutting particular agency budgets in any given year but allowing expenditures generally to rise over time. In sum, the committees adopted and Congress approved an incremental solution. Budgets would not be allowed to fall too far out of balance and, if there were room to increase programs, those increases would be marginal so as not to increase taxes or borrowing. And if conditions were tough, Congress would make the President act first.

The tax committees were able to keep revenues roughly equal to expenditures by virtue first and foremost of the growth of the U.S. economy. Hidden taxes did, however, increase. Individual deductions were eroded, the level of tax payments increased due to "bracket creep" (with people moving to higher tax brackets through inflation-driven higher incomes), and increases in Social Security taxes on individuals were enacted. Thus liberals were able to fund their programs. Conservatives also served their interests by lowering overall rates (although because of loopholes few ever paid the full rates) and by passing necessary adjustments in depreciation and business taxes.[5]

Consensus Unraveling

This system of spending and taxing worked well as long as the economy was expanding and revenues were increasing. The system began to break down as expenditures on nondiscretionary social programs and the Vietnam War increased. President Johnson's policy of "guns and butter" without tax increases was financed by increased borrowing and by allowing the replacement of borrowing authority monies to be reallocated off-budget (Cogan, Muris, and Schick 1994). In 1965 President Johnson added a surtax on income to increase revenues, and in the following election House Democrats lost seats. The reaction to the surcharge was a harbinger of the tax revolt of the 1970s.

The spending side of the equation also became more complicated. In 1969 President Nixon was faced with a serious budgetary problem. Increases in social expenditures, increases in defense spending, and the opposition to the surtax left Nixon with little room to maneuver. The Appropriations Committees found that more and more of the budget was committed to uncontrollable expenditures and, as Schick (1981) shows, members of Congress continued to vote for new entitlements and for expanding old ones by increasing eligibility and indexing them to inflation. These pressures on expenditures and the reluctance to tax directly led to the breakup of the relatively consensual politics of the classical period. In the era of steady growth (roughly 1946–1966), expenditure decisions were decentralized to Appropriations subcommittees and to authorizing committees, while the tax committees could adjust revenues when necessary. As expenditures for entitlements increased and taxes increased due to inflation and the loss of deductions, budgetary decisions became more difficult.

President Nixon's reelection in 1972 and his subsequent decision to impound funds appropriated by the Congress further exacerbated the breakup of the classical consensus. The President's impoundments in effect told the Congress, "I don't care what you appropriate, I will decide what will be spent" (Schick 1981, 135). The conflict between the Republican President and the Democratic House over who controlled expenditures was dramatically altered by Watergate. As the status of the presidency fell, Congress became bolder and, after the 1974 election, changed the budgeting procedure by passing the Budget and Impoundment Control Act of 1974. Extensive details regarding the exact changes brought about by this act can be readily found elsewhere (Sundquist 1981; Shuman 1984; Davidson 1992); for our purpose it is sufficient to state that the new procedure added a new level of activity to an already cumbersome process. Appropriations had been conditioned by authorizations under the classical system. Under the new system both authorizations and appropriations were to be based on budget resolutions. In short, Congress created overarching Budget Committees, which were to coordinate budget policy. In order to achieve this end, Congress created the Congressional Budget Office (CBO) and changed the appropriations procedures. Despite this additional structure, the fundamental underlying problems did not go away. Expenditures for entitlements stayed up and effective tax rates were still increasing.

The choices were tougher and the consensual decisionmaking of the classical period was breaking down under the strain.[6] The number of amendments per appropriations bill (a measure of consensus between the committee and the floor) increased fivefold from 1963 to the mid–1970s. By the late 1970s the increase in amendments was twentyfold over 1963. Stanley Bach of the Congressional Research Service put it this way: "Increases in the number of amendments proposed in recent years, and increases in the percentage of winning amendments, suggests that the [Appropriations] Committee has had increasing difficulty in accommodating to the preferences of the House and in anticipating and settling potential controversies in advance" (Wildavsky 1988, 196). The politics was harder in large part because the economic policies of the past were constraining members' ability to tax and spend. The dilemma would get much worse.

The Budget and Impoundment Control Act of 1974

After the classical period, budgetary politics became a larger part of American politics because the choices faced by Congress became more difficult, thereby forcing Congress to change the rules and procedures by which it considered budget choices. The major change was the Budget and Impoundment Control Act of 1974. Prior to this act, Congress worked within a decentralized authorization and appropriation process wherein substantive committees such as Agriculture and Armed Services dealt with issues and authorized expenditures for programs. These authorizations then went to the Appropriations Committee and its subcommittees where monies were appropriated for authorized expenditures. The resulting thirteen appropriations bills were never combined until the end of the process. In short, Congress had no mechanism for determining the effect of one part of the budget on the whole, nor the effect of the whole budget on the economy.

In the reforms of 1974, Congress established a comprehensive budget process; but in order to keep most members involved they overlaid the existing procedures with the new budget resolution procedures. Congress attempted to keep the decentralized revenue and spending process intact and at the same time to add an integrated system. In Allen Schick's words (1995), "This combination has made for complicated, ever changing relationships between Congress's budget process and its other budget related activities."

The following describes this complicated process as laid out in the 1974 reforms. In passing a budget resolution, Congress specifies budgets for five-to-ten years with binding aggregate budget figures. The main aggregates in the resolution are: total increases or decreases in revenue; total new budget authorities (money that can be spent) and outlays (money actually spent); total loan obligations and guarantee commitments; the deficit (or surplus); and total public debt. The resolution specifies these five levels over twenty functional categories including national defense, energy, health, and Medicare. Allocations to the functional categories must add up to the corresponding budget totals.

Under the rules, the Budget Committees of the House and Senate must present a budget resolution to Congress by April 15 of each year.[7] After adoption of the resolution, the regular authorization and appropriation process works its way through Congress within the constraints imposed by the resolution. In practice, the resolutions do not meet the deadline, and occasionally have been over a hundred days late. There are many reasons why the resolutions are late but the primary reason is political. Given the tough choices and the differences in philosophy between Republicans and Democrats, agreement has been hard to come by. Conservatives do not want to vote for tax increases. Liberals do not want to vote for program cuts and can't get tax increases. Because setting priorities is not easy to achieve, the regular authorization–appropriation process often proceeds without a budget resolution.

The 1974 rules allow Congress to use the so-called "reconciliation procedure" to bring revenue and spending under existing law into line with amounts set forth in the budget resolution. Reconciliation involves two distinct operations: the issuance of reconciliation instructions that set spending limits, and the enactment of a reconciliation bill that changes revenue or spending laws. Reconciliation is an option for Congress and it is used when there are significant revenue increases, budget cuts, or a combination of both. The major budget shifts of 1981, 1982, 1984, 1990, 1993, and 2001 were all enacted through the reconciliation process.

The first stage of reconciliation begins with the budget resolution instructing specific committees to report legislation that changes existing laws. Social Security is exempt from reconciliation procedures as are (in practice) discretionary authorizations. The designated committees then attempt to meet the limits set by the resolutions. If more than one committee is instructed to report legislation, the bills are put into an omnibus reconciliation bill. The rules governing the passage of these bills differ in the House and the Senate but the ability to amend the bills is limited given their complexity. Congress's attempt to solve hard budget problems by layering over a decentralized process with a resolution-reconciliation integrative process did not solve the deficit problem. Nor did the 1974 changes magically make budget problems go away. Rather, these changes increased greatly the amount of time that members of Congress must spend on budget matters.

The reconciliation process *did*, however, bring about one change that has made politics easier. Given the complexity of the omnibus budget packages and the reconciliation process, Senators agreed that no filibusters would be allowed during reconciliation. With regard to the revolving gridlock theory, this means that, if a budget is passed under the reconciliation rules, the gridlock region is defined by the veto pivot and the *median* member in both the House and the Senate. Thus the

President and Congress face a choice of using either the budget reconciliation with its complex processes but a simple majority rule, or the non-reconciliation rules under which filibusters are allowed. A further tradeoff is that the changes made under reconciliation rules often expire after a five-to-ten-year time period. Thus a majority in the Senate must consider a temporary tax or spending change with majority support or a weaker (but permanent) change that can overcome a filibuster threat.

Inflation in the 1970s

The 1970s were characterized by inflation; during the Carter presidency, inflation was particularly high. Inflation had a positive effect on the budget because as inflation rises, wages and prices rise, pushing taxpayers into higher brackets and thus increasing the amount of revenue collected by the government. This increase in taxes collected during the 1970s kept the deficit low relative to the GDP. In fact, every budget projection by the CBO from 1975 through 1980 showed a *surplus* three years down the road. This allowed Congress to somewhat reduce marginal tax rates, increase the personal deduction for tax filers, and speed up depreciation rates for business investments, while simultaneously continuing to fund entitlement programs.

The rise of inflation, however, had a down side from a politician's viewpoint. Taxpayers knew that, despite their higher salaries, they had less real income; and taxpayers on fixed incomes were hurt by increased taxes on private property. During this period the dominant Keynesian economic model was questioned, and supply-side theorists came to the fore. Put simply, the view that economic growth and stability is secured through wise government spending was challenged by the view that economic growth is aided by a private sector less burdened by taxation and regulation. Proposals to cut taxes were generated by academic think tanks, by citizens groups, and by elected representatives. Beginning with Proposition 13 in California, voters clearly signaled that they were very unhappy with increased taxes. Thus while inflation helped keep the deficit low, it also helped trigger a tax revolt across the country.

The rise of inflation in the late 1960s and 1970s raised incomes into new marginal tax rates (the rate paid on the last dollar earned) and shifted the tax burden. C. Eugene Steuerle (1992) has calculated the effect of these changes on marginal and average tax rates for the middle class (at the median income), the poor (at one-half the median), and the well-to-do (at twice the median). Between 1960 and 1980 the average tax rate for those with twice the median income rose from about 12 percent to over 18 percent, while their marginal rate went from 21 percent to over 40 percent. Average taxes for median income earners rose from about 7 percent to just over 10 percent, while their marginal rate dropped from 20 percent to about 18 percent. For those with incomes at one-half the median, average taxes rose from around 1 percent in 1960 to over 5 percent by 1980, while their marginal rate went from near zero in 1959 to about 18 percent by 1980.

Thus the median taxpayer's income tax rate rose only slightly, whereas taxes for those at the lower end (one-half the median) and the upper end (twice the median) increased more substantially. Those at the lower end now paid Social Security and Medicare taxes, while the wealthy saw both their average rates and their marginal rates increase. In addition, state (income) and local (property) taxes more than doubled during these two decades. The tax burden on middle- and upper-middle-class voters had increased to cover the larger entitlement and social expenditures.

These changes in the distribution of taxes, together with the shifts in the budget, moved the United States toward a new era of policymaking—one that was inevitable no matter who had been elected to the presidency or the Congress in 1980. As Steuerle put it, "In this new era, reforming old expenditure or tax rules or meeting new priorities required that trade-offs be made explicitly among many existing programs. Tax reform, for instance, provided for lower rates and tax relief for the poor by reducing expenditures hidden in the tax code" (1992, 3).

These conditions, based on inflation, were most clearly seen in the 1976–1980 period. The percentage increase in the consumer price index (CPI) from year to year during this period was never below 6 percent; it reached 11.3 percent in 1979 and 13.5 percent in 1980. This pushed taxpayers into higher brackets, thus increasing both average taxes paid and the number of people at higher marginal rates. The effect on the government's budget was to ensure a steadily increasing stream of revenue. In fact, as Don Fullerton has so ably shown, *every pre–1981 budget projection showed a surplus in the budget within three years.* "As a result, legislators always seemed to find themselves with surplus revenue that could be used for some combination of increased spending or decreased taxes" (Fullerton 1994, 170). Under these conditions, legislators of either liberal or conservative bent could please constituents. Conservatives could claim that the revenue measures that they enacted lowered taxes (Merrill, Collender, and Cook 1990). Liberals could continue to spend in their programs because analysts had shown that within three years there would be a budget surplus.

The high rate of inflation during these years thus allowed Congress to continue to appear consensual, giving something to everyone. But this behavior was only held in place by bracket creep and higher taxes that were politically unsustainable. Higher average taxes and marginal rates upset voters, while at the state level, inflation caused housing prices to soar, thus raising property taxes at reassessment time.

Tax Revolt and Reagan's 1980 Election

The Democrats under Carter already knew in the 1970s that taxes had to be reduced, thereby putting pressure on expenditures. The Carter administration proposed cutting defense expenditures and shifting the savings to social expenditures. The Soviet invasion of Afghanistan, however, ended this strategy, and Carter proposed major increases in defense in his last two budgets. In addition to this revenue dilemma, the Social Security Trust Fund was in trouble, and it became clear that fixing it would entail increased taxes.

Thus the government faced a situation in which expenditures would necessarily increase given entitlements and the need for a growing defense budget, and revenue would surely decrease given the mood of the electorate. Steuerle (1992, 3) put the dilemma as follows: "The agony of moving to the new era came not from demands that were extraordinary by historical standards, but from the simple requirement that meeting new demands required politicians to identify losers." In the realm of ideas, supply-side economists came to the fore. If it were possible to stimulate economic growth through lower taxes, and if that growth would increase government revenues, then there would not be as many political losers as politicians had feared. This potential solution, articulated by some high-profile Republicans, appeared attractive to voters who were growing less and less comfortable with the status quo.

Taxpayers, first in California and then later across the country, signaled their anger over increased taxes and the "stagflation" that characterized the economy during the Carter presidency. This anger led to extraordinary election results in 1980. The 1980 national elections shifted the presidency and the Congress to the right. The Republicans controlled the Senate for the first time in twenty-six years, and in the House they picked up forty-six seats in the 1978 and 1980 elections. The newly elected members of Congress faced a new policy world. Inflation was over 13 percent; interest rates were over 18 percent; and the unemployment rate remained high as well. Moreover, most budget expenditures were for cash transfer and income transfer programs that are mandatory, and Social Security was expected to be running a deficit within five years. Taxpayers signaled at the ballot box that they wanted tax relief. The choices would no longer be easy. Congress could no longer both reduce certain taxes and continue to fund programs as though the revenue flow were guaranteed to increase. The politics of taxing and budgeting would have to change.

Going into the 1980 elections, the following set of conditions were present, and would squarely face whomever won the election.

1. Entitlements as a percentage of the budget were high and rising, and they were mandatory, not discretionary.
2. Taxes on average had been rising, especially for high- and low-end taxpayers, and effective marginal rates had also risen. Voters across the country had clearly signaled their desires—lower taxes.
3. Defense spending, which had been decreasing as a percentage of the federal budget, was now rising again. The Soviet invasion of Afghanistan together with the Iranian hostage crisis had led President Carter to ask for large increases for the military, and opinion polls showed that Americans favored a stronger military.
4. Members of Congress knew that the Social Security Trust Fund was to be in deficit within the next few years, and that they would have to deal with it.

In short, public policy regarding taxing and spending needed to be addressed regardless of who won the election. Members of Congress faced brutal choices. Taxes had to be reduced because voters wanted them reduced. Expenditures for social programs were mandatory and growing, and the plan to shift money from defense to entitlements was no longer viable. Budgetary matters were about to move from being *part* of governing to being *most* of governing. That is, the politics of taxing and spending would take up most of Congress's time. Finally, the combination of brutal choices and the increased importance of budgetary politics hardened members' attitudes. Conservatives favored cutting taxes and programs; liberals favored raising taxes for the wealthy and corporations in order to fund needed programs. Moderates were fewer in number and were pressured by the harsh economic necessities.

Coalitions for Tax and Budget Reform

Prior to 1981, Congress and the President, liberals and conservatives, could have their cake and eat it too. That is, conservatives got tax cuts passed when pressure mounted, and liberals could vote for the decreases (or not contest them) because they were assured that their programs would continue to be funded. Conservatives could not block increased expenditures because they were in the minority, but were able to appease their constituents with tax cuts and other victories. The 1980 election changed all this. The Congress elected with Ronald Reagan marked a distinct shift in preferences to the right. The Senate was Republican; and the 192 Republicans, together with conservative southern Democrats, made a working majority in the House.

The policy result of this preference shift was that "1981 represents a watershed year in the making of tax policy, from an era of constantly projected surpluses to one of constantly projected deficits. . . . The making of tax policy would never be the same" (Fullerton 1994, 171).[8] The two key pieces of legislation were the Economic Recovery Tax Act (ERTA) of 1981, initiating tax reduction and indexing, and the Omnibus Budget Reconciliation Act (OBRA) of 1981. These acts were passed as a result of the newly elected conservative majority. Republicans hung together and, with the support of very conservative Democrats, changed tax policy dramatically.

The story of how this coalition was formed to bring about substantial tax and spending change is a fascinating one. It is a tale of how gridlock can be overcome through the alignment of preferences in response to a widely perceived problem, and how gridlock can reappear when the same coalition members face conflicting political pressures. That story is told at the start of the next chapter. It brings together the budgetary aspects of this chapter with the preferences and institutions discussed in the previous chapter for a full picture of what can and cannot be accomplished according to the revolving gridlock theory.

For our present purposes, it is sufficient to note that the conservative coalition of 1981 was successfully able to lower individual income tax rates, to index them to inflation, and to cut spending (although not as dramatically as many conservatives would have liked). The first of these changes, lower rates, was a popular change, although the size of the tax cuts signaled that the era of classical budgeting was over. No longer were all sides content with small tax cuts and spending increases held in place through shifting priorities and economic growth. The second change, indexing income tax rates to inflation, meant that tough budget decisions could no longer be avoided through high inflation and bracket creep. And the third point, the moderate but not dramatic spending cuts, signaled the limitations of agreement on budgetary issues. Tax cuts are politically more attractive than tax increases; and spending increases are easier to pass than spending cuts. Thus the true test of the conservative coalition was in slashing the size of government—which was found to be politically difficult.

On the revenue side, then, individual income taxes were cut substantially, although these reductions were phased in over time. On the expenditure side, growth in domestic discretionary spending was held down, but nowhere near as greatly as conservatives in the Reagan administration had desired. Defense spending increased in response to the Soviet threat. And mandatory domestic spending on Medicare, Social Security, could not be cut without changing the nature of their entitlements.

Deficits under Public Scrutiny

The recession of 1981–1983 together with the tax cuts, entitlement growth, and heightened defense spending caused dramatic increases in the deficit. Unlike the previous deficits, these were projected to continue well beyond the three-to-five-year budgeting period. Their size was also much larger than budget analysts had grown accustomed to. If politicians hoped they could continue deficit spending, and continue it at this high rate, they were sorely mistaken. Public attention would soon turn to this issue, and budget politics would become more contentious than ever.

There are a number of ways to demonstrate that budgetary politics constitutes an ever-increasing share of total congressional politics. One can highlight the attention paid to the budget by the media. As the budget becomes a larger part of politics, stories about the budget in the broadcast and print media ought to rise dramatically. Additionally, one can show how over time the nondiscretionary portion of the budget has grown. The larger this "mandatory" percentage of the budget becomes, the less control the President and Congress have over appropriations, leading ultimately to little or no room for new programs. In this section we show that media attention to the budget has grown enormously since 1980, and that mandatory expenditures take up an ever-increasing share of the budget. We tackle this latter issue first.

Through the 1960s, mandatory budget expenditures (including interest on the debt) were about half of the size of discretionary expenditures. The federal government spent about 12–13 percent of GDP on discretionary purposes, including defense, and 6–7 percent on mandatory items (Congressional Budget Office, 2005). When Ronald Reagan took office in 1981, discretionary expenditures were 10.1 percent of GDP and mandatory expenditures were 11.6 percent. By the start of Bill Clinton's presidency, discretionary spending had been squeezed to 8.6 percent of GDP, with 13.5 percent reserved for mandatory expenditures. By the end of the Clinton administration mandatory spending was double the discretionary amount, the exact reverse of the 1960s. As discussed above, the big-ticket items other than Social Security have been Medicare, Medicaid, and interest on the debt.

Mandatory spending growth squeezes the discretionary portion of the budget. The squeeze gets even tighter if one notes that about one-half of all discretionary spending today goes for national defense, leaving less than 20 percent of the total budget for other programs. With over 80 percent of the budget reserved for mandatory and defense spending, those favoring new government programs have less and less of the budget to work with. Environmentalist, agricultural, and business interests must work harder to keep expenditures for the Environmental Protection Agency and the Departments of Agriculture and Commerce at what they deem reasonable levels. Liberal members of Congress have a difficult time pushing new programs, given the budget squeeze and the opposition to serious tax increases. Conservatives, on the other hand, have not been able to make major cuts in the mandatory portion of the budget; thus they are forced to try to cut from the discretionary portion of the budget's non-defense-related expenditures. In short, liberals and conservatives are fighting over an increasingly smaller and smaller part of the budget. Military spending can't go below a given amount; as a result, agricultural, environmental, and other domestic programs are all that are left to fight over. The budget has become more contentious because conservatives can't cut big entitlements and, where they can cut, there are smaller savings. Liberals cannot raise taxes to fund new programs and have to work hard to keep domestic discretionary programs funded at adequate levels.

Given the above circumstances, it is not hard to understand why budget politics has come to dominate Congress and media coverage of Congress. This is reflected in the *New York Times* coverage of Congress and the budget from 1970 through today. During the 1970s the *Times* ran an average of 2,300 stories per year on Congress; about 200 of these stories also focused on the budget. In 1980 the number of stories on Congress rose to 4,700, and from 1981 through 1995 never fell below 5,400 (there were over 7,000 stories each year from 1981 through 1987). The number of stories on Congress *and* the budget rose above 900 in 1979 and thereafter averaged about 1,800 a year.

Figure 3.1 shows the increase in *New York Times* stories on the budget as a percentage of stories on Congress. The increase clearly shows the new importance of the budget in congressional politics. The peaks in the figure represent the major budget battles of 1981 and 1995. In 1981, the stories featured the breakdown of previous coalitions, the major tax cuts, and struggles over spending cuts. In 1995, the stories featured the showdown between Clinton and congressional Republicans, ultimately resulting in the government shutdown. The budget deficit became a constant source of media coverage throughout the 1980s and 1990s, with a

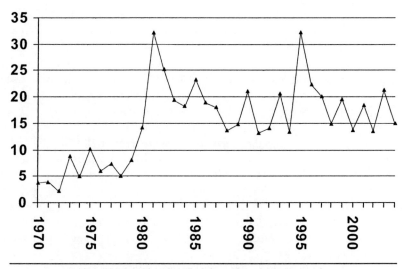

Sources: New York Times articles identified through Lexis-Nexis searches

FIGURE 3.1   Percentage of *New York Times* Articles on Congress Also Dealing with
the Budget

pattern of fewer budget stories in election years and more budget battles upon their return to office in off-years.

Another indicator of the heightened importance of the budget as of the early 1980s is the change in the rules, procedures, and institutional arrangements that govern budgetary politics. As budget decisions became more stark, Congress was forced to move away from the incremental decisions and arrangements that had governed budget politics during the classical period. As we shall see, the adoption of the budget resolution and the increased use of the reconciliation budget testify both to the increased importance of the budget and to the complexity of the decision process.

Tax Increases and Budget Mechanisms

The U.S. economy fell into a severe recession in late 1981 and the effect on the budget was ominous. Revenue was down because taxes were lower and fewer people were employed. Expenditures for programs such as unemployment insurance and food stamps were up. The decrease in revenues plus the increase in expenditures generated a major increase in the budget deficit. Early in 1982 it was clear that the budget would have to be modified. There are only two real ways to reverse deficits: raise taxes or cut expenditures. Cutting expenditures is a conservative response whereas raising taxes is a liberal response. Which way the President and the Republican Senate would move depended upon where they could find the votes.

The budget battles of 1981 showed resolve among conservatives for cutting taxes, but less resolve for cutting spending. Liberal Democrats preferred to raise taxes rather than cut spending, but neither was an attractive option for them, especially after suffering legislative defeat on the budget in 1981. And President Reagan, realizing that he did not have the votes for further spending cuts, was left to strike a deal with the Democratic majority in the House over tax increases. As noted above, press coverage of the budget process remained high after 1981, and many of the stories focused on the deficit. In 1982 and 1984, Reagan agreed to not veto tax increases, as long as they focused elsewhere than on the income tax cuts that he had won in 1981. Moreover, he had to actively advocate for the tax hikes in order to provide political cover for the Democrats in Congress who joined with him in a curious coalition. To secure enough votes for passage, small spending cuts needed to be coupled with corporate tax increases to cobble together enough Republicans and Democrats for passage. This coalition held together to pass the Tax Equity and Fiscal Responsibility Act (TEFRA) of 1982 and the Deficit Reduction Act (DEFRA) of 1984.

Although budgeting of the early 1980s was mainly about taxation, major cuts in 1981 and then increases in 1982 and 1984, the largest shift on the spending side came in the Social Security reforms of 1983. Again, it took an approaching crisis for Congress to take politically difficult actions. This time it was not the overall budget deficit but the looming deficits in the Social Security system that raised concerns. The sizable growth of Social Security came from substantial benefit increases coupled with an aging American population. Neither Democrats nor Republicans wanted to be blamed for making the tough choices needed to address these problems. In a word, Social Security was in gridlock.

Imminent shortfalls were sufficient to push current Social Security policy out of the gridlock region, with liberals and conservatives both realizing that action needed to be taken. Yet neither side wanted to act first, fearing the other would accuse them of harming the venerable institution of Social Security. To overcome this problem, the President and Congress agreed to set up an independent commission, chaired by Alan Greenspan, to make recommendations for reform. Those recommendations provided the basis for the reforms of 1983. With sufficient political cover, Congress passed and the President signed the reforms, which increased the tax rate, gradually raised the retirement age, and infused the Social Security Trust Fund with general revenues. Social Security operates in a way that current workers pay for current beneficiaries. For the first few decades after the 1983 reforms, Social Security was expected to take in more money than it sent out. If that surplus were set aside, it could be used to later pay for the retirement benefits of the Baby Boom population. Because of large deficits in the rest of the budget, however, the government has continually spent that Social Security surplus, filling the "trust fund" with IOUs.

Put simply, even given Social Security reform in 1983 and tax increases in 1982 and 1984, large projected deficits continued. In 1985, members of Congress faced more pressure from the public to address these deficits. Realizing that consensus over tough budget decisions would not be forthcoming without significant changes to the budget process, Congress passed the Gramm-Rudman-Hollings Act (GRH). This act set goals for deficit reduction such that the budget would be balanced by 1991. Each year would be a step toward that goal. If Congress could not meet its yearly target, GRH specified across-the-board spending cuts sufficient to force that target to be met. The reasoning was as follows: if we, as members of Congress, do not make the tough choices needed to raise revenues and hold down spending, the tough decisions will be made for us. And those across-the-board changes will be less favorable than the more politically sound changes we would make on our own.

Thus it was thought that, when faced with this significant threat, Congress would act responsibly. And when economic growth of the 1980s was sufficient to make GRH targets reasonable, Congress held the line. Yet a couple problems arose with this plan. First, coalitions in the House and Senate would only agree to this plan in the first place if they could have some guarantees, including that mandatory spending would not be cut. Second, if circumstances arose to make the deficit reduction target unfeasible, Congress could vote to set aside the automatic spending cuts implied in GRH. Removing the most threatening aspects of the "across-the-board" cuts made members less fearful of them, and the ability to vote against the enforcement of the GRH cuts was routinely exercised. By 1987, when a second Gramm-Rudman-Hollings Act was passed, the balanced budget target date had been amended to 1993. Although GRH put some public pressure on members, it was far from perfect.

In 1986, Congress took one more major attempt at addressing taxes. This time, however, members were mainly focused on the complexity of the system. Over the years there had been so many modifications and loopholes extended into the tax codes that the system was widely perceived as unfair. The 1986 Tax Reform Act was designed to close a number of these loopholes, reduce the complexity of the tax code, and thus move the system toward more equal taxation among those with similar incomes. It was argued that the increased revenues from the closed loopholes and simplification would allow for somewhat lower marginal rates, a change that made voting for the act much more attractive to members of Congress.

Public policy after 1981 was focused on the deficit, and budget politics became contentious. For the 1982 and 1984 tax increases, the same conservatives who had supported Reagan in 1981 defected. That is, after 1981 there was a new status quo point and from 1982 through 1986 centrists in both parties built strong bipartisan coalitions to shift policy generally leftward. The end result was a new gridlock region in which the left could not seriously increase taxes and the right could not decrease expenditures, leaving programs and taxes basically intact. In short, the battles between liberals and conservatives became bitter, or "hardball."

None of this is to say that there were no budget battles during the Johnson and Nixon–Ford eras. Rather, our claim is that policy shifted partly as a result of exogenous conditions (the economy) and the concomitant shifts in public preferences that were reflected in the Congress. Votes were more divisive after 1981—there were winners and losers—and liberals and conservatives became more strident because there was more at stake.

1990 Budget and PAYGO

After the 1986 tax deal, neither liberals nor conservatives had enough votes to advance their agendas. Taxes could not be cut further; spending could not be raised significantly. And neither side wanted to pay the political costs to cut spending or increase taxes much more. This gridlock was made acceptable to the public because the high economic growth rate throughout the 1980s kept the deficits below crisis levels. To secure political support after the tough budget times that included multiple tax increases, presidential candidate George H. Bush pledged, "Read my lips. No new taxes." And with his election in 1988, this pledge set the tone for negotiations with Congress and continued budgetary gridlock.

As is so often the case, external shocks made this status quo budgeting policy unacceptable. Energy price increases following Iraq's invasion of Kuwait and the American response coupled with other economic forces to send the U.S. into a recession in 1990. As 1990 progressed, deficit projections for the coming year rose from under $100 billion to $161 billion to $231 billion. Bush's initial proposal had been to meet the revised Gramm-Rudman-Hollings targets through spending cuts in entitlements, cuts in the capital gains tax (which would generate one-time revenue through taxes on sales of stock shares at the lower rates), and user fee increases. Updated budget numbers made this plan inadequate. Democrats in Congress responded with their own plan, which increased taxes. And Bush was left with no good options.

Serious deficit reduction would require a compromise of spending cuts and tax increases. Democrats in control of Congress could force the President to realize this through the passage of a budget that would force Bush to either: (1) break his no-new-taxes pledge, or (2) come up with such sizable spending cuts that the President's party would face heavy criticism and likely defeat in the upcoming midterm elections. Since his own election was more than two years away, and since the deficit crisis was substantial, President Bush agreed to join Democrats in a budget deal that would raise taxes but also cut spending.

Even with this compromise, gridlock was hard to overcome. The initial deal fell apart, with conservative Republicans and liberal Democrats voting it down to save their own seats. These Democrats were brought back on board by focusing on tax increases more than spending cuts. With no other viable options, President Bush signed the measure. The final deal struck in 1990 would cut the deficit by $500 billion over five years. It also would put in place further budget mechanisms intended to bring about further budget discipline in Congress. Specifically, the 1990 Budget Enforcement Act (BEA) established Budget Caps and Pay-As-You-Go (PAYGO) rules.[9] The Budget Caps would set a top limit on discretionary spending. The PAYGO rules would be even more constraining. Under PAYGO, whenever a proposal was made to increase spending or cut taxes, legislators would have to couple such proposals with offsets of spending cuts or tax increases elsewhere in the budget. Put simply, under PAYGO there was no free lunch. The easy and politically attractive decisions could no longer be made in isolation. Tradeoffs, which had become evident in the 1980s, were now made explicit.

1993 Budget with Unified Democrats

Although the reforms of 1990 were beneficial in terms of holding down the deficit, they came at a political cost. President Bush was held accountable for continued economic hardship and for breaking his no-new-taxes pledge. Facing independent candidate Ross Perot, who focused on budget deficits and fiscal irresponsibility in Washington, and Democrat Bill Clinton, who argued that unified Democratic government was the cure for gridlock, Bush fell to defeat in 1992.

President Clinton faced the same budget landscape as Bush. Entitlement spending was poised to rise dramatically, interest on the debt was crowding out other spending areas, and deficits were still projected far into the future. Two factors made this situation somewhat more manageable, however. First, the fall of the Soviet Union meant that a peace dividend was forthcoming, with decreases in defense spending taking pressure off the budget. Second, unlike Bush, Clinton had not taken a no-new-taxes pledge and could, if necessary, raise taxes.

Republicans in the minority in Congress adopted a political strategy of letting the unified Democrats deal with the continued deficits. Democrats, without sixty votes in the Senate, realized that their only hope of passage of a budget reform was to rely on the reconciliation rules passed in 1974, used in 1981 and occasionally thereafter. Such rules would eliminate the filibuster threat in the Senate, but would still require majority votes, meaning that moderate Democrats would have to vote for tax increases and spending cuts, neither of which were very attractive back home.

Once again, the coalition formation to overcome budgetary gridlock is one worth telling in detail. We do so at the start of Chapter 5. For now, it is important to note that the 1993 Budget Reconciliation Act trimmed another $500 billion off the deficit over the next five years through tax increases and limits on spending growth. It was passed with only Democrats voting for it, meaning that Republicans allowed the Democrats to pay any cost associated with overcome budgetary gridlock this time.

The 1995 Budget Battle

And there were costs to be paid. Moderate Democrats from conservative districts were already becoming scarce, as the distributions of liberal to conservative members illustrated in the Appendix make clear. The 1994 elections made them almost nonexistent. A majority of House Democrats from conservative districts who had supported Clinton on the budget deal and other Democratic priorities were defeated in 1994.[10] This stands in stark contrast to the typical 90–95 percent reelection rates for incumbents. Added to Republican gains in open-seat races, these defeats allowed Republicans to capture the House and Senate in 1994. Just as overcoming gridlock in 1990 had been costly for President Bush, so were the 1993 reforms costly. Since President Clinton was not up for reelection in 1994, Democrats in Congress bore the brunt of public resentment.

If there were to be major budgetary changes after 1994, they would be based around Republican proposals in Congress. President Clinton's budgets were, like many Reagan budgets of the 1980s, treated as "dead on arrival" and ignored. In their first year of governing, congressional Republicans attempted to see just how much power they could exert in this process.

Relying once again on reconciliation procedures, in order to avoid filibusters in the Senate, Republicans went about formulating a budget. In the Contract with America, on which they ran in 1994, they had promised to bring about a balanced budget and solidify it with a constitutional amendment. To be taken seriously, Republicans would need to propose a budget moving significantly in that direction. By the fall of 1995, they had formulated a budget that would be a significant conservative shift, lowering taxes, cutting nearly $900 billion off of projected spending over seven years, and resulting in a budget surplus by the end of 2002.

Sending this budget to the President after the October 1st beginning of the fiscal year meant that a presidential veto would lead to the shutdown of the government. If Clinton vetoed the measure he would then be portrayed as shutting down the government in order to preserve government deficits. Or so the Republicans hoped. But the veto came, and prospects of an override were nonexistent. As became evident over the winter months, public support for the President remained solid while Speaker of the House Newt Gingrich and congressional Republicans were blamed for the impasse. Eventually the Republicans backed down, passing a much less sweeping measure in a compromise with the President. The best that Republicans could hope for was to keep spending growth at or below the level of economic growth, so that spending as a percent of GDP would diminish.

Gridlock and Surpluses

This sort of gridlock, with President Clinton threatening to veto cuts in taxing and spending and congressional Republicans refusing to raise taxes and spending would characterize the rest of the 1990s. Politically, such stalemate was more attractive to all than the costs of overcoming gridlock. The compromise of 1990 had cost President Bush his job, just as the 1993 compromise had been costly to congressional Democrats. Unless immense deficits reappeared, neither side wanted to take the blame associated with raising taxes or cutting spending. And, even if someone had been willing to pay the cost, there were opponents on the other end of the political spectrum with sufficient numbers and institutional structures to stop such proposals in their tracks. Additional changes would be small, would be based on compromise, and thus would not be major victories for either side.

Yet, despite this gridlock (or perhaps because of it), massive deficits did not reemerge. Instead, by 1998, surpluses emerged. Years of economic growth led to a larger American workforce and to more corporate profits. Both of these contributed to increased revenues. The stock market boom, including the bubble of over-priced technology stocks, resulted in revenue gains.[11] And the higher marginal income tax rates adopted in 1990 and 1993 continued to generate more in taxes as incomes rose for most Americans. PAYGO rules helped keep Congress from reversing these positive trends. And the peace dividend from the end of the Cold War allowed a reduction in military spending. While entitlement spending continued to rise, it was offset by defense reductions and soaring tax revenues.

The surpluses of the late 1990s surprised budget watchers who had been dealing with deficit politics for so long. Projections that had shown long-term deficits in the 1980s and beyond now predicted a decade or more of surpluses. Politicians once again saw room for political gain. Republicans took notice that federal revenues exceeded 20 percent of GDP for the first time in decades, and argued for tax cuts. Democrats saw the possibility of new directions for federal spending, including extending health coverage, greater involvement in education, and shoring up the Social Security Trust Fund by putting those surpluses in a "lockbox."

Yet proposals to move budget policies to the right were resisted by President Clinton and movement to the left was a nonstarter in the Republican Congress. It seemed possible to return to a form of consensus budgeting like in the classical period. Yet the animosity of the previous twenty years of picking budget winners and losers meant that compromise was also tough to come by. The best that members could hope for was continued gridlock on budgetary issues. They could, however, ease the pain of the annual budget process by abandoning the Budget Caps and PAYGO processes put in place in 1990. Proposals to do so became more attractive over time.

2001 Tax Cuts

The rise of federal budget surpluses led to debates during the 2000 elections about future government priorities. For those who were used to hearing about the economic threat of budget deficits, stories about the harmful nature of excessive surpluses seemed surreal. Yet politicians are always happy to develop plans to cope with surpluses, as that means new spending and tax cuts—politically attractive options.

The 2000 presidential elections were closely contested, to say the least. When George W. Bush emerged as the winner, his presidency allowed the continuation of a push on policy to the right that had begun with the Republican takeover of Congress in the 1994 elections. Threats to veto conservative measures by the Clinton administration were replaced by strong support from the Bush White House. Because of the surpluses, however, proposals looked very different from those of 1995. Back in the days of deficits, most of the Republican aim had been to reduce spending. In 2001, they could engage in the happier task of cutting taxes.

Nevertheless, just like in 1981 when northern Democrats in Congress argued that the Reagan tax cuts were not sustainable in the long run, liberal Democrats in 2001 were likewise skeptical. They would have preferred a compromise that would bring about some of their budget priorities as well—at a minimum targeting more of the tax cuts to those in lower income brackets. Outside of such a compromise, Senate Democrats would oppose the tax cuts, even to the point of filibustering them.

Realizing this, Republicans in Congress returned once more to the reconciliation rules that would require only a majority vote in the Senate. Even still, compromises needed to be made with moderate Republicans over the size of the cuts and who would receive them. Ultimately, the tax measure addressed many aspects of the tax code simultaneously. Individual income tax brackets were lowered for everyone, including an immediate and retroactive reduction of the bottom 15-percent bracket to 10 percent, and a reduction of the other brackets as well, with the top bracket falling from 39.6 percent to 35 percent by 2006. The "marriage penalty" that led many married people to pay higher taxes than they would have if they had not been married was addressed through a variety of changes including an increase in the standard deduction for married couples. Child tax credits were increased, incentives were given for education savings accounts, and the estate tax (dubbed the "death tax" by conservatives) was phased out over ten years. The cost of using the reconciliation process was that all of these provisions would expire at the end of ten years unless renewed.

As we will discuss in Chapter 6, this shift to the right in the lowering of taxes was one of many moves to the right attempted by the unified Republican government. Limiting the conservative movement were moderate Republicans and Senate Democrats who would exercise their filibustering rights whenever possible. Moreover, these conservative proposals and attempts to keep Republicans aligned behind them caused Senator Jim Jeffords of Vermont to leave the Republican Party and caucus with the Democrats in May of 2001, handing them majority control in the U.S. Senate. The Jeffords switch, while not ultimately modifying policy too drastically, showed the extent of political pressure on members of Congress. If the party asks too much of them, especially when those votes would go against district considerations, they will vote with their districts. When the party keeps insisting and even goes so far as to threaten to punish dissenting members, those party moderates may exercise their option of leaving the party and joining the other side. In so doing, a moderate Republican like Jeffords would become an independent who would support the Democrats.

Part of the reason that the Jeffords switch did not modify policy substantially is that other events intervened. The terrorist attacks of September 11, 2001, would turn American attention away from domestic budget issues to a more pressing crisis. Spending on military and homeland defense purposes became a priority. Further tax cuts to help the country out of the recession that had begun before 9/11 and continued afterward were seen as helpful. Adding to uncertainty and concern, the technology bubble of the stock market burst in 2000, leading to a loss in stock values and fewer government revenues from capital gains.

The combination of all of these events meant that, by 2002, deficits had returned. Whatever partisan unity had been developed in the days after 9/11 was shown to be short-lived. Democrats blamed the Bush tax cuts for the return of the deficits. Republicans directed blame toward the terrorists and the economic recession they had inherited from the Clinton administration. And the public remained more focused on the continued threat of terrorism, the subsequent wars in Afghanistan and Iraq, and the economic slowdown, than on the details of budgeting in Washington. Without pressure from the public, members of Congress were in no hurry to make tough decisions to raise taxes or cut spending substantially enough to balance the budget. And, having let the PAYGO rules expire, they were not required to find offsets for tax cuts or spending increases.

The debate over where the surpluses went will continue for some time. And what to do about the subsequent deficits will be something taken seriously when public pressure returns on this issue. The Congressional Budget Office offered a first pass at how the surpluses turned into deficits (2004 *Congressional Quarterly Weekly Report*, 146). For fiscal year 2003, for example, revenues were down $573 billion relative to projections that had been made in 2001. Of that total, $179 billion was a result of the tax cuts, $155 billion was due to the economic slowdown, and $239 billion was due to the stock market slump. On the spending side, supplemental appropriations for terrorism and defense purposes, and the continual pressure of entitlement spending, meant that a balanced budget was once again far out of reach.

Off-Budget Policymaking

The story we have just told is one of how Congress struggled with new budget realities. Growing entitlement programs displaced other types of spending. Cuts in defense and discretionary domestic areas could only go so far, and are now near their lowest acceptable levels. And the public is very resistant to tax increases. These forces led to the breakdown of consensual budgeting, to an era of winners and losers, characterized by gridlock and deficit politics. Shifts to the right in budgeting followed electoral shifts in 1980 and in the 1994–2000 period. Shifts to the left occurred in 1982–1986. In-between, gridlock held. This stalemate was only overcome when the realities of large budget deficits and an attentive public forced politicians to act. And those actions, in 1990 and 1993, had adverse consequences for President Bush and congressional Democrats. All of this is the story of decades of public budgeting. But the story does not end there. The changes in budget politics have spilled over into other areas of public policymaking.

As noted above, the budget's domination of American politics since 1981 is indicated by the increased coverage given to this issue in the media. Of equal significance have been the side effects of these changes. New policy proposals were harder to come by and major policy changes were forced off-budget—their costs were borne by business, consumers, and state governments rather than by the federal government through taxes. For example, George H. Bush's Americans with Disabilities Act and the 1990 amendments to the Clean Air Act were both off-budget. If, as we claim, American politics had become budget politics as consensus broke down in the 1970s and gridlock took hold in the 1980s, we should expect to see that the number of major policies passed by Congress decreases over this period, and that the ratio of off-budget policies to budget policies increases. That is, as the budget constrains contemporary programs, new policies requiring money will be harder to come by and members will turn to off-budget policies because these don't directly affect the budget numbers.

Defining "major policy" is not an easy thing to do because people disagree about which policies are important; however, David Mayhew (1991) has defined "major policy" by objectively ascertaining the amount of press coverage given to issues before the Congress. His purpose in defining major policies was to determine whether divided government affected policy results. Although our purpose differs, we can use his careful selection of public policies from 1946 through 2002 (Mayhew 2004) to corroborate our point about the declining importance of general policies and the increased importance of budget policies.

Table 3.4 shows these results over time. Beginning with John Kennedy in the 87th Congress (1961–1962) and ending with Richard Nixon's 92nd Congress (1971–1972), on the average eleven major policies per Congress were passed that had direct budget implications. Most of these policies involved domestic discretionary or entitlement expenditures; fewer than 5 percent were tax decreases. In contrast, these same Congresses each passed an average of about six major pieces of legislation that were nonbudgetary. Thus an average of about seventeen significant policies were passed per Congress, and the ratio of budget to off-budget policies was about 2 to 1.

During the Nixon–Ford and Carter years (1973–1980) the number of major budget-related issues fell to just below six whereas the number of major off-budget pieces of legislation rose to more than eight per Congress. In Reagan's first Congress, the budget dominated policymaking: of nine significant pieces of legislation, seven were on-budget whereas only two were off-budget. The 98th and 99th Congresses (1983–1986), in which Republicans controlled the Senate, passed on average four on-budget policies and four off-budget policies. In the Democrat-controlled 100th Congress (1987–1988), the Democrats passed some social legislation such as water quality improvements, aid for the homeless, and catastrophic health insurance that had on-budget implications but in general the amounts passed were quite small because they were at least trying to meet Gramm-Rudman-Hollings restrictions. The amount of significant legislation stayed at about these levels during the George H. Bush presidency. In Bush's first two years (the 101st Congress, 1989–1990) there were five on-budget items and four off-budget items including the Clean Air Act Amend-

TABLE 3.4 Legislation with Budget Consequences and Off-Budget Legislation

Years	Congress	President	Budget-Related	Off-Budget
1961–1962	87th	Kennedy	11	4
1963–1964	88th	JFK/LBJ	9	4
1965–1966	89th	Johnson	15	6
1967–1968	90th	Johnson	6	11
1969–1970	91st	Nixon	14	7
1971–1972	92nd	Nixon	11	5
1973–1974	93rd	Nixon	8	14
1975–1976	94th	Ford	5	9
1977–1978	95th	Carter	5	7
1979–1980	96th	Carter	5	5
1981–1982	97th	Reagan	7	2
1983–1984	98th	Reagan	3	4
1985–1986	99th	Reagan	5	4
1987–1988	100th	Reagan	7	5
1989–1990	101st	Bush	5	4
1991–1992	102nd	Bush	3	4
1993–1994	103rd	Clinton	5	6
1995–1996	104th	Clinton	4	11
1997–1998	105th	Clinton	3	6
1999–2000	106th	Clinton	2	4
2001–2002	107th	Bush	7	9

Source: Mayhew 1991, 2004.

ments and the Americans with Disabilities Act. Starting with the 102nd Congress, and extending through the Clinton administration and up through 2002, *every* Congress passed more pieces of major off-budget legislation than major on-budget legislation. Use of the PAYGO rules and Budget Caps made the formulation of legislation with budgetary consequences untenable.

In sum, the end of the classical budgeting period had two results for major legislation. First, on-budget policies that previously outnumbered off-budget by about 2 to 1 were now much less frequent than off-budget legislation. This trend was enhanced by budget mechanisms like Gramm-Rudman-Hollings and PAYGO that were designed to focus budget issues toward deficit reduction. Second, without the ability to offer targeted tax cuts and district spending benefits, it became more difficult to secure the votes necessary for passage of budget and nonbudget issues alike. From an average of about 17 pieces of major legislation per Congress prior to 1973, the total diminished to about 11 per Congress afterward.

Budgets, Revolving Gridlock, and the Future

Some would argue that budget politics are far too complex to be captured in a model as simple as the one proposed in the previous chapter. Rather than being one-dimensional, budget decisions appear to be particularistic, with each member of Congress trying to bring goodies back to the home district. The reconciliation rules call for majorities, not the supermajorities prominent in the revolving gridlock model. The coalitions that come together often take odd forms, with extreme liberals and extreme conservatives voting together against specific packages. Taxing and spending decisions are extremely complex. In many ways, we would agree with this assessment. But we raise the topic of budgetary politics here and give it prominent consideration because we think it is both crucial to understanding congressional politics today and complementary to the revolving gridlock theory. In the previous chapter, we argued that preferences and institutions, uncertainty and elections, all play a role in determining policy outcomes. We find the same to be the case in budget policy.

In its simplest sense, raising taxes and social expenditures constitutes a policy shift to the left, whereas cutting taxes and spending (other than defense) is a move to the right. In the classical budget period, with the possibility of budget surpluses three to five years down the road, majorities were relatively easy to form. Conservatives supported tax cuts, targeting particular cuts to gain the pivotal members needed to secure majorities or supermajorities. Likewise, liberals supported new programs and expanded spending, securing particular benefits for key members who were needed to vote for their bills. Budget deals could include proposals pleasing both sides—and thus enjoyed broad support and consensus.

Beginning in the 1970s, Congress and the President had to make much tougher budget decisions, as the public began to resist further taxes, entitlements were rising uncontrollably, military spending required new commitments, and Social Security was nearing a crisis. High inflation allowed politicians to mask the need for dramatic action for a short time, but by the 1980 elections it was clear that something had to be done by whomever was elected. The question was whether the pain would be shared, as the benefits had been shared during periods of projected surplus, or whether a coalition would form to move policy strictly to the left or the right. The 1980 elections answered this question: Ronald Reagan's election along with the Republican gains in Congress signaled a shift to the right. In 1981, tax cuts were accompanied by a lower rate of general spending increases,with the exception of defense spending. Liberal to moderate Democrats voted against the tax and budget bills. As the revolving gridlock theory predicts, the pivotal members in this shift were the conservative Democrats near the median in the House.

But the results of the policy change were uncertain. The tax cuts, along with the increases in defense spending and the recession, led budget analysts to predict sizable deficits within the year. Two solutions were possible: the initial Reagan coalition could hold together and propose deep spending cuts, or policy could be moved somewhat back to the left with tax increases. Given the options of either tax increases or spending cuts, there are no longer budget winners, only budget losers. The shifts to the right in 1981 had gone too far, and the only reasonable solutions were the tax increases of 1982 and 1984 and the final consolidation of 1986. The Reagan solution was to raise corporate taxes and plug loopholes, but not to touch income taxes or the indexing provision.

In any era of budget deficits and public pressure to address the deficits, coalitions take odd forms. There is no majority favoring tax increases in both houses of Congress. Likewise, there is no majority favoring spending cuts, especially cuts in major entitlements. As such, when Congress and the President needed to deal with the deficit in 1990 and 1993, they attempted to reach compromises that involved a combination of tax increases and spending cuts. This combined strategy of moving both to the left in raising taxes and to the right in cutting spending pleased no one—at best it spread the pain of cutting the deficit. When politicians can pass the blame off to members of the other political party, they will do so. Democrats were able to direct the blame for the pain of the 1990 budget deal toward President Bush, who had made his famous "no new taxes" pledge. But the unified Democratic government that passed the 1993 budget act had no one else to blame. Politicians bringing home nothing but bad news are unlikely to be reelected. As such, the Republicans lost House seats in 1982, the Senate in 1986, and the presidency in 1992, each following tax increases. But Democrats faced the same tough decisions as Republicans, and passed equally painful legislation.

When surpluses emerged, budgetary politics became attractive again. Spending increases and tax cuts were possible. And again the revolving gridlock theory pointed to the direction of the change. With Republicans in Congress aligned with a Republican President for the first time since their election in 1994, a rightward shift would be expected. As expected, tax cuts were the order of the day in 2001. As all of these examples illustrate, the revolving gridlock theory is helpful in predicting the direction of budgetary changes, as well as explaining when such changes are impossible or very costly.

Looking to the future, politicians confront all of the same budget realities discussed here. There is continual public pressure for low taxes. Indeed, when individual income taxes exceeded 9 percent of GDP in the late 1970s and again in the late 1990s, both times the public voted in Republicans who promised and delivered on tax cuts. There is an entitlements crunch with steady increases projected in Social Security, Medicare, and Medicaid as health care costs rise and the American population ages. According to the Government Accountability Office, Social Security is expected to pay out $3.7 trillion more than it takes in over the next 75 years; for Medicare, the total 75-year deficit is projected at $27.8 trillion (2005 *Congressional Quarterly Weekly Report*, 447). Cuts in defense and discretionary areas, which were favorites in the 1980s and 1990s are now limited. The peace dividend has been secured, but 9/11 showed Americans that it is still a dangerous world. And the discretionary side of the domestic budget has already been reduced significantly.

The politically easy answer for members of Congress is to rely on deficit spending and ignore these problems. We started out this chapter by pointing out that deficits are the norm rather than the exception. And yet, when the deficits grew and the media coverage turned to them, members of Congress had no choice but to act. Public attention, while potentially slow in coming, seems inevitable once again.[12] Government borrowing could dramatically displace private borrowing, leading to much higher interest rates, less private investment, and lower economic growth. Government payments of interest on the debt could crowd out other spending priorities. Or a prescient political entrepreneur could turn the public attention to the deficit before a crisis hits. How this happens is less important than what happens next. After all the changes of the past twenty years, from divided government with a Republican President to unified Democratic governance to divided government with a Democratic President to unified Republican governance, Congress and the President face very similar problems to those of the 1980s. Learning from past decisions, from successes and failures, is crucial for mistakes to be avoided. Those lessons become more clear upon understanding congressional politics of the past quarter century, a task to which we now turn.

Notes

1. For a discussion of how events transform voters' preferences, which in turn transform the political agenda both generally and as it regards racial policy in the United States, see Carmines and Stimson (1989).

2. While we focus here on broad categories of taxing and spending, the actual decisions that lead to these overall figures are of greatest importance. The "microbudgeting" approach studies these decisions in detail. Among the best work in microbudgeting is that of Cogan, Muris, and Schick (1994). See especially Cogan's chapter on the dispersion of spending authority.

3. Due to the decades between the numbers shown in the table, neither of these peaks appears in the table.

4. Some of the best work on the politics of the appropriations process with regard to political parties, the influence of the President, and the delegation of appropriations authority has been conducted by Kiewiet and McCubbins (1988, 1991).

5. For an excellent analysis of the politics of finance in the House Ways and Means Committee, see Manley (1970).

6. See Coleman (1997) for an alternative view of how conflict arose on budgetary issues as of the 1970s.

7. The required date was May 15 prior to the Gramm-Rudman-Hollings deficit reduction act of 1985.

8. McKenzie and Thornton (1996) discuss how the need to cope with the budget deficit has influenced economic policymaking in the United States.

9. See Collender (1991) and Cogan, Muris, and Schick (1994) for in-depth discussions of Budget Caps and PAYGO.

10. See Brady, Cogan, Gaines, and Rivers (1995) for an assessment of the causes and consequences of the 1994 elections.

11. See *Congressional Quarterly Weekly Report* (2004, pp. 130–164) for recent numbers and an in-depth analysis of the politics of the budget process.

12. That the American people see the tradeoffs in spending, taxing, and deficits and form consistent opinions about these tradeoffs is nicely established by Hansen (1998).

4

Republican Presidents and Democratic Congresses

The previous two chapters describe the revolving gridlock theory in detail. Chapter 2 explains how preferences of members of Congress, placed within the institutions of Senate rules, separation of powers across branches, and bicameralism, lead to a gridlock region. Policies near the median in the House and Senate are firmly within this region and cannot be altered to the left or right. Policies that are extreme relative to the preferences of broad majorities in Congress are changed through bills that gain the supermajorities needed to pass. Somewhat more moderate status quo policies can sometimes be modified, but only through the compromises necessary to build large coalitions.

When budget deficits are not seen as a significant problem, such coalitions sometimes can be constructed through concessions on tax and spending issues. When deficits seriously constrain such activities, agreement is tougher to reach and congressional politics then pits winners against losers. Such contentious actions contribute to polarization of party members and to difficult decisions by moderates concerning whether to support their party or to vote with their district. Such polarization results in significant policy gridlock as each side can stop policy movement through filibusters or vetoes. Gridlock can be overcome in these circumstances only through concessions by moderates that leave them electorally vulnerable. Their subsequent electoral defeat contributes further to polarized politics.

These arguments of the past two chapters have thus laid the groundwork for this chapter and the two that follow, illustrating how this story both explains and is rooted in the politics of the 1980s, 1990s, and today. This chapter brings together the spatial theory of Chapter 2 and the budgetary aspects of Chapter 3, with a focus on policymaking over the budget in the divided government era from 1980 to 1992. It tells the fascinating story of how Reagan and the congressional Republicans forged a coalition with southern Democrats in 1981 to bring about significant tax reform and more minor spending cuts. It then explains how and why this coalition fell apart in the face of significant budget deficits. The attempts to cope with these deficits resulted in failed and temporary political coalitions in Congress over the next several years until, ultimately, no further coalitions for policy change on the budget were politically viable. Nevertheless, massive deficits and public demands forced policymakers to form coalitions that were politically devastating to those who joined them against their own electoral interests.

Arrival of the 97th Congress

The revolving gridlock theory presented in Chapter 2 depends on determining the preferences of members of Congress. In this section, we attempt to show how preference shifts resulting from elections can be meticulously documented, leading in the end to conclusions about which individuals became the pivotal members of Congress in 1981.

The newly elected 97th Congress came to Washington in 1981 with a new President and an old agenda—rising entitlements, high taxes, Soviet involvement in Afghanistan, and a rapidly decreasing Social Security Trust Fund. The new Congress differed significantly from the 96th Congress. The Senate was Republican for the first time in twenty-six years; liberal Senators including George McGovern (D, SD), Birch Bayh (D, IN), Gaylord Nelson (D, WI), and Frank Church (D, ID) had been defeated in 1980. They were replaced by conservative Senators like Dan Quayle (R, IN), Robert Kasten (R, WI), Steven Symms (R, ID), Charles Grassley (R, IA), and James Abdnor (R, SD). Among other ways, the ideology of members of Congress can be judged by interest group ratings, like those of the liberal Americans for Democratic Action (ADA).[1] A score of 100 is very liberal in voting in the given year, while 0 is very conservative. The eleven defeated or retired Democratic Senators had a mean score of 55.5 and a median ADA of 50 in 1980. In the first session of the 97th Congress, the Republican Senators who replaced them had a mean ADA score of 6.8 and a median of 5. In short, the election had resulted in a significant shift of the preferences of the U.S. Senate to the right. Also important were the facts that the Republicans were now the majority party, and the preferences of the committee chairs had also shifted to the right.

In the 96th Congress, the Chairs of the Finance, Appropriations, and Budget Committees were Russell Long (D, LA), Warren Magnuson (D, WA), and Edmund Muskie (D, ME). In the most significant change in preferences, Senator Muskie's 1979 ADA score was 53 whereas his replacement in the 97th Senate, Senator Pete Domenici (R, NM), had a 1979 ADA score of 5. Given that the Republicans chose to use the reconciliation procedure, the shift was important because the Budget Committee would set the spending limits during the first budget resolution.

There were also major shifts in important subcommittee chairs. Senator Thomas Eagleton (D, MO) chaired the Agriculture subcommittee of Appropriations in 1980 and his ADA score was 78, whereas his replacement in the 97th Congress, Senator Thad Cochran (R, MS), had a 1980 ADA score of 22. In 1980 the chair of the Interior subcommittee of Appropriations was Senator Robert Byrd (D, WV), whose 1980 ADA score was 56; his replacement in the 97th Senate, Senator James McClure (R, ID), had an ADA score of 17.

Although these shifts are illustrative, more compelling evidence can be obtained by comparing Senate means and medians by election over time. We calculated the mean, median, and standard deviation for ADA scores over all sessions of the Senate from 1969 through 2003.[2] Table 4.1 shows these figures up through the Reagan presidency. During the Nixon–Ford and Carter years the median Republican ADA score was about 17 while in the 1981 session of the 97th Congress the median had dropped to 10. In addition to the drop in the median, the spread of preferences had tightened. Republican ADA scores ranged from 0 to 55 (Weicker, CT, and Hatfield, OR, scored 55), which was the narrowest spread during the 1969–1988 period. Analyzing mean scores and variance shows the same tightening phenomenon at work. The mean Republican ADA score in 1981 was 16.8 with a standard deviation of about 16. Both the mean and the standard deviation show about a 40 percent drop from any Senate scores over the 1969–1980 period. The reduced range and variance of scores around the median and the mean indicate that not only did the center of the party shift to the right but also that the number of liberal and moderate Republican votes was greatly reduced in the first session of the 97th Senate.

Even with this shift to the right in the Republican Party, the Democrats had opportunities to at least delay legislation, and in some instances to successfully filibuster if they could hang together. The election resulted in a shift to the left among Democratic Senators—the median Democratic Senator in the Nixon–Ford and Carter years scored an average ADA of between 56 and 66 while in the first session of the 97th the median had risen to 70. The spread around the Democratic median, however, was the full 100 points, from a conservative 0 to a liberal 100. The variance around the mean increased, meaning that although the median Democrat was a liberal with an ADA score of 70 there were a large number of Democrats far to the right of the median. Three Democratic Senators had ADA scores of 15 or less—Stennis (MS), Long (LA), and H. Byrd (VA)—while another three, Johnston (LA), Bentsen (TX), and Zorinsky (NE), had ADA scores of 20 or 25.

The floor median ADA score in the 97th Senate dropped to 35, about a 10-point drop from the Nixon–Ford and Carter years. There were twelve Senators near the floor median, with ADA scores between 30 and 40. Of the twelve, eight were Republicans and four (Heflin, Nunn, Boren, and Cannon) were Democrats, in contrast with many more Democrats near the median previously. Clearly the 97th Senate was more conservative and under Republican control. The median voter was twice as likely to be a Republican as a Democrat, and, if a Democrat, then a conservative one. The Republicans were a tightly clustered conservative group, whereas the Democrats ranged from very conservative to extremely liberal.

The 1980 elections brought the Republicans to the majority in the Senate and shifted preferences to the right, resulting in a majority for more conservative policies. In addition to the Republican majority, there were a sufficient number of

TABLE 4.1 ADA Score Summary (Senate)

	Nixon 1969–1972 Averages	Nixon/Ford 1973–1976 Averages	Carter 1977–1980 Averages	Reagan 1981	Reagan 1982	Reagan 1983	Reagan 1984	Reagan 1985–1988 Averages
Republicans								
Median	18	17	17	10	15	15	15	11
Mean	27.4	28.7	26.2	16.8	25.1	22.1	25.8	20.4
Standard Deviation	27.6	29.0	22.5	16.0	23.6	19.5	24.9	23.7
Democrats								
Median	63	66	56	70	70	75	75	78
Mean	56.9	59.0	54.2	65.1	67.7	68.3	74.0	71.6
Standard Deviation	31.5	28.8	23.4	26.7	24.5	21.7	23.3	21.9
Entire Senate								
Median	42	52	44	35	45	40	50	48
Mean	43.9	46.7	43.1	39.5	44.7	43.3	47.5	46.2
Standard Deviation	33.2	32.4	26.8	32.5	32.0	30.9	34.1	34.2

conservative Democrats to ensure that the filibuster could not be used often or effectively. In short, the Democrats in the 97th Senate were badly split, with conservative Democrats reading the election as a mandate for a policy shift to the right. A second factor increasing the prospect for a conservative policy shift was that President Reagan would be setting the agenda. This meant that even liberal to moderate Republicans like Cohen, Heinz, Mathias, and Weicker were reading the election results as a Reagan-right mandate.

One way to show this effect is to look at those Senators who were in both the 96th and 97th Senates and to compare the shift in the direction of their ADA scores. Technically, the scores are not comparable because they are calculated over different votes. However, if we simply ask whether Senators in both Senates have become more or less conservative, the results will be indicative. The expectation is that the Republicans will become more conservative across the board whereas the Democrats will split, with northern Democrats becoming more liberal and southerners (on the average) becoming more conservative. Because ADA scores only indicate the percentage of times a member voted liberally, we broke the results down as follows: major change, measured as at least two votes in the 97th Senate (10 ADA points) more conservative or more liberal than in the previous Senate; slight change, measured as one vote (5 ADA points) more conservative or liberal; and no change from the 96th to the 97th Senates. Of the thirty-five Republicans in both Senates, only two (Pressler and Hatfield) changed in a liberal direction (one major and one slight). Eighteen Republicans changed by more than two votes to more conservative positions; nine shifted to the right by one vote; and six did not change from the 96th to the 97th Senate. In sum, the analysis is consistent with the notion that the Republicans present in both Senates read the results of the 1980 election as a mandate for a conservative shift, and their voting patterns followed suit. Even considering that the votes were over different issues, these results show that Republicans strongly supported conservative positions on a range of issues after the 1980 election.

There were forty-five Democratic Senators who served in both the 96th and 97th Senates. The hypothesis is that the Democrats, unlike the Republicans, will split and go both directions—liberal and conservative. Fourteen of the forty-five (31 percent) did not change direction; of the remaining thirty-one Senators, twenty became more liberal while eleven shifted to the right. Sixteen Democrats voted significantly more liberally (at least two votes) while seven, mainly southerners, became significantly more conservative. The eight Democrats exhibiting slight changes in directions split evenly: four more liberal and four more conservative. In sum, Democrats read the 1980 election in different ways, splitting about two to one in favor of adopting more liberal positions, whereas Republicans overwhelmingly read the election as a signal to shift to the right.

The 1980 House election yielded somewhat different results. The Republican Party gained a net of 33 seats, taking them to 192 total seats in the 97th Congress. Although this was their highest total in over a decade, the Republicans still needed to hold all their members and convince twenty-six Democrats to vote with them in order to achieve the 218 votes needed for a majority. The House elections shifted the preferences of members to the right, because the Democrats who lost or retired were on the average more liberal than the Republicans who replaced them. The shift to the right was not as significant as in the Senate for a number of reasons. First, the Democrats were still the majority party and as a result the conservative shift did not *appear* as dramatic. Second, the chairs of the major committees were either returned or replaced by similarly minded Democrats. These factors dictated that House Democrats still controlled the machinery and timing of the institution, and that old-line Democrats like Rostenkowski (IL), Dingell (MI), Wright (TX), and O'Neill (MA) would control the Democrats' response to the Republicans' budget policies. Without a majority and with Democrats in control of the House's machinery, the Republicans' major battles would be in the House. The gain in seats gave conservatives a chance at winning but it would be harder than in the Senate.

While these details get at the heart of the political scenario as members entered the 97th Congress, the extensive findings can be boiled down to a simple preference shift. Figure 4.1 illustrates the 1980 election results in the format introduced in Chapter 2.

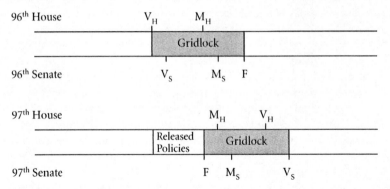

FIGURE 4.1   The 1980 Elections

The 96th Congress, under President Carter, faced gridlock from the veto pivot in the House to the filibuster pivot in the Senate. The House was more liberal than the Senate. The President was a Democrat, and thus the gridlock region extended to the left. The possibility of filibusters in the Senate constrained policy movement to the left, whereas the President's veto and the difficulty of overriding such a veto in the liberal Democratic House stopped policy movements to the right.

The 1980 elections shifted the median in both the House and the Senate to the right, with Republican gains in both chambers. The most dramatic shift in the gridlock interval, however, came as a result of the presidential election. No longer would the threat of a presidential veto extend the gridlock region to the left; now the region would extend toward the conservative preferences of Ronald Reagan. The gridlock region for the 97th Congress was defined by the filibuster pivot in the

Senate and the veto pivot, also in the Senate. This meant that the gridlock region shifted dramatically to the right, releasing policies that formerly had been held in place by the preferences of a Democratic Congress and a Democratic President with veto powers. Republicans could seize on these released policies, shifting them to the right, back into the gridlock region.

The constraint on policy change would generally be the filibustering of Democrats in the Senate. However, with regard to budget issues, Republicans could opt to use the reconciliation rules that would prevent budget resolutions from having to gain supermajorities in the Senate to overcome filibusters. As such, with regard to budget issues, the President was constrained not by the filibuster in the Senate but by the need to construct a majority in the Democratic House. Pivotal members on nonbudgetary issues would be conservative Democrats in the Senate, and on budget issues they would be conservative Democrats in the House. Thus the new President looked to southern Democrats to round out his new coalition.

Turning Election Results into Policy Outcomes

Given the dilemma facing the country in 1981—high entitlement expenditures, a much-needed increase in defense spending, voter anger about taxes, the drying up of the Social Security Trust Fund, and a stagflated economy—it was clear that a tax cut, increases in defense spending, and cuts in some programs would be forthcoming. The debate would be over *how much* to cut taxes, *how much* to increase defense, and *which* programs should be cut back. President Reagan had the first move; between his inauguration and State of the Union Address, the President and his director of the Office of Management and Budget (OMB), David Stockman, worked the Hill to prepare members for the magnitude of the cuts. Stockman's "Black Book" revealed that the President would ask for $50 billion in spending cuts. Among the targeted programs were the National Endowment for the Arts, Social Security benefits for students, food stamps, comprehensive employment training, research on synthetic fuels, and urban development. In tandem with these program cuts, the President also proposed the adoption of the Kemp-Roth tax cut—a 10 percent cut in income taxes in each of three years—and a $50 billion increase in defense spending.

In his State of the Union Address in February, President Reagan warned of a "day of reckoning" if Congress did not act immediately to cut taxes and expenditures. Reagan promised to maintain the safety net for the truly needy. He proposed the 10–10–10 tax cut effective July 1, 1981, and cuts in eighty-three programs ranging from food stamps to mass transit grants to dairy price supports. The assumption underlying these proposals was clearly supply-side economics. Cutting the size of government would unleash creativity in the private sector, stimulating economic growth and offsetting potential losses in tax revenues.

Stockman and the President chose to use the reconciliation process discussed in Chapter 3 to push the policy shifts through Congress. Roughly, the process calls for the House and Senate Budget Committees to first pass resolutions placing limits on expenditures within functional categories and instructing committees to reconcile their decisions with the aggregate totals in the budget resolution. After passage of the resolution, the regular appropriating and taxing process would go to work. The decisions made by the committees would result in two bills: an appropriations bill addressing all the cuts and the increase in defense, and a tax bill. The consolidation of all these issues under the reconciliation rules enabled the President to appeal to the American public just before the voting, rather than having to deal with thirteen regular appropriations bills spaced out over time.

Democratic opposition to the tax cuts and spending cuts was immediate. They did not question that these cuts would be made; they questioned the magnitude. Their strategy was to appear responsible before the electorate while waiting to sort out the potential effects of Reagan's proposals. Representative Rostenkowski put it best: "We are still debating exactly what it was that voters expressed at the ballot box last fall" (1981 *Congressional Quarterly Weekly Report*, 377). Reagan and Stockman understood from the start that they would need conservative Democratic support, so their House lobbying activity focused on southern Democrats. House Speaker Thomas P. (Tip) O'Neill and the Democratic leadership also focused on southern Democrats. For example, Representative Hefner's proposal to increase defense spending by $6.6 billion more than Reagan's proposal was meant to entice southern Democrats to vote for the Democrats' budget.

Securing Spending Cuts

Republicans in the Senate pressed ahead on the resolution and in March the Senate Budget Committee voted unanimously to approve a reconciliation resolution cutting $36.4 billion from Carter's 1981 budget plan (thus less than the original $50 billion plan, but still a noticeable cut). Republicans "exhibited unprecedented solidarity" whereas Democrats "squabbled openly around the conference table" (1981 *Congressional Quarterly Weekly Report*, 499). Ten separate Senate committees were given reconciliation orders. On April 2, 1981, the Senate passed a budget resolution that cut $36.9 billion in expenditures, and assumed revenues based on Reagan's 10–10–10 tax cuts. The House Democrats meanwhile were developing their own counter-proposal, which featured a smaller, one-time tax cut and expenditure cuts that were $19.4 billion smaller than those proposed by the Senate resolution. Even though the Democratic proposal was less severe than Reagan's request, it represented "a major rightward shift by the majority party in the House" (1981 *Congressional Quarterly Weekly Report*, 622).

Representatives Phil Gramm (D, TX) and Delbert Latta (R, OH) proposed a substitute for the Democratic plan that was much closer to the Reagan budget; but the Gramm-Latta proposal was defeated 13–17 by the Budget Committee. The Budget Committee, however, did not represent the floor. On May 7, 1981, the House of Representatives voted for the Gramm-Latta substitute. Sixty-three Democrats joined Republicans to support what was essentially the basic Reagan proposal. The vote "provided cold, hard proof that the fragmentation among the Democrats . . . is extremely serious" (1981 *Congressional Quarterly Weekly Report*, 783). Given this decisive victory in the Democrat-controlled House, the House–Senate conference agreed and both bodies passed the budget resolution. The resolution was a victory for Reagan's policies because it included $36 billion in budget cuts, assumed a $53.9 billion reduction in taxes (a 5–10–10 cut), and instructed committees to reconcile their numbers with the resolution.

But the battle was not yet over. The committees, particularly in the House, would not all meet their instructions and there would be a series of votes on the final omnibus reconciliation bill. In addition, the House and Senate tax committees had to draft bills to actually reduce taxes since the budget resolution is not binding in law. "The first true test of how serious Congress is about cutting federal spending in the budget will be how the committees respond to their reconciliation instructions" (1981 *Congressional Quarterly Weekly Report*, 839). The Democratic strategy in the House was to hope that the President's popularity fell or that economic conditions deteriorated such that deep cuts in the budget would become untenable. Interest groups pushing to reverse budget cuts turned to the committees.

In late June, House Republicans were faced with major problems, as seven of fifteen committees were short on their reconciliation proposals. The Republican-controlled Senate had already presented a reconciliation package that remarkably exceeded the first resolution by trimming $39.6 billion (the goal was $35.1 billion). Several House committees, however, failed to meet the targets in agriculture (Agriculture), impact aid for school districts (Education and Labor), park acquisition (Interior), funding for the arts (Appropriations, Interior subcommittee), Medicaid (Energy and Commerce), and subsidized housing (Banking, Finance, and Urban Affairs), among other program areas. Republicans had to choose between accepting the committees' results or pushing for an alternative that cut expenditures to a level consistent with the first resolution. The alternative plan was referred to as Gramm-Latta II, and the vote would be tough because now it was a vote to actually cut whereas the first vote was advisory.

The crucial budget reconciliation votes would occur on the rule under which the bill would be reported and on the actual Gramm-Latta substitution. Roughly, the Democrats wanted a rule that would force Republicans to vote separately for every cut greater than what the committees had proposed. Republicans wanted one vote—up or down—on the whole package. The Republicans, with the support of very conservative southern Democrats, prevailed on the rule, and on June 26 the House accepted the Gramm-Latta substitute by a 217–211 vote. The Gramm-Latta bill cut $38.2 billion in 1982 and was compatible with the Senate bill. The majority favoring Gramm-Latta was composed of a unified Republican party together with conservative Democrats. Figure 4.2 shows the array of House Democratic support for President Reagan's policies by ADA score. The results show that the more difficult the vote, the further right the Democrats supporting the action were. Cutting taxes is much easier to vote for than cutting programs and, as can be

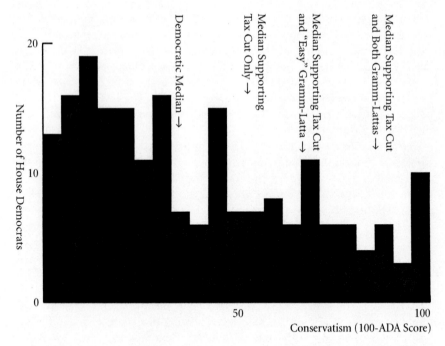

FIGURE 4.2   House Democratic Support for Reagan (1981)

seen (and as described below), Democrats supporting both the tax cut and the first Gramm-Latta substitute (which was not binding) were more conservative than those who only supported the tax cut. The twenty-nine Democrats supporting Reagan all the way on tax cuts and the tough Gramm-Latta II proposal were very conservative indeed.

Tax Cut Politics

The first budget resolution had accepted the broad outline of the Reagan tax policy, and it seemed clear that the Republican Senate would not present much of an obstacle. Regarding passage of the tax bill, in the House of Representatives there were two major concerns to be addressed: (1) should the cuts be multiyear or one-time; and (2) who should benefit from tax relief? Senator Dole's Finance Committee proposed a 25 percent cut with 5 percent the first year followed by 10 percent cuts in each of the next two years. House Democrats insisted that the main beneficiaries be those with annual incomes of $20,000 to $50,000. The tax bill also included a drop in marginal tax rates and additional retirement and business-related breaks. The debate, however, would center around the multiyear proposal and the question of who would benefit.

The Republican Senate proposed a three-year, 25-percent tax reduction package that did not target "middle income earners" in any specific way. The Senate also approved indexation beginning in 1985, which meant that bracket creep would be eliminated. The House Democrats countered with a two-year, 15-percent-total cut in individual taxes skewed to provide most of the relief to those earning less than $50,000 annually. Their alternative allowed a third-year cut if certain conditions were met. Given that Republican unanimity for the three-year Reagan–Dole proposal guaranteed only 192 votes, the bill was still 26 votes shy of passage. Under these circumstances, the President began to court the members of the conservative Democratic Forum. The forum consisted of forty-seven Democrats of whom forty-four were from southern and border states.[3] Kent Hance (TX) and Charles Stenholm (TX) were among the House leaders of the Democratic Forum. In short, in order to pass, the tax bill would have to appeal to the median voter, who was surely in this group of forty-seven conservative Democrats. On the liberal side, Rostenkowski and Jones were leading the battle for those favoring a one-time cut aimed at earners with incomes below $50,000. The liberals, too, knew that to win they had to woo conservative southern Democrats. The shift to a two-year, 15-percent tax cut was indicative of this strategy.

Liberal Democrats were more than a little annoyed by the Republicans' wooing of conservative Democrats. Representative Moffett (CT) sought punishment for Democrats voting too often with Republicans. Representative Long, the chair of the Democratic caucus, openly spoke of disciplining maverick Democrats. The Democratic leadership, however, refused to agree to any sanctions largely because they knew they would need the help of conservative Democrats in the future for other purposes. The fate of the Reagan tax bill would be decided by members of the Democratic Forum. Representative Hance told Rostenkowski that he would carry the President's bill—a three-year, 25-percent individual tax cut (5–10–10) with significant tax cuts for corporations—to the floor. One important side issue was indexation of the individual income tax. This would involve indexing taxes, like entitlements, to inflation so that inflation could not force wage earners into higher brackets. The Senate included indexation in its tax bill. On each of the crucial indexation votes in the Senate, a bloc of conservative Democrats voted with the Republicans.

With the Senate firmly in place and the House outcome in some doubt, President Reagan on July 27, 1981, appealed to the public, arguing that the tax cuts were as crucial as the budget cuts he had won a month earlier. In the House, "both the President's and the Democrats' bills have been laden in recent weeks with myriad benefits and sweeteners for different groups of taxpayers, as each side has sought to put together a coalition of support" (*New York Times*, July 27, 1981). Needless to say, the arguments for these sweeteners were complicated and arcane. The point is that the benefits were offered to southern and border-state Democrats who were on the fence between the Reagan bill and the Democratic bill. The President's speech cut through the distracting complications by focusing on the need for a major tax cut. Reagan also made a plea for indexing, arguing that without it taxes would rise automatically over the long run.

On July 29, 1981, the House of Representatives voted 238–195 to adopt a bill close to Reagan's original proposal, sponsored by Conable (R, NY) and Hance in place of the Democratic bill drafted by the House Ways and Means Committee. Forty-eight Democrats voted with Reagan whereas only one Republican (Jeffords, VT) opposed. Thirty-seven of the defecting Democrats came from the South; Texas accounted for eight defectors and Georgia seven. In conference, Senator Kennedy kept the Senate in session for two days trying to send the bill back to committee to remove the breaks for big oil. In the end, the basic Reagan package survived: a three-year (5–10–10) individual income tax reduction with income taxes indexed after 1985; a major increase in the depreciation allowance for corporations; and a major reduction in the top corporate tax bracket (from 70 to 50 percent). In sum, the President's basic tax package had carried the day.

Our thesis has been that the 1980 elections shifted the preferences of the U.S. Congress to the right and that the major policy shifts of the Reagan revolution were achieved in the Senate by virtue of the Republicans' majority status (with conservative Democratic support) and in the House by garnering votes from the conservative Democratic Forum. Figure 4.1 shows the shift in the gridlock region, leading to the establishment of conservative Democrats as the pivotal voters. Figure 4.2 shows the array of Democratic preferences in the House and indicates the positions of key Democratic defectors. The broad array of Democratic preferences from very conservative to very liberal highlights the difficulty of organizing unified Democratic action. Representative Hefner validated this phenomenon when he said: "Even when the Democrats are together, we're still fragmented. We're a party made up of liberals, moderates and conservatives. We don't have the luxury of the Republicans, who know exactly who their constituency is" (1981 *Congressional Quarterly Weekly Report*, 786). The Reagan victory was achieved by the unified Republicans plus conservative Democrats; Senator Breaux (D, LA) said that his vote couldn't be bought but "it can be rented" (1981 *Congressional Quarterly Weekly Report*, 1169).

As was hypothesized in the previous two chapters, the shift in preferences and pivotal members after the 1980 elections released spending and taxing decisions from a state of legislative gridlock. The movement was to the right, for lower taxes and lower spending. This shift was moderated by pivotal members—southern Democrats in this case. The votes of the pivotal members were secured by moderating policy somewhat (from 10–10–10 tax cuts to 5–10–10, and from $50 billion in spending cuts to less than $40 billion), and by including sweeteners in the tax and budget bills.

Adjustments and Solidification of Policy

As described in Chapter 2, after policies have been brought inside the gridlock region, we should expect little change. Absent exogenous shocks, electoral shifts, or new realizations, previous coalitions will hold, allowing no further movements to the left or right. Following the major budget changes of 1981, budget politics over the next two decades would be characterized mainly by minor adjustments and gridlock. The main exogenous shocks would be in terms of recessions in the early 1980s and early 1990s. Both would contribute to large budget deficits that gained public attention. Prior to 1994, electoral shifts would be less significant than in 1980, with small moves to the left in Congress in the 1980s. Because of the recession, deficits, and electoral shifts, tax policy would be modified somewhat to the left in 1982 and 1984, and leveled out in 1986. Budget decisions would be complicated by contentious deficit politics and by new mechanisms introduced in 1985 and 1990. Ultimately, budget policy would be solidified in a status quo that could not be significantly altered other than by politically costly deficit reduction measures, until 2001. This section tracks the adjustments and solidification of budget policy in the 1980s.

After 1981: Reagan's Shift on Taxes

In 1982 taxes were raised far more than expenditures were cut because a majority in favor of cutting expenditures could not be established, leaving the tax increase as the primary weapon of deficit reduction. In short, the second session of the 97th Congress was not as hospitable to conservative ideas as was the first session. With a sour economy and a lower level of support than in 1981, Reagan could not appeal to the public as before to pressure members of Congress to support his conservative agenda. Because tax policy was now shifting to the left (favoring increased taxes), we expect to find the majority for the new policy to differ from the majority formed for the 1981 tax cuts and reconciliation budget. We expect conservative Republicans to be the major opponents of the 1982 tax increases.

Interest rates and inflation dropped during 1982, but at a price. Unemployment reached 10.8 percent by late 1982 and industrial production continued to decline. The recession that had begun in 1981 appeared likely to continue for quite a while. The budget deficit was projected to be about $180 billion in 1983 with an annual deficit of over $300 billion by 1988. Representative Latta summed up the problem simply in January 1982: "The honeymoon is over."

Democrats in the House were reluctant to take up the tax issue, given the upcoming 1982 elections. Members were leery of voting for tax increases and then having the President campaign against them as tax-and-spend liberals. Thus in an unusual fashion Representative Rostenkowski, Chairman of the Ways and Means Committee, chose to wait until the Republican Senate and the President had acted. In the Senate, President Reagan's call to plug tax loopholes and require a minimum corporate tax was treated as insufficient.

The Senate Finance Committee proposed (on an 11–9 straight party vote) a $98 billion tax increase: $21 billion in the first year, $34 billion in the second, and $43 billion in the third. The bill raised taxes on corporations, cut back some business benefits given in the previous year's bill, and established a minimum tax on high-income individuals. The committee attached its bill to H.R. 4961, a minor tax bill passed by the House in 1981, thereby meeting the constitutional requirement that tax bills must originate in the House. Committee Democrats advocated repealing the 1983 individual tax cut (10 percent). The Senate voted on July 23, 1982, to accept the Finance Committee's report by a 50–47 vote. Several amendments to cut the 1981 tax reductions were defeated on the floor largely because Senator Dole assured his colleagues that repealing the 1981 tax reductions would guarantee a presidential veto.

In the House, the Ways and Means Committee was having trouble agreeing on what to include in their own revenue agreement, so on July 28 they agreed to go directly to conference on the Senate bill, and the full House agreed to go along with this proposal. The advantage of this strategy was that members anxious about their reelection bids would not be voting on a Democratic plan but rather on a Republican plan, and the Republican Senate and President could be held responsible for the tax increase.

The battle in conference took eight full days and was painful. Increasing taxes and cutting spending in an election year are not popular activities among members of Congress. Battles over restoring the 1981 cuts in welfare and limiting Medicare reimbursements and Medicaid co-payments highlight the policy differences between Democrats and Republicans and between House and Senate. In the final analysis, $17.5 billion in spending cuts over three years was accepted. On the tax side, the chief battle was over the proposed $38 billion increase in corporate taxes. The Democrats prevailed by dropping the indexation of taxes on capital gains, defeating Republican liberalization of capital gains taxes, and increasing the minimum tax on wealthy individuals.

Final passage of the 1982 Tax Equity and Fiscal Responsibility Act (TEFRA) depended upon President Reagan's willingness to lobby on its behalf. Although in principle Reagan did not like increasing taxes, he had prevented any increase in personal taxes; the indexed 5–10–10 tax cuts would stay intact; and some of his original loophole-closing proposals made it to the final package. Without Reagan's backing, Democrats would not deliver the votes needed for passage, while with Reagan's public sponsorship they could cleanly run for reelection saying that they had supported the President's bill. In order to assure Democrats that he was committed to the bill, the President promised to send personal letters to all who supported it, thus giving the Democrats electoral cover. The question then became whether Reagan could convince enough Republicans to support the bill. To this end the President went to the Hill and pressured Republicans to support the 1982 tax increases. On the crucial votes, from the Rousellot (R, CA) motion that the law was unconstitutional to final passage, only 75 to 88 Republicans voted with about 150 to 170 Democrats to pass the bill. A majority of Republicans voted against the President and the compromise. In the Senate the bill also passed, but 11 Republicans voted against it and 9 Democrats sided with the majority to fashion a 52–47 victory.

To sum up, the downturn in the economy along with the 1981 tax cuts had created a large deficit that had to be brought under control; the director of OMB, his deputy, and other Reagan strategists clearly indicated that no further "real" expenditure cuts were possible. The administration decided that raising business taxes and closing loopholes were preferable to losing part of the individual income tax cut. Thus, in order to cut the deficit, the compromise proposal adjusted tax policy to the left, away from the 1981 status quo. Since Senators' and House members' preferences were fairly stable, the majority for the leftward shift differed from the majority that had passed the key items of the 1981 Reagan revolution a year earlier.

In line with the revolving gridlock theory, we would expect that the Republicans who defected from the President would be the most conservative. Likewise, Democrats who voted for the President's tax and reconciliation bills in 1981 and against the 1982 deficit reduction act would be the pivotal moderate to conservative Democrats. On the Republican side, stalwart conservatives like Barry Goldwater (AZ) and Jesse Helms (NC) voted against the tax hike. The median 1981 ADA score of Republican defectors was 5 while the mean was a scarcely higher 10.4. The story in the House was the same. Eighty-eight Republicans voted for the tough Gramm-Latta bill and the tax cut in 1981 and then deserted the President on the 1982 tax increase; twelve Democrats followed the same voting pattern. The median ADA score of these Republicans and Democratic defectors was about 7 while the mean was 10. In short, in both the House and Senate, the 1982 coalition to increase taxes was "middle-to-left" or "middle-out" (with some liberal Democrats refusing to join the coalition in order to either force moderate Republicans to vote for tax increases or gain further concessions in exchange for their votes), whereas the 1981 "cut-taxes-and-spending" crusade had been a middle-to-right coalition of Republicans and very conservative Democrats.[4]

The 1980 elections had allowed for a significant shift to the right in tax policy. The coalition for this shift was conservative, made up of both Republicans and southern Democrats. When the economy declined in 1982, budget deficits indicated that the tax cuts had gone too far, leaving policy to the right of the median in both the House and the Senate. However, preferences and constraining institutions prevented a full shift back to the left. When the President supported shifts back to the left, Congress was able to move policy back toward the median members. When the President opposed the shifts, there would be gridlock. Reagan promised to veto legislation that attacked his 5–10–10 indexed individual income tax cuts, and there certainly were not enough votes to override this supermajority constraint. As a concession and a response to the budget deficits, Reagan agreed to tax increases elsewhere. A coalition in support of such a policy would have to come from the left, with conservative Republicans deserting. In order to avoid the blame for the tax hikes, House Democrats forced the President and the Republican Senate to initiate the proposals. This new coalition responding to the ballooning deficit would cooperate in another tax increase in 1984 but then find no further common ground after the 1986 tax act.

The Refinements of 1983–1986

As noted by media coverage of Congress and by in-depth analyses, public policy from 1983 to 1986 was focused on tax and budget policy. But such a focus would bring about no radical change but rather a shift slightly to the left. In 1983

Congress passed an adjustment to Social Security that raised taxes. In 1984 Congress again passed a tax increase, the Deficit Reduction Act (DEFRA), and in 1986 Congress passed a major tax act. The politics behind these changes can be explained as follows: (1) the 1982 elections shifted Congress to the left; (2) attempts by liberals to significantly raise taxes failed as did attempts by conservatives to cut expenditures (other than defense); and (3) the 1986 tax act was a continuation of the policies begun in 1981. Congressional politics had become budgetary politics, and budgetary policy could no longer be shifted in any dramatic fashion because neither the liberals nor the conservatives had the votes to do so.

The 1982 elections to the U.S. Senate produced little change. Newly elected Senators Trible (VA) and Hecht (NV) replaced Democrats, while the Democrat Bingaman (NM) replaced a Republican, yielding a one-seat Senate gain for the Republicans. The 98th Senate would be much like the 97th Senate. In the House elections there was a shift to the left as the Republicans lost twenty-six seats to the Democrats, primarily in the southern and border states, in the Midwest, and in the Northeast. Moreover, the Republicans who lost had been supporters of the President's policies. To compare these results with the congressional changes faced by Reagan's immediate predecessors after two years in office, President Carter lost eleven Democrats in 1978 and President Nixon lost twelve Republican seats in 1970.

One way to think about the 1982 elections is that President Reagan's policies were very conservative and put at risk those Republicans who came from moderate districts. A President puts at risk those congressional members furthest from his own policy proposals. Republicans from moderate districts like Jim Leech (IA) had constituencies that were likely to oppose some of Reagan's policies. These representatives face a dilemma. If they vote for the President's policies they will face an electoral opponent who will paint them as too conservative for the district. If, on the other hand, these representatives vote against the President, they will fall out of favor with the White House. Figure 4.3 shows the district preferences of these vulnerable members.

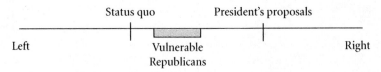

FIGURE 4.3   Vulnerability in Republican Districts

Due to pressure from their party in Congress or from the White House, Republicans feel that they sometimes must vote with their party even in cases where they should rightly vote against the party because of the preferences of their constituents. In doing so, they are putting their seats at risk.

Brady and Cogan (1998) support this theory over a variety of elections from 1954 to 1996.[5] For example, they find electoral vulnerability and losses in 1982 for moderates who supported Reagan's early policies, and in 1994 for moderate and conservative Democrats who supported Clinton's early proposals (analyzed in Chapter 5). In order to determine if district characteristics and voting support played a role in the 1982 election, Brady and Cogan analyzed the election results for Republican incumbents in the House. The results support the claim that Republicans who came from the least conservative districts and who voted with the President were the most likely to be defeated in 1982. In short, the Republicans from moderate districts who voted with Reagan paid a price, whereas the so-called "Gypsy Moth" Republicans (who voted against Reagan after the 1981 Christmas break) were reelected. Once again, the point is clear: members of Congress who please their constituencies are most likely to get reelected; and sometimes voting for the district means voting against the party.

The new House in 1982, with 269 Democrats and 166 Republicans, was more liberal than the 97th House. Attempts to further roll back spending for social programs and governmental services were doomed to fail. President Reagan's economic performance ratings fell to 30 percent; the "voting scores for the 57 newly elected House Democrats [were] the most liberal since the class of '46" (Palazzolo 1992, 148). As George Miller observed, "Last fall's election really put the leadership on the cat bird's seat" (Palazzolo 1992, 149). Moreover, from the 98th through the 100th Congresses, the Democratic leadership made sure that the Budget Committee was stacked with liberal Democrats. (In 1983 no Democrat with an ADA of less than 50 was appointed.)

The 1983 budget was Reagan's first full budget not reliant on Carter baselines. It included large cuts: the Department of Energy was to be dismantled, many programs such as Amtrak were to be zeroed out, Urban Development Action Grants (UDAG) were zero funded, and the Environmental Protection Agency (EPA) was cut. But Congress was not responsive. We interviewed top-ranking Reagan OMB personnel regarding the political limits on spending changes. One knowledgeable participant claimed: "[It is] not fair to say that we had reached the outer edge of the spending envelope. But any more that could be done was marginal because: (1) the recession was deep; (2) it was coming on to the 1984 elections and the mandate had worn off; and (3) the interest groups that lost in 1981 had regrouped."

Another Reagan appointee said that in 1983 and 1984 the stumbling blocks were Waxman (D, CA) in the House on Medicare and Medicaid; Weicker (R, CT) in the Senate on Health and Human Services (HHS) and harbor matters; Cohen (R, ME) on rural housing; and Stafford (R, NH) on educational programs. Senators Dole (R, KS), Packwood (R, OR), and Baker (R, TN) set the parameters for debate. In short, conservatives no longer had a majority and policy shifted slightly back to the left. Expenditures would not be cut, defense would receive less than Reagan wanted but more than the House wanted, taxes on corporations would be raised, and tax loopholes would be plugged; the 5–10–10 indexed individual income taxes, however, would not be touched. The political coalitions necessary to pass the slight shift were middle-out coalitions. Across a whole set of votes from the 1983 budget resolution through the 1984 DEFRA tax hikes, the twenty-one Republican Senators who supported the compromises had a median ADA score of 50 and a mean of 50.8. The cast was familiar: Weicker, Cohen, Percy (IL), Mathias,

Danforth (MO), Andrews (ND), Kassebaum (KS), Chafee (RI), Gorton (WA), Stafford, Hatfield (OR), and Packwood (OR), to name a few. The Republicans not voting for compromises had a mean ADA of 12.4 and a median of 7.5; they included Helms and East (NC), Wallop (WY), and Kasten (WI). Democratic supporters of the compromises were familiar moderates such as Chiles (FL), Dixon (IL), Bradley (NJ), Moynihan (NY), Sasser (TN), and Bentsen (TX). On the House side, the story was the same. The conservative Democratic caucus split over the compromises whereas moderate-to-liberal Democrats and moderate Republicans voted for compromise. The Republicans who voted against Reagan in 1982 voted against him again in 1984. In sum, after 1981 the readjustment to increase taxes was passed by middle-out or middle-to-left coalitions in stark contrast to the middle-to-right coalition that had passed the major 1981 conservative legislation.

The 1986 Tax Act

Many have interpreted the 1986 Tax Reform Act as a reversal of previous practice. Birnbaum and Murray (1987) and Beam, Conlan, and Wrightson (1990) argue that the 1986 act was true reform. Our interpretation agrees with Fullerton, namely that the 1986 Tax Reform Act "was indeed important legislation. But the direction of tax policy-making had really changed by 1981" (Fullerton 1994, 190). The politics of the 1986 act had already been established by the switch to the right in the 1980 election, Reagan's conservative legislation of 1981, and the two adjustments again raising taxes in 1982 and 1984. The Tax Reform Act of 1986 was the result of four developments that pushed the tax code together; Fullerton lists these developments as follows. First, supply-siders continued to affect tax policy. Calls for a flat tax or a modified flat tax were gaining ground. Second, the tax system had become too complicated both in terms of its legal complexity and the amount of time it took the "average" taxpayer to fill out the forms. Third, public confidence in the tax system was low, in large part due to reports that large corporations and wealthy individuals paid no taxes. Fourth, marginal effective tax rates were shown to have high disparities between different types of assets or financing (see Fullerton 1994, 192ff.). Note that the issues of progressivity and considerations of revenue are missing from this list.

The most politically interesting feature of the 1986 tax reform was that, perhaps foreshadowing future PAYGO procedures, the proposals were to be revenue neutral—compromises could not simply be struck by lowering taxes. Whether this could be accomplished while meeting the goals of the reformers was unclear, as one compromise after another fell apart. The goals of the tax legislation that culminated in the 1986 act were lower marginal tax rates, less complexity, similar tax burdens for those with similar income, and a more efficient allocation of resources. Senator Bradley was probably the first to formulate this overview and to push it in the Bradley-Gephardt fair tax proposal of 1982. The Bradley-Gephardt plan was not taken too seriously in 1982; however, the Reagan 1984 reelection campaign staffers were worried that Walter Mondale would endorse the plan and gain an advantage in the 1984 election. The President thus announced that the Department of the Treasury would conduct a study on taxes, but that it would not be due until after the election. The Treasury report, like the Bradley-Gephardt proposal, endorsed a modified flat rate (of 15, 25, and 35 percent rates) on individuals and a shift of $150 billion from individual taxes to corporations (a rise to a 33 percent rate). In short, the relevant proposals were revenue neutral, distributionally neutral, and designed to level the playing field.

The Treasury proposal was opposed by business and other interests because they saw it as restricting capital investment. Senator Packwood, the chair of the Finance Committee, said that he liked the tax code as it was, and the American public was indifferent to the reform given its complexity. Secretary Baker modified the Treasury proposal by reducing indexation and integration, strengthening the acceleration of depreciation allowances, and restoring tax breaks for oil and gas and other benefits. Baker kept the 15, 25, and 35 percent brackets, although in order to make the proposal revenue neutral he added a windfall recapture tax.

On the House Ways and Means Committee, Chair Dan Rostenkowski restored (under pressure) additional benefits that caused the top rates to go to 38 percent and shifted $140 billion over five years from individual to corporate taxes. House Republicans led by conservatives and aided by southern Democrats killed H.R. 3838 on a procedural vote. Again, as in 1982 and 1984, President Reagan went to the Hill encouraging Republicans to keep reform alive, and promised to veto the bill if changes were not made in the Senate. The Senate Finance Committee increased excise taxes, reduced corporate taxes below the levels proposed in the House, and killed the rise to 38 percent in the top personal rate. The result was a projected revenue shortfall, and Packwood stopped the mark-up, thus momentarily halting tax reform. The Finance Committee then proposed a top rate of 27 percent plus a surcharge, but ensured higher real revenues by fully taxing capital gains and disallowing some "passive losses." The House-Senate conference raised the top personal rate to 28 percent (actually 33 percent for the highest income brackets for whom a 5 percent surcharge could be applicable), ultimately securing passage and the President's signature.

The summary results of the tax changes from 1981 to 1986 are as follows: (1) marginal tax rates were reduced; (2) politicians now paid serious attention to estimates of revenue impact, in which revenue considerations dominate all discussions of tax reform; and (3) the five-year budget had been established as the primary budget-planning vehicle. These changes all began with the 1981 Economic Recovery Tax Act, modified by the 1982 and 1984 tax bills. "The new era of tax policy was in effect as of August 1981, but its first products were not evident until TEFRA in 1982 and DEFRA in 1984. These bills closed loopholes, slowed depreciation, and started to level the playing field. By 1986, in these respects, the Tax Reform Act of 1986 was simply more of the same" (Fullerton 1994, 206).[6]

The politics of budget formulation also shifted during this period. Any President facing the U.S. economy in 1980 would have had to address tax reform, Social

Security reform, defense increases, and spiraling entitlement expenditures. The major shift in policy was the 1981 ERTA bill, which was passed by the newly elected conservative majorities in the House and the Senate. The revenue shortfalls generated by the recession caused the President to favor eliminating loopholes, shifting taxes to corporations, and leveling the playing field. In order to achieve these ends and keep the reduced average and marginal tax rates, the politics shifted to the center and those who were crucial in passing the 1981 reform were most opposed to the 1982, 1984, and 1986 reforms. The election of 1982 was particularly important for the expenditure side of the equation because the twenty-six Republicans who lost in the House had been supporters of the 1981 budget changes. From 1982 through 1986 it was clear that the votes to seriously decrease expenditures were no longer there, and there were also not enough votes to increase individual income taxes. Thus it seems clear that by 1986, budget policy either had been perfected or was mired in gridlock. Despite the fact that future budget deals would need only bare majorities based on reconciliation rules, between the House and the Senate no majority agreement could be reached, either for tax increases or for spending cuts. Deficits became institutionalized and the national debt grew.

The passage of the 1986 tax act was the culmination of the 1981 Reagan tax revolution. The dramatic lowering and indexing of individual income taxes over the 1981–1986 period had dropped average taxes and dramatically decreased marginal tax rates. The original decrease was a direct result of the 1980 elections, which shifted the preferences of both the House and Senate to the right, and it was conservatives who passed the 1981 tax policy. The recession of 1982–1983 resulted in high deficits, and as a result Congress twice passed significant tax increases. President Reagan beat back Democratic attempts to shift taxes to individuals (through dropping the last two years of the 1981 act's tax cuts) by threatening vetoes that would have been sustained. The 1982 and 1984 tax increases were restricted to corporations and to closing loopholes, and both were passed without the support of the conservatives who had passed the 1981 tax cut. Individual income tax cuts were built into the 1986 tax act and were now untouchable.

The issue of expenditures did not go as well for the President. The 1982 election had shifted the House somewhat back to the left, and it was clear that there was no majority for dramatic cutbacks in expenditures. Twice the Office of Management and Budget (OMB) put forward tough budget resolutions and twice they were dead on arrival. The best that can be said on the expenditure side is that the *rate of growth* in expenditures was slowed (Cogan, Muris, and Schick 1994). In effect, after 1986 it was clear that taxes could not be raised without dire consequences for the politicians proposing the raises, and expenditures could not be cut—in other words, the deficit was here to stay. Until 1997, no five-year budget projection since 1981 had shown a budget surplus, whereas every five-year budget projection prior to 1981 showed a surplus starting two or three years out.

In the period from 1986 to 1992, then, we begin to see how the dominance of the budget combines with preferences and constraining institutions to lead to policy gridlock. After highlighting the failure of the Bush election in 1988 to produce a change in the gridlock region, we will turn to an analysis of the 1990 budget act. This budget deal was a strong indication that consensual politics was dead with regard to budgetary issues.

The Gridlock of George H. Bush

In an important sense divided government became an issue when George H. Bush was elected President (Fiorina 1996). Prior to Bush's victory, the Eisenhower, Nixon, and Reagan presidencies could be dismissed as circumstantial. That is, Ike won because he was a war hero, Nixon because the Democrats were badly divided in 1968, and Reagan because of economic stagflation. With Bush's victory over Dukakis, scholars, journalists, and others began talking about divided government as a permanent feature of American politics. Most political scientists focused on why voters elected divided governments.[7] Some focused on the consequences of divided government; and it was these scholars who coined the term "gridlock."[8] Forgetting the variants, the gridlock theme was essentially the same—divided government produces policy stagnation. Thus the analysis of Reagan's last two years and George H. Bush's four years points to a quintessential period of gridlock—a Democratic Congress and a Republican President with few legislative achievements between them.

The 100th Congress following the 1986 elections returned the Democrats to majority status in the Senate and brought James Wright to the speakership of the House. Given control of the Senate and bright prospects for winning the presidency, the Democrats, especially Wright, wanted to establish a policy position that distinguished them from Reagan. The Democrats passed an $18 billion sewage treatment bill and an $88 billion transportation bill over Reagan's veto. They also passed the small ($443 million) Homeless Shelter Act and a $30 billion housing bill. In addition, Speaker Wright pressed for a larger role in U.S.–Central American policy. Despite the Democrats' victory in the 1986 elections and Speaker Wright's aggressive use of his office, not many objective observers would give the 100th Congress high marks for significant legislation. President Reagan's actual and threatened vetoes and the Gramm-Rudman-Hollings sequestration threats helped define the "gridlock region," which left little room for major changes in budget resolutions and appropriations bills. There were no individual or corporate tax increases and no major cuts or increases in expenditures.

George H. Bush's presidency did not give rise to many significant domestic policy shifts. The Gulf War, the collapse of communism, and the defeat of the Sandinistas in Nicaragua were the major events of the Bush presidency. All were based on exogenous shocks, rather than electoral shifts in the gridlock region. On the domestic front, the major legislation was off-budget. Interviews with Bush OMB officials generated comments like, "We knew that if he was going to do anything for the environment and education and keep the Reaganites we would have to figure out how to do it without adding to the budget," or "They [the Reaganites] never trusted us so we had to be especially careful on how we created a kinder, gentler America." The Clean Air Act amendments and the Americans with Disabilities Act were both carefully crafted to be off-budget, as was the minimum wage increase.

Theoretically it is not surprising that George H. Bush had few initial legislative victories. Policy gridlock typically is overcome by major shifts in the gridlock region through elections. With a switch in the party of the President, the boundaries of the gridlock region change, with the filibuster pivot replacing the veto pivot and vice versa. The less-restrictive supermajority constraint of the filibuster often dictates that some policy areas (where legislation was vetoed by previous Presidents) are released for movement toward the President's position. Because Bush replaced another Republican President, he did not have this advantage and was therefore handicapped from the beginning by a lack of issues that he could successfully act upon. At best, policy change could come through Bush's refusal to veto legislation that Reagan had vetoed, but this would result in policy shifts to the left, away from the majority of his party. In addition to the fact that the President's position had remained almost the same from Reagan to Bush, the makeup of Congress was largely unchanged by the 1988 elections, so no new policy initiatives could be expected from a change in congressional preferences. Along with the deficits that discouraged tax cuts and new expenditures, there was little room for President Bush to maneuver on the domestic agenda. Figure 4.4 shows the identical gridlock regions for the 100th and 101st Congresses; as usual, V represents the House and Senate veto pivots, F the Senate filibuster pivot, and M the medians.

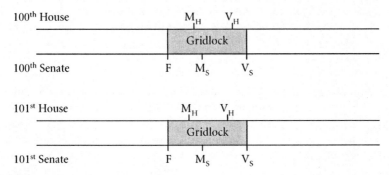

FIGURE 4.4   The 1988 Elections

Although George Bush won the 1988 presidential election by a relatively comfortable margin of 54 to 46 percent over Michael Dukakis, the congressional election results differed very little from those of the 100th Congress, in which the Democrats retook the Senate and increased their House majority. In the 100th House the Democrats held 258 seats to 177 for the Republicans whereas in the 101st House the Democrats actually increased their number to 260, reducing the Republicans to 175. There were 230 Democratic incumbents up for reelection in 1988 and 218 of them won, meaning that all of the leaders of the Democratic 100th House would be back. Moreover, in districts where both Bush and Republican House candidates won, the President ran behind the congressional candidate (receiving lower vote share) 85 percent of the time. In short, the 1988 congressional elections returned to Washington the Congress elected in 1986 plus some new Democrats. Thus, unlike all Republican Presidents of the twentieth century save William Howard Taft, George Bush's victory had actually generated a loss for his party. In the Senate the numbers stayed the same from the 100th to the 101st Senate—55 Democrats to 45 Republicans. The President faced a Congress dominated by Democrats who had felt *no* effect from his personal victory over Dukakis.

In our view, the major policy battle during the Bush presidency was the 1991 budget deal (which was voted on in 1990 prior to the midterm election). Bush's now-famous "no new taxes" pledge in his acceptance speech at the Republican Convention; his breaking the promise; and the subsequent defeat, impasse, and passage of the budget are a classic example of our view of how "gridlock" operates. We now look at this turning point in Bush's domestic presidency with the intention of showing how the consensual bipartisan coalition strategy, which had been successful in the classical budgeting period, failed in this new era of budgetary dissensus.

The 1990 Budget Crisis

Since the 1981 tax act, the idea that individual income taxes were as high as they should be was the majority position. Politicians who attempted (or even strongly advocated) raising these taxes had (like Walter Mondale) been defeated; the median position in the Congress was to leave income taxes alone. The 1982, 1984, and 1986 tax acts had not violated this principle. Corporations paid higher taxes and loopholes were closed, but average and marginal tax rates were lower in 1987 than they had been in 1980. The budgets for 1987, 1988, 1989, and 1990 were not problematic. Nobody was up to changing the provisions of the 1986 act and there were not enough votes to cut expenditures. In addition, given the growth of the economy, the deficit as a percentage of GDP had declined to manageable proportions.

Seven years of "Republican growth" came to an end in the second year of the Bush presidency. The Iraqi invasion of Kuwait was a precipitating event and the resultant rise in energy prices helped lead to a downturn in the economy. The slowing economy, along with the savings and loan crisis and bailout, caused consumers to delay purchases and markets to become cautious. With this general slowdown, government revenues also slackened, whereas expenditures continued to grow—unemployment compensation, food stamps, and other programs demanded the same if not higher levels of funding. It was clear by March 1990 that the budget deficit would be larger than predicted in the 1990 budget and larger than allowed under Gramm-Rudman-Hollings rules. This was the economic context of the budget crisis.

The original Gramm-Rudman-Hollings proposal of 1985 called for a balanced budget in 1991. In 1987 Congress revised this target year to 1993. The early-year targets were relatively easy to meet with the help of accounting practices, budget gimmicks, and other tactics. But over time it became more difficult to meet the targets and, as the economy slowed in 1990, the projected deficits grew even larger. The Gramm-Rudman-Hollings target for 1991 was in fact a $64 billion deficit. If Congress were to meet this target, some tough budget decisions would have to be made.

The downturn in the economy presented problems going into the 1990 elections. The economic slump and the ever-increasing deficit meant that achieving Gramm-Rudman-Hollings targets would be difficult without substantial expenditure cuts and/or tax increases. The Republican experience of the early Reagan years had taught congressional members that opposition to taxes was good politics whereas cutting popular expenditures was bad politics. Democratic members knew that many government programs—Social Security and Medicare especially—were popular but that raising individual income taxes was not popular. Thus, as Gary Jacobson (1990) argues, the public elected Republican Presidents committed to "no new taxes" and Democratic Senators and Representatives committed to increasing popular social programs. It is obvious that elections generating these kinds of preferences guaranteed continued deficits. If programs are popular and the taxes necessary to pay for them are not popular, the only way to have it both ways is to increase the deficit. In short, put off the tough decisions to the future, and certainly until after the next election. The Gramm-Rudman-Hollings solution to the problem was to set targets and, if they were not met, then cut spending across the board (excepting certain mandatory programs such as paying the interest on the debt) to satisfy the deficit reduction numbers. More importantly, this scheme allowed members to look like they were fiscally responsible—"I voted for and support Gramm-Rudman-Hollings"—while fighting to keep expenditures up in areas deemed important to their constituents.

President Bush's 1991 budget proposed expenditures of $1.23 trillion and revenues of $1.17 trillion for fiscal year 1991, leaving a deficit of about $64 billion, right at the Gramm-Rudman-Hollings target. The Bush administration claimed that without this budget the deficit would be about $100 billion, thus prompting the need for $36 billion in deficit reduction. Bush proposed that $19.5 billion of this reduction should come from revenue increases, with the main increases coming from a reduction in the capital gains tax (thus inducing stockholders to sell shares, increasing their taxable income for 1991); user fees; and the imposition of Medicare taxes on state and local government employees. All of these arguably could be justified without breaking the "no new taxes" pledge. The rest of the $36 billion was to come from cuts in Medicare and other entitlements plus a $4 billion cut in defense, relative to the baseline projections.

The Congressional Budget Office (CBO) released its own analysis, which differed greatly from the Bush budget. The CBO numbers showed a $161 billion dollar deficit for 1991. The difference in the budgets was due to the CBO's less-rosy assumptions about the state of the economy, and their inclusion of the savings and loan bailout in their calculations. Meanwhile, the Democratic House took up the budget issue and passed its own resolution 218–208, with no Republican voting in favor. The House resolution called for $1.24 trillion in outlays and $1.17 trillion in revenues, thus meeting the Gramm-Rudman-Hollings requirements. The House budget, however, differed greatly from the Bush budget in priorities, weighing tax increases much more heavily than spending cuts. The Democratic Senate could not reach an agreement on a budget resolution and in frustration voted for the House resolution. Then both bodies told their Appropriations Committees to get to work.

Given the different preferences shown in the budgets, working out a solution would have been difficult under any conditions. The slowdown in economic growth exacerbated the problem and both sides agreed to a budget summit in May. Little was achieved as each side lectured the other on budget matters. Then, with the effects of the economic downturn becoming more obvious, on June 26, 1990, President Bush made his fateful reversal to allow tax increases as part of the budget deal. And on July 16, Richard Darman, the director of OMB, said that the deficit for 1991 could reach $231 billion.

Under these conditions, even with concessions on taxes from the President, the going was tough. Finally, on September 30, one day before $85 billion in automatic Gramm-Rudman-Hollings cuts were to kick in, the summit participants announced that they had made a deal. The agreement was a $500 billion deficit reduction package over five years beginning with $40 billion in 1991, and new budget procedures (mainly Pay-As-You-Go [PAYGO] and Budget Caps) to stop congressional backsliding on agreements.[9] Specifically, the deal would cut defense and discretionary (nonentitlement) expenditures by $182 billion over five years; cut entitlements and farm subsidies by $186 billion; and reduce interest payments by $165 billion by restructuring the national debt. On the tax side, the deal would impose a 10 percent surcharge on earned income over $1 million; raise the top marginal tax rate from 28 to 33 percent; raise the alternative minimum tax from 21 to 25 percent; increase the Medicare tax base from $51,300 to $100,000; and forgo for one year the indexing of tax brackets mandated under Reagan's 1981 tax legislation. Thus the budget deal looked like a compromise—and it was. The negotiators were moderate Democrats, and they agreed to budget cuts and new budget procedures while the President and the congressional Republican leadership agreed to tax increases.

The fact that the leadership of both parties supported the compromise signaled that the majority-building strategy was to be bipartisan. Each party's leaders were to secure a majority of their congressional party in support of the bill, thus ensuring passage. As noted in the previous chapter, deficit-fighting coalitions took odd forms in 1982, 1984, and 1986. The need to raise taxes scares off the most conservative members, whereas some types of tax increases and spending cuts frighten away liberal members. Members of Congress look first to their home districts to see if they can afford to vote with their party. The right wing of the Republican Party was the first to react this time. They viewed the increase in individual taxes as a betrayal of all they had won under the original tax act of 1981. Liberal congressional Democrats were unhappy, too, over the regressive taxes on alcohol, gasoline, and tobacco, and over the cuts in Medicare. President Bush went public with a TV appearance à la Reagan, pleading for support. Public opinion turned against the

President and the "Deal." Ed Rollins, a political consultant to the Republican Congressional Campaign Committee, advised Republicans to run against the President's deal. The Congress as an institution also suffered, with over 70 percent of the public disapproving of the Congress's role in budgetary politics.

It became clear, given the public reaction, that a majority of the Republicans in the House would not vote for the bill, at which point liberal Democrats also felt free to vote against it. The final vote was 254 against and 179 in favor. Of the Republicans, 71 voted yes whereas 105 voted no. On the Democratic side, 108 voted for and 148 voted against. Given our reasoning about gridlock, the opposition should be characterized by more conservative Republicans and more liberal Democrats voting no. Republicans voting against the budget had a mean ADA score of 15.4, while those voting for the budget had a mean ADA score of slightly over 20. Democrats voting against the budget had a mean ADA score of 75.9, while those voting in favor had a mean ADA score of 63.8. Thus the ideological wings of both parties voted down the compromise deal.

There were also district and electoral factors at play in the vote. Most importantly, the level of competition an incumbent faced for reelection was directly related to the vote, with those facing tough challengers more likely to vote against the deal (Jacobson 1993). Challengers to both parties' incumbents saw the deal as an important issue that they could use in their campaigns to unseat incumbents. Republicans challenging Democratic incumbents could claim that voting for the deal meant new taxes, whereas Democratic challengers could say that a "yes vote" cut popular programs like Medicare. A *Congressional Quarterly* survey found that over four hundred challengers said that they were opposed to the deal.

Following the budget deal's defeat, Congress sent President Bush a continuing resolution to keep the government going, and the President vetoed it, shutting down parts of the government and further angering the electorate. The Congress in haste reactivated the original House resolution, with majorities of Republicans in both the House and the Senate voting against it. In three weeks Congress put together a package that, after conference, dropped the 10 percent surtax (but in its place limited personal deductions), increased the top rate on taxes to 31 percent and not 33 percent, limited itemized deductions to 3 percent at the margin for top earners, and set the top capital gains rate at 28 percent. The new budget package cut popular programs less and counted on tax increases more than deficit reduction through cuts in entitlements. The new deal maintained many of the new budget procedures such as PAYGO and Budget Caps. The bill (H.R. 5835) passed the House by a 238-to-192 margin. The leftward shift of the second bill (more taxes, fewer cuts) resulted in liberal Democrats and moderate Republicans voting in favor. Democrats supporting the new bill had a mean ADA of 72.6 while those opposing were at 61.4. Republicans voting against the bill had an average ADA of 14.3 and those voting in favor had an average ADA of 32.1, though there were few Republicans voting yes. President Bush, falling in popularity and taking the blame for the government shutdown and budget deficits, signed the measure.

One obvious question arising out of the revolving gridlock framework is, given that the final deal shifted policy to the left of the original compromise, why didn't conservative Republicans vote for the initial deal, which was closer to their preferences? The answer lies in what is "revolving" about the revolving gridlock theory. Concisely, they *couldn't* vote for the early package. A vote for the initial compromise would have been a triumph over gridlock and would have secured a policy more to the Republicans' liking, but would have been opposed by their constituents and therefore would have led to their demise at the polls. Gridlock in budget matters occurs when there is lack of support among the electorate (and thus among the politicians) for any particular mechanism—tax increases or budget cuts—that would lower the deficit. Members of Congress who focus more on ending gridlock than on catering to their districts' preferences will lose their seats and thus will be unable to end gridlock in the long run. Those who prolong gridlock will be generally considered inept or self-serving and will debase the entire institution of Congress, but they will be viewed in a favorable light by their constituents and therefore will be reelected.[10] In 1990, President Bush focused on limiting budget deficits and ending gridlock. This meant breaking his promise to the American people, and it led to his electoral defeat in 1992.

Thus the events of the 1990 budget deal fit well with our scenario of preferences, supermajority institutions, and tough budget decisions. The 1988 election resulted in the victory of a Republican President and the continuation of a Congress that, since the 1986 elections, had been controlled by the Democrats and that was decidedly left of the President. President Bush's major domestic legislative achievements in 1990—the Americans with Disabilities Act and the Clean Air Act amendments—were both off-budget. With the rise in oil prices generated by the Gulf War, the economy stalled and the deficit grew. The President's original budget proposal met the $64 billion Gramm-Rudman-Hollings targets, but only by making rosy economic assumptions about growth. Then in the summer of 1990 the President called for a budget summit in which tax increases would be on the table. The summit—composed of Democratic congressional leaders, Republican congressional leaders, and administration officials—devised a five-year, $500 billion reduction package that increased taxes and cut expenditures (roughly equally divided). The legislative strategy was for a majority of both parties to pass the package, making the deal bipartisan and in the process protecting both the President and incumbent members of Congress. The right wing in the Republican Party objected strenuously to the deal on the grounds that tax increases betrayed the Reagan revolution of 1981. When it became clear that these conservative Republicans could not assemble a majority, they joined with liberal Democrats who were opposed to the cuts in entitlements to defeat the deal. The Gingrich–Dellums coalition, pairing the conservative Georgia Republican with the liberal Democrat from Berkeley, was indeed unlikely. However, this left–right coalition was anticentrist, capable only of voting *against* proposals. Clearly, they could work out no budget deal of their own; they were allied only because for their own reasons they favored the status quo over the proposed budget deal. President Bush's veto of a continuing resolution to keep the government running resulted in general opprobrium for the President and the Congress. The quickly-put-together budget that did pass emphasized taxes more than cuts in expenditures and was essentially passed by

Democrats. Gary Jacobson (1993) has shown how both preferences and potential electoral vulnerability heralded the votes on the budget.

Explanations of Policy Outcomes

In the 1990 congressional elections nine Republican incumbents lost their seats, and in six open-seat Republican districts Democrats came away winners. With Republicans taking back fewer seats, the 102nd Congress was like the 100th and 101st—Democratic and to the left of the President. The domestic legislative agenda was characterized by inaction and presidential vetoes of congressional legislation. In all, President Bush vetoed twenty-four bills including two tax acts, the family leave act, a bill addressing China's most favored nation status, and campaign finance reform. Typically, Congress would pass legislation such as campaign finance reform and minimum wage increases that it knew the President would veto, and enough Republicans would then vote with the President to sustain his veto. In terms of the revolving gridlock theory, Congress passed legislation sufficiently left of the status quo point that was in turn vetoed by the President, and one-third or more (overwhelmingly Republican) members of Congress voted to sustain the veto, thus leaving policy at the status quo point or in gridlock.

Our interpretation of events from 1981 to 1992 is not unique. Many commentators and scholars have described the period in similar terms. Charles Stewart's analysis of tax policy (1991, 163–164) in the 1980s argues that:

> Tax policy in the 1980s was guided by the confluence of changing preferences and institutions. As the decade began, discontent with taxation had reached a high level, and a president was elected promising to cut taxes in a particular way. Uncertainty among congressional Democrats . . . along with Republican gains in both the Senate and the House, provided an influx of individuals . . . intent upon lowering taxes with a supply side flavor. . . . After 1981 the story was completely different. While the 1981 tax cut was not a policy equilibrium, it was nearly so: given the configuration of policy preferences in the House and Senate, along with institutional vetoes, room to maneuver in negotiating tax policy had shrunk dramatically. . . . Stalemate in tax policy, which is half the stalemate in balancing the federal budget, is a product of the 1981 tax reform and the constitutional system of institutions sharing power.

Mathew McCubbins's analysis of U.S. budget deficits (1991, 103) tells much the same story. He concludes his analysis as follows:

> Once the deficits of the 1980s were in full bloom, the check Ronald Reagan held over increases in revenue was sufficient to prevent Congress from enacting a tax increase. The compromise required to overcome the mutual checks held by the House Democrats and the Senate Republicans over each other's spending programs led to increased spending on nearly every function of government [in the

post–1981 period]. Republican threats to veto tax increases will keep budget deficits in the headlines for some time to come.

Other work in regulatory politics (Romer and Weingast 1991) and welfare policy (Ferejohn 1991) share the same view. Namely, the 1980 elections yielded a congressional majority and a President intent on cutting personal income taxes, and this shift in member preferences resulted in a new tax policy. The shifts in 1982, 1984, and 1986 respectively increased corporate taxes, closed loopholes, and finalized the basic 1981 reforms. After the 1982 elections expenditures continued to rise (albeit at a slower rate) and the combination of congressional preferences and supermajority institutions yielded no major shift in budget policy. The rise in the deficit during the Bush presidency led Bush to agree to tax increases that were unpopular with much of his party in Congress, resulting in the fiasco of 1990. Ultimately, of course, the tax increases (especially in light of Bush's theatrical 1988 campaign promise of "no new taxes"), together with an anemic domestic program, led to Bush's defeat in the 1992 presidential election.

We do not disagree with other analyses demonstrating how various policies in the 1980s resulted from congressional preferences and institutional arrangements. Indeed, we have argued the same case. The details may differ—for example, we give Reagan a greater role than Stewart (1991) does—but the broad story is the same. We do, however, have a different emphasis. In all of these legislative matters, member preferences and constraining institutions such as the filibuster and the presidential veto determine policies. Granted, party affiliation also plays a role. Democratic members of the House and Senate are generally more liberal than their Republican counterparts. However, our emphasis is less on the party affiliation and more on the policy preferences of the members; we do not care whether the 218th House voter is a southern Democrat or a northeastern Republican because in our view those members' positions and not their party determine policy.

This may not seem to be a significant difference, yet that is where the revolving gridlock theory truly begins to differ from many others. The major difference is that the election of a unified government—a Democratic President and Congress, for example—need not lead to policy shifts unless the election dramatically shifts congressional preferences as it did in 1980. In fact, as we argue in the next chapter, the election of Clinton in place of Bush was not accompanied by a correspondingly significant change in Congress, and the Clinton 1993 budget package—especially the tax increase—cost the Democrats their House and Senate majorities. Below, we briefly outline the reasons why scholars and other observers believed in the early 1990s that divided government caused gridlock, and why unified government would end it.

Studies of Divided Government

With the election of George H. Bush in 1988, the President was a Republican for the fifth time in the last six elections, whereas the House was still Democratic.

Divided government had become the normal state of affairs in American politics. Electoral scholars were not surprised by the results because, as Rosenstone (1983) had shown, a generic Republican candidate would always beat a generic Democrat at the presidential level, and a host of congressional scholars, most notably Gary Jacobson (1990), had shown that Democrats will win House elections, ceteris paribus.[11] The Bush victory did, however, produce one surprise. Although divided government at both the federal and state levels had been common in the post–World War II era (Fiorina 1996), scholars and commentators began to see such government as a problem. James Sundquist (1988) was arguably the first to elaborate this theme by claiming that divided government was inefficient and irresponsible; and, because it was apparently here to stay, he further argued that we needed a new theory of governance. Other scholars followed suit, roughly divided into two groups: those who disliked and condemned divided government and those who more objectively examined why Americans elected divided governments and what it meant. The Committee on the Constitutional System, Lloyd Cutler (1988), and Ginsburg and Shefter (1990) fall into the former category. Cutler believed that divided government increased budget deficits whereas Ginsburg and Shefter partly attributed the deficit, trade and foreign policy problems, and increased congressional investigation of the executive to divided government.

The *Congressional Quarterly* and the *National Journal* quickly picked up on this issue and other journalists followed suit. Thus by the time of the 1992 election divided government had become part of the normal vocabulary of American politics. In fact, in October 1992, a majority of Americans felt that a unified government would be better than divided government. (That the question was even asked demonstrates the attention now being paid to this issue.) Bill Clinton's victory in 1992 ended twelve consecutive years of divided government and the issue faded from the media spotlight, only to reemerge to some extent in 1995.

Leadership and Gridlock

Another tier of literature on the Bush presidency arose when scholars began to assess the lack of policy achievement during the Bush years. These reassessments focus on leadership, presidential style, and the organizational ability of the President. This kind of critique has deep roots in political science; leading works in the field are Richard Neustadt's *Presidential Power* (1960); Fred Greenstein's *The Hidden-Hand Presidency: Eisenhower as Leader* (1982); Tom Cronin's *The Presidency Reappraised* (1977) and *Rethinking the Presidency* (1982); and Terry Moe's work on the institutionalized presidency (1985, 1993). In all of these works the focus is on determining the bases of presidential power, the President's bargaining style, his standing in public opinion, and the way he organizes his White House staff and the cabinet. The sum of these various factors can, in a sense, give some indication of the quality of presidential leadership.

We do not deny that such variables have an effect on a presidency and on the President's electoral chances. We do, however, argue that most of these studies undervalue the role of the preferences of members of Congress and the use of supermajority institutions in determining presidential policy success. To be sure, most scholars adopting this approach mention that President Bush faced Democratic Congresses, and Neustadt goes so far as to point out that Presidents get elected on the basis of coalitions that have little to do with the policy problems they face. Heclo (1977), Greenstein, and Cronin point to the President's relationship to the bureaucracy as a crucial element in presidential leadership, and we do not deny a role for bureaucratic interests in determining policy. We differ in that our emphasis is on the President's role as a proposer of policy and as a frequent user, either by threat or action, of a supermajority institution—the veto. And we claim that congressional preferences, the location of the status quo policy, and the proposed policy's location are the more-important determinants of what is called "presidential success." Our argument is somewhat more consistent with Steve Skowronek's contention (1993) that the political opportunities of the time shape the President's policymaking ability; we differ in that we specify congressional preferences and supermajority institutions as the main variables affecting presidential ability. In this way, we are sympathetic to Charles Jones's work (1994), which seeks to place the presidency in the larger political context of a constitutionally separated system.

A good example of a work that has a different focus from our own is Bert Rockman's essay on the Bush presidency (1991). Rockman asks three questions in his essay: "First, what are a president's inheritances or legacies, and how do these constrain him. . . ? Second, how does the president relate to the presidency as a corporate enterprise? The third question asks how the president carries out his personal leadership role" (3). Answering these questions allows Rockman to assess the Bush presidency and to conclude that "George Bush showed himself to be an effective maintaining president" (31).

Other analysts of the Bush presidency speak of copartisanship (Jones 1991, 1994); the cooperative style of leadership (Quirk 1991); and the "Let's Deal President" (Campbell 1991). Each of these analyses starts with some form of the "President as leader" premise and each comments on the 1990 budget deal. It is illustrative to examine how these views differ from that produced by the revolving gridlock theory. Jones (1991), after reviewing the events leading up to the first Bush budget deal (the one that failed), argues: "Neither Bush nor congressional leaders were seemingly prepared for this outcome, in spite of signals that it might occur. . . . To propose increasing taxes and cutting programs is to touch the nerve ends of party differences. The achievement of getting a plan at all was overshadowed by its defeat on the House floor" (61). He concludes his analysis with: "Focusing only on the delay involved, or the compromise made, or the stalemate that results, fails to acknowledge the change in politics that has occurred" (64). Again we agree with much of what Jones has to say, especially the emphasis on the use of the presidential veto and the nature of the bargaining between the President and the Congress. The revolving gridlock theory, however, places a greater emphasis on the preferences of individual members and on the fact that the final policy is decidedly within the gridlock region. Moreover, the edges of this region were determined by conservative Democrats as part of a liberal coalition, once Bush had agreed not to veto all tax increases.

Colin Campbell (1991) attributes much of the budget debacle to the President's strategic errors, which were not simply errors in judging the preferences of the Republicans in Congress. "He [Sununu] then proceeded to fuel the suspicions of the Democrats who feared that the 'no preconditions' pledge might constitute a trap forcing them to come forward with proposals for new taxes that the administration would then bat down" (214). In short, the President's staff had not been unified and disciplined in regard to the 1990 budget; thus the debacle. Paul Quirk (1991) argues that: "The results on the deficit under Bush would indicate whether a moderate, pragmatic president pursuing a cooperative strategy would get a better result [than Reagan]" (77). Quirk argues that in the budget deal Bush was too flexible about ends while being rigid regarding means. Specifically, he argues that Bush was flexible about deficit reduction as an end and rigid in regard to the means, especially in regard to capital gains (75–77). "While seeking to achieve or at least project that reduction, Bush declined to modify his stand on taxes" (77). Quirk characterizes the final budget deal in this way: "Agreement had been reached, not by resolving differences in a manner that served long-term common interests, but by sweeping difficult choices under the rug" (79).

Note that in both Campbell's and Quirk's interpretations the President had made strategic errors in tactics (Campbell) and in bargaining (Quirk). Our view is that given the status quo on taxes and expenditures, especially entitlements, there was no viable supermajority in Congress for either serious tax increases or expenditure cuts, and thus interpretations using leadership strategies and tactics to explain the policy results are flawed. President Bush, given the preferences of his party, should have been even more rigid on the tax side as a means to deficit reduction. His flexibility on taxes cost him the original budget deal and left him with a party that was uncommitted to his candidacy during the 1992 election. The final budget deal was passed by the Democratic majority and emphasized tax increases over entitlement reductions. In short, our view is that leadership, although certainly an important concept, is hard to define and extremely limited as an explanatory variable once context has been taken into account. In regard to divided government, these leadership essays all focus on cooperation and either explicitly or implicitly argue that good choices can lead to results even under divided government.[12]

Given the above views regarding divided government and leadership, many political scientists, journalists, and insiders felt that electing a unified government with decent leadership would get the country moving. Those who had argued that divided government caused irresponsibility and was unrepresentative believed that the 1992 election would result in an end to gridlock. Clinton's campaign had featured an end-of-gridlock theme and his State of the Union Address in 1993 did the same. Democratic members of Congress hailed an end to gridlock; the result would be reduced deficits, fair and comprehensive health care policy, campaign finance reform, an increase in environmental legislation, tax cuts for the middle class, a family leave act, and many other cherished aims. Why did they believe that this would all happen? With the President and the Congress representing the same party, preferences are aligned, and both the legislative and executive branches have incentives to cooperate because policy success leads to electoral success. The veto pivot shifts to the "correct" side of the policy space (from right to left in 1992), and the President has the good fortune to lead a majority rather than a minority party. All this would be true if the election had resulted in the alignment of presidential and congressional preferences, and if Congress were a majoritarian institution, without filibusters in the Senate. If the preferences are not aligned and policy proposals are too far from the preferences of the median voter and the filibuster pivot, then the President's programs will fail and gridlock or the perceived failure of presidential leadership will result. Furthermore, if the preferences of Congress have not shifted and the President chooses to avoid proposing anything that a majority doesn't initially favor, gridlock again ensues. We claim in the next chapter that the congressional elections of 1992 did not shift preferences in Congress—and thus the likelihood of major policy change was slight, regardless of the fact of unified government.

Elections and Legislator Preferences

As we highlighted in Chapter 2 and have emphasized in Chapters 3 and 4, it is our belief that the preferences of members of Congress, along with the institutions in which they operate, determine policy outcomes at the federal level. The most effective way to change these preferences is by replacing the members themselves in elections. Elections give voters a chance to respond to the policies (or to the lack thereof) that legislators have enacted in the U.S. republican system. Only with major shifts in the preferences of congressional members can we expect breaks from gridlock.

One way to compare the membership of Congress over time is to examine how members have voted on a variety of issues in each Congress. As discussed previously, interest groups such as the ADA publish scores that demonstrate how liberal or conservative members are in a particular year.[13] In our Appendix, we include graphs of these ADA scores over time for the House of Representatives. These scores are meant to provide a better picture of how elections and politics over time have led to congressional members' changing preferences. A quick glance across these graphs lends great support to the revolving gridlock theory that we have presented in the previous chapters. As the first two graphs (Figures A.1 and A.2) illustrate, prior to the 1980 elections, the real ADA scores are seen to be relatively flat, with legislators widely dispersed from liberal to conservative.

The 1980 elections featured a conservative shift (toward lower ADA scores). The 1981 budget deal divided the Democratic Party in the House, with southern Democrats supporting the Reagan budget. By 1984, the ADA scores appear to be more bipolar than flat. There is a cluster of conservative Republicans at the low end, with liberal and moderate Democrats making up a second, though more diverse, lump on the high end. In between these two extremes are the moderate (mostly northeastern) Republicans and conservative Democrats, typically from the South. Above we claimed that the conservative Republicans held together as a group whereas the Democrats were more divided; and some Republicans from moderate districts needed to support less-conservative positions in 1982 and 1984 to retain their seats. This would explain the distribution of ADA scores shown in Figure A.3. The pivotal members necessary to break gridlock, given the bipolar nature of this distribution, are more spread apart than prior to the 1980 elections. This leads to a larger region of gridlock, where no policy changes are possible.

This bipolar distribution continues to be evident throughout the remainder of the Reagan and Bush administrations, as shown in Figures A.5 and A.6. Due to the lack of a center, it is not surprising that middle ground was difficult to find and that politics became more contentious. With the rise of budgetary politics, the liberal and conservative camps became more divided and pronounced. Some middle ground was found in 1986, as the tax laws were simplified, although this period is still shown to be fairly bipolar by the ADA scores.[14]

In the next chapter, we will show how the 1992 elections led to very few changes in the preferences of members of Congress. The 1994 elections, however, were a significant change, with many Democrats from conservative districts replaced by Republicans. Although policies were still held in place through Clinton's vetoes, the loss of moderate members, the large number of conservative Republicans, and the polarization of legislative politics are all evident in the ADA score distributions of Figures A.6 and A.7. The bimodal distribution that had begun in the 1980s is here more pronounced than had been seen in Congress in quite some time. As discussed in Chapter 6, with President George W. Bush's election in 2000, the rightward shift in preferences in 1994 could now result in some rightward policy shifts, especially on taxes. Again, budget politics would be characterized by winners and losers and by the use of reconciliation rules to avoid Senate filibusters. These actions solidified the polarization of congressional politics, as illustrated dramatically in Figure A.8. We turn now to how this polarization of preferences, coupled with supermajority institutions, leads to significant constraints on policy change, even under unified governance.

Notes

1. The ADA score is the member's ranking constructed from a set of roll call votes chosen by the Americans for Democratic Action to represent issues important to liberals. Thus if there were twenty such roll calls and a member voted with the ADA all twenty times, that member's score would be 100. Conversely a conservative member who never voted with the ADA would receive a score of 0.

2. Because ADA scores are based on twenty different votes each year, comparing them over time could lead to some biases and inconsistencies. Groseclose, Levitt, and Snyder (1999) attempt to deal with these inconsistencies by setting up an "inflation index" to construct "real" ADA scores. Such adjustments are small relative to the broad story we are telling here. Moreover, we feel that there are underlying reasons behind

some of the yearly ADA shifts that are lost by the Groseclose, Levitt, and Snyder adjustments. For our purposes, we mean to use these scores only to demonstrate that in 1981 the Republicans held together as a conservative group and the Democrats splintered, with southern Democrats joining the Republican coalition.

3. With the attempted passage of the Fair Labor Standards Act of 1938, the northern and southern wings of the Democratic Party differed on issues other than race. At various points the conservative (mainly southern) Democrats were part of the Conservative Coalition, the Reagan Democrats, and so on. The press has referred to them at different times as the conservative Democratic Forum, the Conservative Democratic Caucus, or Blue Dog Democrats. The point, however, is not the name but the fact that there have for some time been conservative Representatives within the Democratic Party.

4. This type of "middle-out" coalition appears from time to time. In such a coalition, despite the fact that they might approve of a policy change, extreme members may refuse to vote for the package in order to gain greater concessions or to get members of the other party into political trouble for voting on a difficult issue. When these extreme members hold secure seats, this type of voting is likely to be more prevalent. As a result, amendments moving bills either left or right must be carefully crafted to ensure that there are not too many defections from the extremes on either side. This phenomenon does not adapt to the revolving gridlock theory very well, as we assume that these extreme members will vote for all changes that support their preferred policy positions. And, indeed, we expect that they would vote for such a change if they were focused only on the ultimate bill pitted against the status quo, instead of on electoral gains for their party in other districts or on future compromises if the current bill were to fail.

5. See Canes-Wrone, Brady, and Cogan (2002) for a recent, more comprehensive version of this argument and analysis.

6. The U.S. tax code had been riddled with special loopholes and specific taxes built up over four decades such that the special circumstances of 1986 allowed the bundling of and then the elimination of tax loopholes, thus simplifying the tax code. One might expect that over time Congress and the President might seek to reinstate loopholes and special taxes, and indeed they have done that via increased tax rates and surcharges on individual income, child tax credits, and passive real estate losses. However, it is our belief that such loopholes and taxes are harder to come by under deficit conditions than they were in the postwar boom economy. Furthermore, the establishment of PAYGO and Budget Caps in 1990 show that the Congress recognized its need to restrain itself regarding special taxes and loopholes. Nevertheless, loopholes and tax credits still are adopted, especially when needed to forge a coalition for bill passage. Our belief is that a tax simplification measure like that of 1986 will arise from time to time when so many special exceptions have been incorporated into the tax code that it is seen as unfairly skewed once again.

7. See Cox and Kernell (1991), Jacobson (1990), and Fiorina (1996).

8. See, in particular, Cutler (1987) and (1988); Sundquist (1988), (1993), and (1995); Ginsburg and Shefter (1990); Mayhew (1991); and Jones (1994). On a more technical note, see Alt and Lowry (1994), Krehbiel (1996), and Epstein and O'Halloran (1996).

For more recent studies of gridlock and stalemate, see Binder (1999) and (2003), Jones (2001), Krutz (2000), and Wilkins and Young (2002).

9. The 1990 Budget Enforcement Act shifted attention from the Gramm-Rudman-Hollings fixed deficit targets to adjustable deficit targets. The idea was to treat deficit problems caused by the economy (downturns) differently than problems caused by legislation. Roughly, the three main features of this act were: (1) capping the discretionary budget (both authorities and outlays) through Budget Caps; (2) Pay-As-You-Go rules for revenue and direct spending; and (3) budget rules for direct and guaranteed loans. See Collender (1991) for additional details. For an excellent analysis of microbudgeting aspects of PAYGO and Budget Caps, see Cogan, Muris, and Schick (1994).

10. This is related to the phenomenon known as Fenno's Paradox (Fenno 1975). John Hibbing and Elizabeth Theiss-Morse (1995) present this type of argument in a more general form, leading to a judgment of Congress as a "public enemy," with survey analysis to support their case.

11. See also Erikson (1989) and Fiorina (1991b).

12. Hibbing and Theiss-Morse's work (1995) argues that citizens want leaders with strong principles, who are noncompromisers. Thus Bush would have been better off not to have compromised on the 1990 budget.

13. Because these scores are based on different votes every year, scholars have attempted to find ways to make vote comparisons over time. Keith Poole and Howard Rosenthal (1991a, 1997) have studied immense numbers of votes from all Congresses to gain some sense of voting over time. Groseclose, Levitt, and Snyder (1999) attempt to adjust the ADA scores to make them consistent over time. They generate what can be called "real" ADA scores. Both of these methods produce results that are consistent with what we argue here.

14. Fiorina (2005) questions the conventional wisdom that the American public is as divided and polarized as is Congress (or as it is portrayed in the media).

5

Clinton and the
Rise of the Republicans

Does unified government bring about policy change or unified gridlock? The theory laid out in Chapter 2 is strongly supported by the years of divided government of the Reagan and Bush presidencies. The institutional structures of government, including the filibuster and the veto, along with the individual preferences of members of Congress, have led to policy gridlock. This gridlock was exacerbated by the specter of continued budget deficits. An analysis of the unified government of the Clinton administration in the 103rd Congress provides a more substantial test of the revolving gridlock theory, set against competing theories predicting that unified party control would be sufficient in its votes and vision to overcome partisan gridlock. In the first half of this chapter we analyze the major policy proposals made by President Clinton in his first two years. We focus on the gridlock region and the pivotal members of Congress, leading to firm predictions about the results of these proposals. Across the board, the compromises that were struck in Congress and the final policy results provide strong support for the revolving gridlock theory.

These policy changes (or lack of change) and the politics surrounding Clinton's proposals partly explain the 1994 election results, bringing back divided government, although this time with a Republican Congress and Democratic President. Just as Democrats in 1993 were convinced of their imminent legislative successes, so too were Republicans in 1995 elated. But the revolving gridlock theory urges caution. In the early years of the Clinton presidency, proposals needed to appeal to members near the median or the filibuster pivot (often quite conservative) to pass; following 1994 they had to appeal to veto pivot (often quite liberal). Yet Clinton was not making conservative proposals; nor were Republican proposals to the 104th Congress liberal. To succeed, each of these proposals had to be modified. Legislation was successful only where that modification was successful. And, as expected, status quo policies beginning in the gridlock region remained there.

This chapter follows the Clinton presidency through three stages. First, we examine the President's proposals under unified government, and how they needed to be changed to appeal to pivotal members of Congress. Second, we see the same process for proposals made in the Republican House after 1994. Finally, we illustrate the resignation of both sides that gridlock would continue. Throughout, we emphasize the importance of budget politics, with a focus on the 1993 budget reconciliation and the 1995 budget battle. But we now are well positioned to also examine non-budgetary issues, from family leave legislation to health care reform to Constitutional amendments. Ultimately, we are able to judge the effectiveness of the revolving gridlock theory—and of the Clinton presidency—across dramatically changing political circumstances.

Legislators' Preferences
Entering Unified Gridlock

Our strategy in previous chapters regarding a left–right continuum was to use the Americans for Democratic Action (ADA) scores. In this chapter we will vary that strategy to show that our argument is robust. That is, if we use different measures of liberalism–conservatism and still get the same median Representatives and Senators, then (1) our use of ADA scores is justified and (2) our explanation holds irrespective of the measure used.

One non-ADA strategy for determining Senators' preferences is to choose a legislative arena—say, environmental politics—and to use the League of Conservation Voters index to array the members. We could repeat this procedure for other legislative arenas such as labor and small business. This method poses problems in that some legislation we might want to study encompasses several dimensions that cannot be isolated in any one vote or set of votes. Budget reconciliation, for example, features grazing rates, gas taxes, agricultural assistance, and many other policy arenas that are not voted on separately. Therefore we have arranged Senators and Representatives in two ways. First, we took the members' scores for eighteen separate ratings, converted them such that the lowest scores are conservative and the higher scores are liberal, and then averaged across all eighteen measures, ranking the members from conservative to liberal.[1] Second, we took the same eighteen measures, calculated which five or six Senators and Representatives were closest to the median on each rating scale, and tabulated the frequency of their median positions; for example, Charles Robb (D, VA) was at or near the median on four of these issue measures. Tables 5.1 and 5.2 give these frequency measures for the 103rd Congress, at the start of the Clinton administration.[2] For the Senate we also calculated the filibuster pivot. Table 5.3 shows the liberal-to-conservative rankings of Senators in the 103rd Congress, based on their combined scores on these eighteen measures in the 102nd Congress.[3] And Table 5.4 shows the liberal-to-conservative rankings of Senators in the 103rd Congress based on ADA scores, for a comparison.

The findings are hardly surprising to anyone familiar with the U.S. Congress. The Senate frequency measure in Table 5.1 reveals results one would expect to find in looking for median members of Congress. Democrats with three or more

TABLE 5.1   Frequency Indexed in Median Group (103rd Senate)

Frequency	Name
7	Nunn
5	Exon, Ford, Packwood
4	Breaux, Cohen, DeConcini, Heflin, Hollings, Johnston, Robb, Specter
3	Bingaman, Bumpers, Jeffords, Shelby
2	Boren, Bradley, Byrd, Chafee, Conrad, D'Amato, Hatfield, Pryor, Reid, Smith
1	Fourteen others

Frequency is the number of ratings in which this Senator appeared in the group of five to seven Senators at or near the median-rated member. Ratings used were: AAUW, ACLU, ACU, ADA, ASC, BIPAC, CCUS, CFA, COPE, LCV, NAM, NCSC, NEA, NFIB, NFU, PCCW, TEAM, UAW.

TABLE 5.2   Frequency Indexed in Median Group (103rd House)

Frequency	Name
9	Charles Wilson
8	Michael Andrews
7	Dave McCurdy
5	Sherwood Boehlert, Chet Edwards, Lee Hamilton, Joseph McDade, Stephen Neal, J. Pickle
4	Glen Browder, Robert Cramer, Dan Glickman, Timothy Roemer
3	Tom Bevill, James Bilbray, M. Carr, Gary Condit, George Darden, Glenn English, Larry LaRocco, William Lipinski, Marilyn Lloyd, Ronald Machtley, Constance Morella, Norman Sisisky, Ike Skelton, Christopher Smith, John Tanner
2	Cooper, Derrick, Dooley, Fish, Gibbons, Gordon, Leach, Moran, Murtha, Ortiz, Sarpalius, Slattery, Spratt, Whitten
1	Fifty-five others

Frequency is the number of ratings in which this House member appeared in the group of eleven members at or near the median-rated member. Ratings used were: AAUW, ACLU, ACU, ADA, ASC, BIPAC, CCUS, CFA, COPE, LCV, NAM, NCSC, NEA, NFIB, NFU, PCCW, TEAM, UAW.

ratings as median were primarily from southern or border states (nine of twelve), with the others being from the Midwest (Nebraska) or the Southwest (Arizona and New Mexico). The four Republicans in this category were Packwood (OR), Cohen (ME), Specter (PA), and Jeffords (VT). The most liberal and conservative Senators from Table 5.3 do not show up on the frequency scale.

TABLE 5.3   Preference Ordering of Senators (103rd), Liberal to Conservative
(high numbers are more liberal, combining eighteen ratings)

Left of Median			*Right of Median*	
Wellstone	91.0		Johnston	61.5
Sarbanes	90.8		Nunn	60.7
Metzenbaum	90.6		Cohen	57.4
Leahy	90.5		Specter	56.5
Simon	90.3		Breaux	56.5
Levin	89.8		Packwood	53.7
Kennedy	89.2		Hollings	53.7
Harkin	88.6		Chafee	51.0
Akaka	88.4		Heflin	50.9
Moynihan	88.3	About 2/5th pivot →	Boren	47.3
Wofford	87.4		Shelby	46.8
Kerry	87.1		Durenberger	45.6
Mikulski	86.7		D'Amato	42.3
Riegle	86.5		Danforth	29.8
Lautenberg	86.1		Roth	29.3
Biden	85.7		Bond	27.5
Rockefeller	85.1		Murkowski	26.4
Pell	85.0		Gorton	25.8
Mitchell	84.9		Kassebaum	25.3
Glenn	84.9		Grassley	24.5
Sasser	84.7		Warner	22.8
Baucus	83.2		McCain	21.5
Bradley	82.6		Coats	20.6
Inouye	82.5		Thurmond	19.0
Dodd	80.6		Simpson	18.7
Daschle	80.5		Cochran	17.6
Kerrey	79.8		Brown	16.9
Byrd	78.9		Smith	15.9
Kohl	77.0		Mack	15.8
Bryan	77.0		Burns	15.5
Bingaman	76.9		Pressler	15.3
Graham	75.5		Lugar	14.9
Lieberman	75.4		Domenici	14.0
Reid	75.4		McConnell	14.0
Bumpers	74.3		Lott	12.9
Conrad	72.8		Hatch	12.3
Pryor	71.8		Dole	12.3
Jeffords	70.3		Craig	10.5
Robb	70.0		Wallop	10.4
Ford	69.0		Gramm	9.1
Exon	67.9		Nickles	8.3
Hatfield	62.7		Helms	7.1
DeConcini	61.6			

Ratings used were: AAUW, ACLU, ACU, ADA, ASC, BIPAC, CCUS, CFA, COPE, LCV, NAM, NCSC, NEA, NFIB, NFU, PCCW, TEAM, UAW.

TABLE 5.4   ADA Ordering of Senators (103rd), Liberal to Conservative
(high numbers are more liberal, using 1993 ADA scores)

Left of Median			Right of Median	
Wellstone	100		Ford	60
Metzenbaum	100		Byrd	55
Feingold	100		Hollings	55
Sarbanes	95		Chafee	55
Leahy	95		Exon	50
Levin	95		Johnston	45
Lautenberg	95		Nunn	45
Kohl	95		Specter	45
Boxer	90		Roth	45
Kennedy	90	About 2/5th pivot →	Cohen	40
Harkin	90		Breaux	40
Akaka	90		Packwood	35
Moynihan	90		Heflin	35
Kerry	90		Shelby	35
Bradley	90		D'Amato	35
Murray	90		Danforth	35
Moseley-Braun	85		Kassebaum	35
Simon	85		Bond	25
Wofford	85		Stevens	25
Mikulski	85		Murkowski	20
Pell	85		Gorton	20
Mitchell	85		Grassley	20
Glenn	85		Coats	20
Baucus	85		Simpson	20
Inouye	85		Burns	20
Feinstein	85		Domenici	20
Riegle	80		McCain	15
Biden	80		Brown	15
Bumpers	80		Smith	15
Conrad	80		McConnell	15
Sasser	75		Faircloth	15
Dodd	75		Hutchison	13
Daschle	75		Warner	10
Kerrey	75		Thurmond	10
Robb	75		Mack	10
DeConcini	75		Pressler	10
Durenberger	75		Lugar	10
Campbell	75		Dole	10
Rockefeller	70		Coverdell	10
Bingaman	70		Gregg	10
Pryor	70		Helms	10
Boren	70		Bennett	5
Graham	65		Kempthorne	5
Lieberman	65		Lott	5
Mathews	65		Hatch	5
Hatfield	65		Craig	5
Dorgan	65		Wallop	5
Bryan	60		Gramm	5
Reid	60		Nickles	5
Jeffords	60		Cochran	0

As can be seen in Table 5.3, the averaged scores show that roughly the 38th to the 52nd Senators are in the interval from the filibuster pivot to the floor median. There are nine Democrats and five Republicans in this region. The most conservative Senators are to no one's surprise: Helms (NC), Nickles (OK), Gramm (TX), and Wallop (WY). The most liberal are all Democrats—Kennedy (MA), Metzenbaum (OH), and Wellstone (MN).

In Table 5.4, we included the same type of listing of Senators, this time using only ADA scores. The findings are remarkably similar. The same names show up as the most liberal and most conservative. And those near the filibuster pivot point are again Republicans and southern Democrats—Breaux (D, LA), Cohen (R, ME), Heflin (D, AK), Packwood (R, OR), and Roth (R, DE). To calculate exactly how similar our combined measure of eighteen ratings is to the commonly used ADA ratings, we looked at the correlation between measures. The coefficient of correlation between our measure and the ADA measure over the same time period was 0.98 and between our measure and Roll Call ratings was −0.82, where any numbers near 1 and −1 represent almost identical measures. Our ranking of Congress on a left–right continuum thus appears to be robust when tested against different measures of liberalism and conservatism.[4]

It is not surprising that members of Congress can be aligned from liberal to conservative consistently across a broad range of topics. Poole and Rosenthal (1998) study every roll call vote taken in Congress and find that a single dimension can account for about three-fourths of all voting decisions. Krehbiel (1998, esp. chaps. 7, 8) offers an excellent review of why, theoretically, a simple pivotal voter model along a single dimension might not explain policy outcomes, due to factors such as partisanship, agenda setting, and presidential persuasion. However, his findings and his ultimate conclusion that the model predicts well in the face of many obstacles testifies to the robustness of the use of the single-dimensional model. These studies, along with our compilation and comparison of various rating systems, lend credence to the view that members of Congress can be modeled as having preferences along a single-dimensional continuum.

Given the establishment of such a continuum, we can begin to see who should be influential in making the deals necessary to break gridlock. Due to the election of a Democratic President, movement to the left on policy would be constrained in the 103rd Congress by those members at or near the two-fifths pivot, as shown in Tables 5.3 and 5.4. This represents a loosening of constraints due to the removal of the presidential veto—since Clinton would sign some legislation that Bush had vetoed. However, in order to secure major policy shifts, Bill Clinton would have had to come to office with like-minded members of Congress. This was certainly not the case given the 1992 elections. Figure 5.1 illustrates the changes in the gridlock region accompanying those elections.

The 103rd Senate had thirteen new members (including the winners of special elections like Senator Feinstein of California). Arrayed from left to right they included two liberal Democrats (Boxer, CA, and Moseley-Braun, IL); two moderate-to-liberal Democrats (Murray, WA, and Dorgan, ND); two moderate Democrats

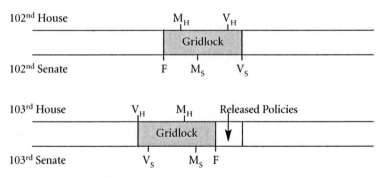

FIGURE 5.1   The 1992 Elections

(Feinstein, CA, and Feingold, WI); and Ben Campbell (CO), the most conservative Democrat elected. The new Republicans ranged from moderate (Bailey-Hutchison, TX, and Gregg, NH) to conservative (Bennett, UT; Kempthorne, ID; and Faircloth, NC), with Coverdell (GA) in between. Thus the thirteen new members fell on either side of Senator Campbell—who became a Republican in the next Congress—creating no shift right or left from the 102nd to the 103rd Senate. More importantly, given the institutional structure of the filibuster, all six of the newly elected Republicans looked to be to the right of the filibuster pivot (as shown in Table 5.4) and would therefore be a constraint on policy movements to the left. Although in the 1992 Senate elections four seats changed parties—two Democratic incumbents were defeated, as were two Republican incumbents—with each party holding its open seats, there was no change in party advantage. The Democrats went into the 103rd Senate elections with fifty-seven seats and they came out with fifty-seven seats. In sum, Bill Clinton would face a 103rd Senate not any more favorable to his position than the 102nd Senate.

In the House, the Democrats' percentage of all votes (50.8 percent) fell to its lowest level since 1980. They won 59.3 percent of all House seats, again their lowest total since 1980. From the 102nd to the 103rd House, the Democrats lost ten seats. Twice as many Democratic incumbents (sixteen) lost their seats compared to Republican incumbents (eight). The Democrats who lost their seats or left Congress after the 102nd Congress had an average ADA score of 67, and on average they had supported Republican Presidents 32 percent of the time. Democrat winners had slightly lower ADA scores and had supported Bush 35 percent of the time. Thus the Democrats who left Congress were slightly more liberal than those Democrats who retained their seats. The Republicans who replaced these Democrats were on average very conservative, with ADA scores of 15 to 20, about 50 points more conservative than the people they replaced.

In all, the Senate in this first unified government in many years was about where it had been in the divided and gridlocked government that had preceded it; in fact, the 103rd unified House was to the right of the previous House. President

Clinton faced a Senate perhaps more willing to filibuster moves to the left and a more conservative House with ten more Republican seats, and conservative Republicans at that.

Nevertheless, the 1992 elections gave hope to many political commentators, scholars, and politicians who believed that unified Democratic governance would end gridlock. The Committee on the Constitutional System and the Brookings Institution sponsored a conference on February 24, 1993, the results of which are compiled in James Sundquist's volume, *Beyond Gridlock?* (1993). Although the participants were mixed in their predictions, a number of them believed that politicians were in the best position in a long while to break gridlock. Thomas Mann noted that "the return of unified party government is especially significant in 1992 as contrasted with 1960 and 1976. This time it follows an extended period of divided government—and conflictual divided government, which was really quite different from earlier experiences" (Sundquist 1993, 13). Sundquist shared Mann's "optimistic outlook," asking, "If the government cannot succeed in the present configuration, when can it possibly ever succeed? As Joan Quigley, the former official astrologer, might have said, the stars are really aligned right for the next four years" (25). The view from Howard Paster, Clinton's assistant in charge of congressional relations, was equally rosy: "That we can now, with a Democratic majority on the Hill and a Democrat in the White House, govern successfully, I think will be borne out" (15). And former Representative Thomas Downey noted what many of his former colleagues in Congress were saying: "We have a Democratic president and there is really not much that we have to do now. Now that we have eliminated divided government we will have eliminated gridlock" (45–46). Of course, such optimism proved to be premature.

In the following sections we will discuss the major legislation attempted by the 103rd Congress. This analysis serves two purposes: to show with concrete examples that congressional policymaking is determined by individual preferences rather than by strong parties; and to demonstrate "unified gridlock," in which the policy changes that *are* made are at most incremental, always being drawn away from the original proposals of Clinton and median members of the Democratic Party in order to capture the median floor voter or the filibuster pivot.[5] One view of a strong party theory would argue that the names we would see in the press would be near the Democratic median. Senators such as Glenn (Ohio) and Sasser (Tenn.) would be engaged with the party leadership in attempts to hold the party together to get enough votes for the passage of legislation, and policy would be moved to their preference points. However, the revolving gridlock theory argues that the names we will run across will be those of the crucial members at the institutional pivot points: Breaux, Boren (D, OK), and Nunn (D, GA) will be key players in legislation requiring a simple majority, whereas Senators such as Durenberger (R, MN) and Specter (R, PA) will play pivotal roles in votes where the filibuster can be used to halt the passage of legislation. The latter of these two possibilities is what we see time and time again in looking through the individual pieces of legislation: the bills must be changed to accommodate the median or the filibuster pivots. Those proposals that do not move sufficiently to the right do not pass. Those that do pass hardly represent an end to policy gridlock.

Policies Needing a Simple Majority for Passage

The 1974 Congressional Budget and Impoundment Control Act and various "fast track" procedures have limited the ability of Senators to filibuster some budget and trade bills. When the President supports such legislation, the constraint caused by a reduced "gridlock region" is that of a simple majority in both the Senate and the House. The median voters are thus pivotal. In the analysis that follows, we argue that initial Clinton proposals on the 1993 Budget Reconciliation Act and NAFTA needed to be modified to the right to appeal to these constraining pivotal members.

The 1993 Budget Reconciliation Act

On February 17, 1993, in his first State of the Union Address, President Clinton proposed an economic plan containing a wide array of budget cuts and tax increases. The media focused on the proposals for taxing the rich and for instituting the BTU (British Thermal Unit) energy tax as the highlights of the plan because these taxes, together with additional corporate taxes, would generate an extra $236.2 billion over the next five years (*New York Times*, February 18, 1993). The administration claimed that the reconciliation bill would reduce the budget deficit by $500 billion over the coming five years, with new taxes accounting for over half of the proposed deficit reduction. The Clinton proposal squared well with liberals in his party. Taxes on the upper 1 percent of income earners pleased liberals; the BTU tax on all fuels pleased environmentalists; and the increase in corporate taxes and limits on the tax deductibility of executive pay also pleased the liberal wing of the party. Moreover, the spending cuts came mainly from defense and the federal bureaucracy ($160.8 billion), with another $60.3 billion in savings theoretically coming from reduced health care costs at no loss in quality.

Thus the President's initial policy was clearly at or near the median Democratic Party position in both the House and Senate. Proponents of the theory of divided government featuring strong parties would have to predict passage of this plan with little modification. The Democratic Party could act en bloc to get the policy passed and signed. However, this is not what happened. The final reconciliation budget differed from the original, decreasing the tax hike and increasing spending cuts. And the major players forcing these changes were moderate Democrats such as Breaux and Boren. Due to the 1974 budget rules, the 1993 final reconciliation budget did not need to prepare for the possibility of a Republican filibuster; rather, fifty votes for Clinton's bill as proposed would secure passage in the Senate. In the end no Republicans voted for the legislation. The changes in the final budget were thus meant to accommodate the moderate Democrats who could threaten to join the Republicans to defeat the measure.

By the end of April newspapers were reporting that the President would not "recognize large parts of [his] tax plan by the time Democrats in Congress finish with it" (*New York Times*, April 30, 1993). Among the first changes were the President's investment tax credit worth $28 billion and the proposed 36 percent corporate tax rate (a 2 percent increase). The Chairs of the House Ways and Means Committee (Dan Rostenkowski; D, IL) and the Senate Finance Committee (Daniel P. Moynihan; D, NY) eliminated the investment tax credit (ITC) and reduced the corporate tax increase to 1 percent. Rostenkowski said, "I'm not going to fall on my sword for an ITC that no one wants" (*New York Times*, April 30, 1993).

The energy tax turned out to be the most controversial part of the President's proposed tax increases. Senators and Representatives from northern states did not like fuel taxes on oil used for home heating, whereas farm-state Senators opposed fuel taxes on ethanol (made from corn) and western Senators opposed gasoline taxes because many of their constituents drove long distances to work. In addition, industries like aluminum that use large amounts of energy to produce their products organized in opposition to the BTU tax. In order to cope with the increasing opposition, the Clinton administration had by mid-May modified its plan in the following way: tax collection was shifted from utility to consumer, the farm use of diesel fuel was to be taxed at a lower rate, propane gas was to be taxed at a lower rate, and boat and jet fuel used in international travel were to be exempted. The hydroelectric power and oil industries, among others, were still seeking exemptions in early June.

The House passed a reconciliation bill in early June by a vote of 219 to 213, but many Democrats from energy and farm states voted for the bill only after being told that it would be amended in the Senate. These Democrats had good reason to believe that the bill would be modified there. On May 20, a bipartisan coalition led by Senator Boren and including the Democrat Johnston (LA) and Republicans Cohen (ME) and Danforth (MO) proposed an alternative budget plan that junked the energy tax. Thus going into the Senate the President's plan faced severe opposition first on the Finance Committee where Boren was a swing vote and then on the floor where it seemed quite possible that eight Democrats could side with the Republicans and vote down any bill that included a fuel tax. On June 7, 1993, the majority leader, Senator Mitchell (D, ME), and the Finance Chair, Senator Moynihan, met with the President and told him that his reconciliation budget was in danger of being killed in the Senate due to opposition to the energy tax provisions. The next day Secretary of the Treasury Lloyd Bentsen revealed on the *McNeil–Lehrer News Hour* that the energy tax emerging from the Senate wouldn't be based on BTUs. By June 10, President Clinton was considering a proposal by Senator Breaux to replace the $70-odd billion energy tax with a $40 billion tax on gasoline and a $30 billion cut in Medicare. The $40 billion gas tax would be raised by taxing an additional eight cents per gallon. This new proposal immediately generated a reaction from the liberal wing of the party. Senator Rockefeller (D, WV) and Representative Mfume (D, MD), the head of the Black Caucus, objected to both the gas tax and the cuts in Medicare. Representative Waxman (D, CA) said, "It seems everybody is supposed to jump through hoops to satisfy conservative Democrats. But they have to face the fact that there are other Democrats who won't go along with more cuts" (1993 *Congressional Quarterly Weekly Report*, 1463).

While the energy tax component was being jettisoned, there was activity across the board in the Senate on the President's reconciliation budget. Conservative Democrats were trying to (1) decrease the individual tax rates for 1993; (2) decrease the tax rates for Social Security recipients; and (3) increase cuts in Medicare and Medicaid. The final package passed in the Senate represented moderate Democratic positions and was more conservative than the President's bill—tax increases were significantly reduced while expenditures were cut deeper.

The House–Senate conference began work on the final reconciliation bill in June and completed its work in early August. The final package limited the energy tax to a 4.3-cent tax on a gallon of gasoline, made a $55.8-billion cut in Medicare payments, and raised the Social Security tax kick-in to $44,000 for couples and $34,000 for individuals. Thus moderate and conservative Democrats were able to eliminate the BTU energy tax and set limits on social spending, moving policy away from the President's original proposal. The Senate bill was more centrist than the final bill as liberals led by the Black Caucus, Bernie Sanders (Indep., VT), Henry Waxman, and others reinstated funding for enterprise zones, slightly reduced the Senate cuts in Medicare and Medicaid, expanded the earned income tax credit, and passed a $2.5 billion increase in food stamp funding. Nevertheless, on the whole it seems clear that the final result was considerably more conservative than the President's original proposal.

The final bill that passed Congress and was signed by the President bore a remarkable resemblance to the bill that had passed in the 101st Congress in 1990. Both bills called for savings of half a trillion dollars over five years. Both contained tax increases on individual incomes in the highest brackets and spending cuts on defense. The same areas that were left alone in 1990 maintained their untouchable status in 1993. This is no surprise. Because the members of Congress and their positions did not change dramatically between 1990 and 1993, the bill outcomes are expected to be in the same range as before. The difficulty that Clinton faced, however, was that some of these tax increases and spending cuts were not merely extensions of the 1990 plan, but expansions of it. The taxing and spending cuts gouged deeper than before. As such, Clinton faced greater struggles in securing votes than would otherwise have been the case. Analysis of the 1994 election results shows that a vote for the Clinton budget deal was equivalent to the sacrifice of a congressional seat in a number of districts. Brady, Cogan, Gaines, and Rivers (1995) find that those members in districts with low Clinton support in 1992 were severely hurt by casting votes in support of Clinton on the 1993 budget deal. These members were placed in a tight spot on the vote. If they voted against the President, the bill would be defeated and Democrats everywhere would be hurt for continuing gridlock.[6] If they voted for the budget, they could count on Clinton's support in the 1994 elections, if the President's endorsement could even be considered an asset in their reelection bids. As Clinton's popularity plummeted, the decision to vote against the majority of their constituents' preferences on the budget deal came to haunt these Democrats.

Without the support of most of the Democrats in Congress, Clinton's budget deal would have failed. The revolving gridlock theory predicts that without substantial changes in the preferences of members of Congress, major new legislation is unlikely to succeed. In order to succeed, liberal or conservative proposals must be made more moderate by appealing to the preferences of Representatives and Senators in a narrow band near the median. Indeed, the 1993 budget proposals, in the end, were made more conservative than Clinton had initially intended in order to appeal to just these members. They had to gamble that a bid to support Clinton and bring an end to gridlock would make up for a budget vote that their constituents disfavored. The 1994 election results show that this gamble did not pay off for many Democrats.

NAFTA

The North American Free Trade Agreement was negotiated by Ambassador Carla Hills during the Bush administration; thus the framework of the treaty had already been established when President Clinton took office. During his presidential election campaign, Clinton had said that he would support NAFTA if side agreements on labor and the environment could be reached. Clinton's original idea was to create North American labor and environmental commissions with the power to levy fines and sanctions. However, Clinton walked a tightrope on NAFTA; in order to pass the treaty he had to have Republican support, and such support would disappear if the side agreements on labor and environment were too tough. Even with the trade agreement being placed under the 1991 fast-track rules, thus eliminating the threat of a filibuster, the President was not guaranteed a simple majority. Yet without the tough side agreements, labor unions and environmental groups would oppose the treaty. The negotiations for side agreements began on March 17, 1993, and on August 12, after five months of wrangling over the nature of the side agreements by the Mexican and Canadian governments, as well as the AFL–CIO and environmental groups, Ambassador Mickey Kantor and the Mexican and Canadian negotiators worked out a deal. The three countries agreed to create trinational commissions to deal with environmental and labor disputes. Disputes not resolved by the commissions would be forwarded to an arbitration panel with the power to recommend trade sanctions against Mexico and the United States. In the case of complaints against Canada, Canadian Courts would impose penalties.

Opponents led by Representative Richard Gephardt (D, MO) said that the side agreements (1) failed to name a funding source for pollution cleanup along the U.S.–Mexican border; (2) did not go far enough to protect U.S. producers; and (3) did not include the possibility of trade sanctions against Mexico for failing to pay their workers a fair wage. The AFL–CIO president said that the agreements relegated workers' rights and the environment to commissions with no real power of enforcement (1993 *Congressional Quarterly Weekly Report*, 2212). It was clear from the reaction of Representative Gephardt and the AFL–CIO that the President had chosen a strategy to keep Republican votes and pick up moderate Democrats, rather than appeal to the Democratic Party median.

In the weeks that followed, questions of funding border cleanups were answered and the amount and source of monies for worker retraining were debated. At one point President Clinton proposed a tax to provide the billions necessary for worker retraining. Minority whip Newt Gingrich (R, GA) immediately sent the President a note saying that House Republicans would not support NAFTA with such a provision in the enabling legislation, and the plan was dropped. In the crucial House vote, 132 Republicans voted for NAFTA along with 102 Democrats. The point is quite clear—Clinton's early support hinged on the creation of the trinational commissions with subpoena powers and sanctions, and such a policy was not acceptable to the Republicans. At every stage of the game, from renegotiating the NAFTA treaty to the side agreements to funding pollution cleanup and worker retraining, Clinton and Kantor took positions that diverged from the center of their party in an attempt to keep the support of the Republicans and the moderate-to-conservative Democrats. The final treaty and the final vote clearly reflect this appeal to the floor median member's preferences.

In both of our cases addressing majority-win institutions—the 1993 budget reconciliation and the North American Free Trade Agreement—the President's original policy inclination was to the left of the floor median. In both cases the final policy output was close to the median floor position, with the President calling for support of these centrist policies. In both the House and Senate the crucial votes came from Senators and Representatives at or about the median—Breaux, Boren, Johnston, and DeConcini (D, AZ) in the Senate; and Stenholm (D, TX), Wilson (D, TX), and other conservative Democrats in the House. When the Senate version of the budget act passed, it was liberals such as Rockefeller, Waxman, and Mfume who objected to the reduced tax increases and enhanced expenditure cuts. The final bill gave liberals some cover by adding enterprise zones, additional food stamps funding, and an $8 billion cutback from the Senate's Medicare cuts, but the overall result clearly shows a rightward policy shift toward the floor median.

The negotiations on NAFTA followed the same pattern. The Clinton administration (1) proposed, then rejected renegotiating NAFTA; (2) proposed creating trinational commissions on environmental and labor issues that had subpoena powers as well as the ability to apply sanctions and enforce them, then dropped meaningful sanctions, allowing Canada out completely; and (3) proposed a tax for funding worker retraining, and then also dropped that idea. At each stage, pressure from Republicans, who asserted that they could not vote for a NAFTA with strong trinational commissions and new taxes, brought the policy closer to the floor median. On the final vote, Clinton sided against a majority of his party in order to get NAFTA through the Senate.

Old Legislation Vetoed by Republican Presidents

It is relatively easy to predict the outcome of legislation for which there exists a majority in the House favoring the policy but not a supermajority sufficient to override a presidential veto. For House members, the election of a Democratic President eliminates the Republican presidential veto threat for bills like family leave and motor voter registration; thus these bills will most likely easily pass. The Senate presents a more interesting case because there is still a filibuster pivot (that is, a three-fifths supermajority is necessary), thus keeping the policy from drifting too far left. Here we would predict that if the President's policy is too liberal there will either be a filibuster or the credible threat of one, and the policy will have to be modified to break the filibuster.

Family Leave

The Family and Medical Leave Act (H.R. 1, S5) was introduced in the Congress on January 5, 1993, and on February 5, one month later, President Clinton signed the bill into law. The eight-year legislative history of the bill is of some interest.[7] Five times Senator Dodd (D, CT) had reported family leave laws from his committee and two of these had reached the White House only to be vetoed by President Bush. The first bill to make it to the White House (1990) applied to businesses with at least fifty employees (which exempts 95 percent of U.S. companies but covers about one-half of the work force) and granted leaves of twelve weeks. President Bush vetoed the bill and neither the House nor the Senate had enough votes to override the veto. In the 102nd Congress a bipartisan effort sponsored by Senators Dodd and Bond (R, MO) changed the family leave legislation to make it attractive to moderate Republicans. The deal exempted the top 10 percent of employees in each company, covered only workers who had worked over 1,250 hours the previous year, and allowed employers to demand medical opinions and certifications regarding leave. This bill passed the House and Senate, but was again vetoed by President Bush. The Senate overrode the veto 68 to 31, whereas the House narrowly sustained the veto 258 to 169.

The family leave bill was again introduced in 1993 and, because the bill already had majority support from the previous Congress, the only question was whether a filibuster was possible. Given that the Senate had overridden the Bush veto in 1992 it was clear that a family leave law would pass. The Senate passed a bill similar to that of 1992 by a vote of 71 to 27, and the House approved the Senate version by 247 votes to 152. Democrats like Pat Williams (MT) claimed that passage signaled an end to gridlock. Note, however, that the bill had already been amended to accommodate moderate Republicans, and that the 1993 bill kept all those Bond-Dodd compromises and thus enjoyed the same amount of support as in 1992. The only change from 1992 to 1993 was that the veto pivot had changed dramatically from anti-family leave to pro-, such that the House could pass the legislation with a majority and the Senate could pass the legislation with sixty votes. Clearly the institutional arrangement requiring a two-thirds majority to override a veto affected results. The surprising result is that the bill wasn't strengthened again to the level of the bill that found its way to the White House in 1990. No longer were the changes between 1990 and 1992 needed to override a veto. The Family and Medical Leave Act had been modified to bring along Republicans in the previous Congress, and Clinton submitted that modified bill rather than a more liberal bill featuring lower numbers, longer leave, and paid leave, as many in his party would have preferred.

Motor Voter

On July 2, 1992, President Bush vetoed the so-called Motor Voter Registration Act, and on September 22 the Senate failed to override the veto. The newly elected 103rd House immediately reintroduced approximately the same bill (H.R. 2) and, on January 27, 1993, the House Administration Committee cleared the way for floor consideration. The House voted for final passage on February 4, 1993, by a vote of 259 to 160. This bill made voter registration easier by tying registration to driver's license applications. In addition, the bill required states to provide uniform voter registration through the mail. Its most controversial proposal required that registration forms be made available at various state and federal offices that provide public assistance, such as welfare and unemployment outlets. Republicans in the House objected to the bill on the grounds that it would cost states money to administer the act, that the bill encouraged the registration of illegal aliens, and that the availability of registration materials was targeted to register potential Democratic voters.

The swift passage of the Motor Voter Registration Act in the House was not to be duplicated in the Senate, where the Republicans could threaten a filibuster. Democrats led by Senator Ford (KY) claimed they had enough votes to cut off a filibuster, because they had garnered sixty-two votes in the attempt to override the veto in 1992. However, this time around Republican Senators knew that there would not be a presidential veto to back them up. Republican leaders made good on their filibuster threat on March 5 when they mustered the votes to delay debate on the bill (52 to 36). The threatened filibuster won the following: the provision to require registration at welfare and unemployment offices was dropped, as was a provision requiring the registration of some welfare recipients. With this reform won, five moderate Republicans supported the bill, and it passed the Senate 62 to 37. The bill that emerged from conference (and ultimately passed) tilted toward the more centrist Senate version.

New Legislation Requiring Supermajorities

In the cases of both family leave and motor voter legislation, previous Congresses had passed bills only to see them vetoed by President Bush. Congress had previously modified the bills to meet pivotal voter preferences, and they became law under Clinton due to the loosening of institutional constraints. These circumstances, however, do not necessarily apply to new legislation introduced by President Clinton. We now turn to an analysis of the job stimulus package and health care to show that, even with new legislation, preferences and constraining institutions determine policy results.

The Jobs Bill

Shortly after his inauguration, President Clinton began to hint at a jobs stimulus package designed to get the economy going. During his State of the Union Address in 1993, President Clinton proposed a $16.3 billion package, with $4 billion going to unemployment benefits, $3 billion to highway programs, $2.5 billion for block grants to state and local governments, $1 billion for a summer youth program, $500 million for Head Start, and the rest for miscellaneous programs under $350 million apiece. The House immediately went to work on the Clinton "jobs bill," which moved forward as a supplemental appropriations bill. On March 9, 1993, the House Appropriations Committee passed the Clinton plan virtually unchanged. Conservative Democrats led by Stenholm (TX) met with the President to ask for a leaner package. Speaker Tom Foley (WA) called a March 11 meeting of the Democratic Caucus and after the meeting told the press that there was strong opposition to delaying or downsizing the jobs bill. The House voted on March 19 to approve the jobs bill at $16.3 billion; House leadership gave Clinton credit for hardballing the conservative Democrats' attempts to change the bill (1993 *Congressional Quarterly Weekly Report*, 649).

The bill's fate in the Senate was another story. Even before the House had passed the bill, Senator Simpson (R, WY) had promised that Republicans would filibuster the bill unless changes were made. Senator Byrd (D, WV) made it clear that he would strongly defend the President's package; however, Democratic Senators Boren and Breaux were pushing to modify the President's proposal. Senator Byrd used an unusual tactic to wrap the bill in a suit of amendments by "treeing" the bill such that amendments to the bill could only be offered after the bill had been defeated. This maneuver clearly upset Republicans and kept Senate Democrats like Boren from proposing amendments to the bill. By late March the President had two problems: (1) moderate Democrats did not like the bill as it was and were being prevented from amending it, and (2) Republicans were united in opposition to the bill. The President responded by speaking out against Democrats who were overly concerned with the deficit (*Wall Street Journal*, March 24, 1993). During the period before spring recess, Republicans attacked the bill as pork for urban Democratic constituents; Byrd and liberal Democrats countered by railing against Republicans, whereas moderate Democrats sought compromises to ensure the bill's passage. Republicans filibustered the Clinton bill and, over the first two weeks of April, Clinton tried to woo moderate Republicans (Specter, D'Amato, Jeffords), but they held to the filibuster. On April 22, President Clinton gave up on the bill, settling for a $4 billion extension of unemployment compensation.

The point is again clear—the President proposed a bill too far to the left of the filibuster pivot to pass. The ultimate result was that the bill pleased neither moderate Democrats nor the filibuster pivots. They preferred the status quo (the absence of a jobs bill) to the liberal jobs bill that had been proposed. Senator Byrd's attempt to maneuver the bill through the Senate solidified Republican opposition and disturbed key Democrats. Again, we have seen how preferences and constraining institutions are the primary factors responsible for policy results. Despite both the President's and Senator Byrd's many appeals for party unity, a strong partisan Congress did not emerge to support the jobs bill.[8] The same story would be retold over President Clinton's most major legislative initiative—health care reform.

Health Care[9]

The Clintons hoped that health care legislation would be the crown jewel of their first Congress. President Clinton involved First Lady Hillary Rodham Clinton in gathering information and formulating policy, using horror stories about the uninsured to make the case for reform. Clinton argued that the objective of a balanced budget could only be achieved by controlling health care costs through a major overhaul of the entire health care system. The combined efforts of the first family brought the issue of health care to the forefront of the American agenda for several months. As with most of the Clinton policy proposals during the 103rd Congress, the proposal for health care reform seemed significantly more liberal than the median member of Congress would have desired. The highly regulatory Clinton plan established universal coverage of all Americans as its major goal. As the plan was brought into light, it became quite evident that the trillion-dollar Clinton proposal was far out of line with the preferences of the average American, as well as of the median members of Congress. Vote counters noted that the plan would have received only a handful of supporters in Congress.

Although the health care plan never made it to the floor of Congress, the committee debates and backroom dealings are well documented (Brady and Buckley 1995; Broder and Johnson 1996; Hacker 1997; Matsui 1995; Skocpol 1996). Hacker argues that Clinton and his advisers naively thought that managed competition would appear liberal to liberals and moderate to moderates. Skocpol argues that Clinton's health care plan failed because of Reagan's anti-government legacy, the deficit, and the fact that Clinton spent critical time and energy on NAFTA (an issue that antagonized liberals and labor groups). Broder and Johnson provide an excellent description of the policy process but conclude (wrongly in our view) that the political system cannot handle such major reforms. Although these studies are valuable in their attention to detail, they are crucial in showing how politicians, scholars, and journalists can miss the broader policy picture. For a Clinton proposal to be successful, it must appeal to conservative Democrats and moderate

Republicans at the filibuster pivots. Thus any focus on the loss of liberals and labor groups shows how far off the mark the discussions and proposals were.

As with other major legislation in the 103rd Congress, more conservative plans would need to be considered to appeal to the median members and to overcome potential conservative filibusters. The policy proposals of President Clinton and members of the 103rd Congress gave different emphases to the three issues of cost, quality, and coverage. Each of the plans can be located on a liberal–conservative continuum according to how many people are covered and who is expected to pay for care, as illustrated in Figure 5.2. On the left of the continuum is the most liberal of the proposals, the single-payer plan, which would cover all Americans by a direct cost to taxpayers. On the far right of the continuum is the Gramm plan, which does not increase coverage and serves basically as a minimal reform of the insurance industry. The status quo is at or near the filibuster pivot in the Senate, characterized by about 85-percent coverage via Medicare and Medicaid programs and private insurance companies, with emergency access for all.[10]

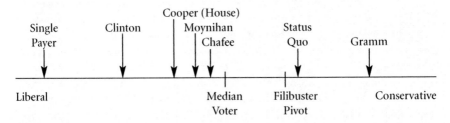

FIGURE 5.2   Health Care Proposals in the 103rd Congress

Given the position of the status quo, a successful proposal could not be to the left of the median voter. The Clinton plan was just that. Universal coverage was the major goal of Clinton's strongly regulatory plan. The expansion of coverage to include the last 15 percent of the public essentially would be paid for by an indirect tax on employers—the so-called employer mandate. The combination of universal coverage and employer mandates locates the Clinton plan to the left of the median voters. When the Congressional Budget Office (CBO) reported the cost of the proposal, and hearings further exposed the estimated numbers, it was clear that the Clinton plan was going nowhere. With maybe thirty votes at its peak of success, the Clinton plan failed to accommodate the preferences of conservative Democratic members at the median (let alone moderate Republican filibuster pivots), and represented a far-too-costly alternative to the status quo.

A somewhat more moderate plan was proposed by Representative Cooper (D, TN) but, like the Clinton plan, proved too costly to attract the necessary votes. Various House committees (such as the Energy and Commerce Committee) had even more difficulty producing proposals with broader appeal and thus were unable to bring bills to the floor. Even if such bills had reached the floor, their passage in the

House was unlikely. Representatives were reluctant to vote on health care prior to the more-conservative Senate. House members did not want to repeat their performance on the budget bill, when they were forced to vote on the BTU tax only to have it later stricken from the Senate version. Given the dim prospects for passing health care legislation in the House, attention turned back to the Senate.

The Senate Finance Committee was expected to produce the bill with the greatest chance of success. This committee, chaired by Senator Moynihan, was viewed as the most representative of the Senate, including both moderate Democrats and Republicans—the key to building a majority. Moynihan's attempt, put forward as a Chairman's mark, was a diluted version of the Clinton plan: a 45-percent increase in the tobacco tax, full deductibility for the self-employed, a requirement that insurance companies cover preexisting injuries and persons who change jobs, and increases in the number of pregnant mothers and children covered by Medicaid. The Moynihan plan sacrificed universal coverage, but increased the funds available to the plan through taxes and greater costs to employers. As information became available on the cost and complexity of Moynihan's plan, it too was eliminated as a viable challenger to the status quo. In many ways, it appeared as if no plan could actually pass through Congress.

As the chances of passing a health care bill in the 103rd Congress diminished, Majority Leader Mitchell called for a bipartisan coalition to salvage reform. The group of moderates, headed by Senator Chafee, proposed expanding coverage without requiring employer mandates. Even this bipartisan compromise failed to make it to the floor. The Chafee plan may have been more attractive to the median voters in Congress than the other proposals, but two factors ensured its defeat: (1) the pro-business filibuster pivot voters in the Senate, and (2) the plan's late entrance into the debate. By the time the Chafee bill had been introduced, members were uncertain whether voters even wanted substantial reform. In late 1994, after a year of debating the Clinton plan and its less-complicated alternatives, Congress officially abandoned health care reform without so much as a floor vote.

Aggregate Analysis

Table 5.5 surveys the results of the legislation we have analyzed. In the case of each proposal requiring only a simple majority for passage, the policy moved toward the floor median. News stories on the budget act featured moderate Democrats such as Boren, Breaux, Nunn, Johnston, and DeConcini; and House Democrats such as Stenholm, Wilson, and Andrews, as the major determiners of the final product. On legislation where supermajority institutions came into play, the names most frequently mentioned were Republicans—Specter, Cohen, Chafee, Packwood, Hatfield, Jeffords, and Durenberger—who of course controlled the filibuster pivot. On motor voter, the job stimulus package, and health care the difference between victory and defeat was in large part due to the compromises made on motor voter, which passed, and the lack thereof on the jobs bill and health care, which failed.

TABLE 5.5 Summary of Legislative Changes in the 103rd Congress

Type of Legislation	Bill	Presidential Proposal	Provisions	Changes	Pivotal Members
Majority only	1993 Budget Act	Left of floor median	1. BTU energy tax 2. Not many cuts 3. 36% top rate on individuals	Eliminate BTU $60 billion in cuts 33.5% top tax rate	Breaux Boren Nunn
	NAFTA	Left of floor median	1. Renegotiate 2. Trinational commission sanctions 3. Tax for worker retraining	Not renegotiated No real sanctions Dropped	Johnston DeConcini Stenholm Wilson
Supermajority Old	Family Leave	Republican filibuster point	1. 12 weeks coverage 2. Companies >50 employees 3. Exempt 10% 4. Full-time employees	None; the President supported a package worked out in 1992	Bond
	Motor Voter	At floor median	1. Registration required in welfare offices	Dropped/modified	Durenberger Specter
New	Job Stimulus	Left of floor median	1. Urban spending 2. Youth summers 3. Pell grants 4. Unemployment	Dropped Dropped Dropped Passed	Boren Breaux
	National Service	Left of floor median	1. $650 million 1st year 2. 5-year authorization 3. $10,000 education awards	$300 million 3 years $4,725	Chafee Kassebaum Packwood
	Health Care	Left of floor median	1. Universal coverage 2. Employer mandates	Dropped Dropped	Cooper Andrews

The family leave bill passed most easily, largely because the President submitted the compromise worked out in 1992. Had the President submitted a bill further to the left as with the 1987–1988 bills, Senators would have filibustered to pull the legislation rightward. And national service legislation passed only after shifting far enough to the right to appease the moderate-to-conservative Senators. In sum, the examination of the major legislation attempted during Clinton's first years has shown two things: (1) the bills that pass Congress are characterized by their appeal to the preferences of institutionally placed pivotal members, and not by their partisan appeal; and (2) gridlock continues under unified government in the form of significant limits on change away from the status quo.

It is also evident that budget divisiveness played a huge role in producing unified gridlock. No Republicans supported the 1993 budget deal, and conservative Democrats forced a number of concessions before they went along with the package. Family leave and motor voter legislation passed the costs off to business and to state and local governments. The programs that would be costly to the federal government were scaled back or killed: the job stimulus package proposed at $16.3 billion was reduced to a $4 billion unemployment compensation extension; and the health care bill, argued at one time to cost one trillion dollars, was abandoned entirely.[11]

Switcher Analysis

Thus far we have considered the possibility that policy is the result of parties, preferences, and institutions. We have argued that members' preferences, in combination with the supermajority institution of the filibuster, largely accounted for policy results in the early years of the Clinton presidency. Partisanship, here defined as the attempt to enact legislation at the median party position, did not seem to influence policy results. In majoritarian issues (the budget act and NAFTA implementation) the policy moved toward the median voter, whereas in nonmajoritarian issues policy moved further to the right in order to secure the cloture vote of the filibuster pivot. Additionally we found that the initial Clinton proposals were to the left of the floor median or the filibuster pivot, and that policies move toward pivotal voters because members' preferences on issues dominate.

However, as is well known, Presidents and others can and do offer congressional members benefits unrelated to the issue at hand in order to gain the members' votes on the pertinent issue. During the final week preceding the NAFTA vote, stories about President Clinton "buying" votes via the treasury were common. It is clear that Presidents and party leaders can offer congressional members policy concessions and favors unrelated to the issue at hand to get them to vote their way. Snyder (1991), Groseclose (1995), and Groseclose and Snyder (1996) have modeled this process and shown that optimal coalition building is characterized by the proximity of the legislation's position to that of the legislator's preference. The President or party leader will focus efforts on members at (or close to) the floor median (and pivotal positions) rather than on those strongly favoring or opposing the policy in question. Efforts targeted at legislators close to the pivot are more likely to succeed in changing the vote because of the near indifference of these members, whether the deal entails changing the bill or making off-issue compromises. Accepting this reasoning allows us to test the revolving gridlock theory more generally on legislators who, in the course of decisionmaking, first vote one way but later switch to the opposite position. There are numerous kinds of votes, such as successive cloture votes, pre- and postconference votes, and successive votes on rules, where "switchers" can be identified.[12]

We wish to test the hypothesis that in the 103rd Congress the switchers were those members near the predicted pivot points. On the budget vote, because this vote was majoritarian in both the House and the Senate, we expect those changing their votes to be located at or near the middle of the left–right continuum, rather than at the party medians. Concretely, this means that David Boren and John Breaux are more likely to switch than Carol Moseley-Braun. Furthermore, because the filibuster pivot is crucial to our theory as it relates to most other legislation, we expect that switchers there will tend to be to the right of the floor median in the Senate, and specifically at (or near) the three-fifths filibuster pivot. That is, because coalition building in the Senate is a supermajoritarian process, the President and party leaders will have to reach across the partisan divide to obtain the sixty votes necessary to overcome a filibuster.

Using Roll Call's ranking of Senators in the 103rd Congress, Figure 5.3 graphs switchers in 1993.[13] Three things are clear. First, although a baseline model of random switching might predict that this graph would be flat because everyone is equally likely to be the target of a coalition-building effort, the actual graph is remarkably peaked. Switchers are much more likely to be moderates than extremists. Second, as predicted, most of the switchers are to the right of the Senate

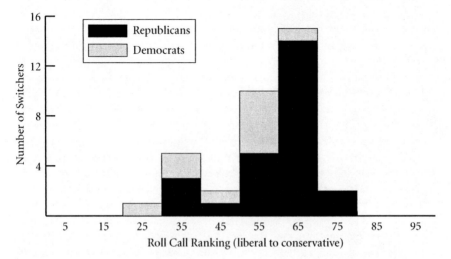

FIGURE 5.3   Switchers in the Senate (1993)

median. Clinton cannot simply count on a Democratic majority; he must make concessions or otherwise induce moderate Republicans such as Specter, Jeffords, and Hatfield to vote with him. Third, this pattern of switchers near the filibuster pivot holds for both Democrats and Republicans.

Switching Across Time

Although the foregoing analysis is specific to unified government and to the 103rd Congress, a similarly revealing exercise can be conducted in the few cases where nearly identical pieces of legislation were addressed by successive Congresses. Of these, the most salient is undoubtedly "fast track" and NAFTA.

In spring 1991, President Bush was pushing for an extension of the fast-track procedures for trade bills. The only major trade bill looming on the horizon was NAFTA, and the discussion thus focused on the use of fast-track procedures for the NAFTA trade negotiations. Without fast track, negotiators would be unable to make the binding agreements necessary for progress toward NAFTA. Supporters of fast track argued that NAFTA would die without these procedures, and many opponents voted against it for just that reason. However, on May 23, 1991, the House voted 231 to 192 to extend the fast-track procedures, and the Senate followed suit on the following day. As the votes in 1991 seemed to be based on the positions congressional members took on NAFTA generally, a comparison with their votes on the passage of NAFTA in 1993 does not seem unreasonable. The actions leading up to the mid-November votes have been discussed above. The resulting votes were both pro-NAFTA: 234 to 200 in the House and 61 to 38 in the Senate.

The crucial consideration in the use of the trade bill as a test of partisanship versus preferences is that the party leader, Clinton, lined up in opposition to the preferences of many members of his own party in the final vote. Had the Democratic President taken a typical Democratic position, party and preference would have remained aligned and no test could be constructed that would discriminate between the two hypotheses—a preference-driven Congress or a partisan one.

The comparative ability of partisan versus preference descriptions of the two NAFTA-related votes can be determined via simple cross-tabulation. Institutional mechanisms such as the filibuster do not play a role here because the votes were filibuster- and veto-proof. For Democrats and Republicans alike, any of four vote combinations (two nays, NN; two yeas, YY; or a mix, NY or YN) may, and in fact did, occur. A simple first pass at the votes, shown in Tables 5.6 and 5.7, asks: What percentage of vote combinations are consistent with the hypothesis that voting on these free-trade issues is based on preferences? The assumption is that solid free traders (YY) and strong protectionists (NN) qualify, whereas legislators switching away from Clinton (YN) or toward him (NY) were near the point of indifference and thus susceptible to influence by the President, interest groups, shifts in constituency opinions, and so on. The answer is found on the diagonals of the two tables: 77 percent (36/47) of Democrats' vote combinations and 79 percent (30/38)

TABLE 5.6   Cross-Tabulation of Senate Trade Votes (Democrats)

1993 NAFTA Vote

		No	Yes		
1991 Fast-Track Vote	No	20	7	27	7/27 = 26% Attraction
	Yes	4	16	20	4/20 = 20% Nonretention
				47	

TABLE 5.7   Cross-Tabulation of Senate Trade Votes (Republicans)

1993 NAFTA Vote

		No	Yes		
1991 Fast-Track Vote	No	3	3	6	3/6 = 50% Attraction
	Yes	5	27	32	5/32 = 16% Nonretention
				38	

of Republicans' vote combinations can be attributed to consistent preferences alone. Votes on NAFTA in 1993 followed votes on fast track in 1991 quite closely.

This need not be an argument for preferences and against parties, as party and preference are correlated. The question is: Can a partisan-based theory or a preference-based theory better predict the behavior of those who did not vote consistently—the switchers over time? If unified government breaks "partisan gridlock," as these theories claim, then it must be because an executive in unified government is better positioned to harness his party's strength in the Congress.

More specifically, the switching behavior that we observe on the off-diagonals in Tables 5.6 and 5.7 should be significantly asymmetric. For example, focusing on Democrats, a partisan-based unified government theory predicts that, with the unified government of 1993 (as opposed to the divided government of 1991), Bill Clinton—as President, party leader, and free trader—should pick up a much greater percentage of erstwhile Democratic protectionists than he should lose of erstwhile free traders. The former (nay-yea, or NY voters) are rallying to the cry of their party's standard bearer who at long last occupies the White House. The latter (YN voters) are deserting him in a time of need, and to make matters worse they had not deserted Republican George H. Bush two years earlier.

We can make such comparisons of switchers in two ways: within the President's party and across parties. A partisan-based theory would predict that within the Democratic Party Clinton's attraction rate (percentage of former Ns to switch to Y) would exceed his nonretention rate (percentage of former Ys to switch to N). Additionally, across the parties, a partisan-based theory would predict a higher attraction rate among Democrats than among Republicans, and a higher nonretention rate among Republicans than among Democrats. These three comparisons can be made in both the House and the Senate, for a total of six comparative tests of the partisan theory on this issue. None of these provides strong evidence of partisan-based vote switching.

The data for Democratic switchers on NAFTA provide the only bit of support for the partisan-based theory. Bill Clinton's attraction rate was an unimpressive 26 percent; only seven of twenty-seven Democrats switched to their President's position. And his nonretention rate, counting the Democratic switchers to protectionism, was nearly as high: four of twenty (20 percent). The predicted asymmetry appears, but ever so barely. It appears that the effect here of having a Democratic President is a gain of one or maybe two Democratic votes in the Senate. One more defector would have put these percentages at nearly identical levels—about one in four would switch each way.

The cross-party comparisons are even less supportive of the partisan-based unified government theory. Clinton's attraction rate among Democrats was significantly lower than that among Republicans. He picked up half of the Republicans who had opposed fast track under Bush, but only had an attraction rate of 26 percent within his own party. And his nonretention rate was actually higher among Democrats than among Republicans. Tables 5.6 and 5.7 show Clinton losing 20 percent of previous Democratic trade supporters, whereas he only lost five of thirty-two Republicans (or 16 percent) who had supported fast track. Both of these sets of results run counter to the partisan theory. Statistically speaking, we cannot reject the null hypothesis of members switching without regard to the party of the President.

For both Democrats and Republicans, the same analysis was replicated for the House, with almost identical results. Democratic switching differences are even closer to zero in the House than in the Senate; Republican switching differences run contrary to what the partisan-based theory of unified government predicts. Of the six comparisons made in both the House and Senate, none provided strong support for the partisan model and a few even ran counter to that model. As we mentioned above, depending on the positioning of the President and the status quo, it is often not possible to discern partisan voting from preference voting, because the two may be in alignment. With this test we have the forces of party and preference in conflict, and no asymmetrical partisan switching is found. This raises doubts about the use of party affiliation as a standard by which to predict voting patterns, beyond knowing the preferences of the legislators.

Finding no support for the strong partisan-based model, we are left to question who these switchers are. A preference-based model allows further explanation of this switching phenomenon. As in the case of switching votes during the course of legislative action on the individual bills noted above, these across-session switchers are also those who are near the pivotal median point. Whether their votes were the easiest to influence one way or the other, or whether their constituencies were fairly equally balanced and just tipped in one direction or the other, these switchers fall squarely between the solidly anti-NAFTA and solidly pro-NAFTA legislators. The mean ADA score for the free traders (YYs) in the Senate was 41.0, for the protectionists (NNs) 72.5, and for the switchers 60.1, just about the median member's score.[14]

The logic here seems very straightforward. Clinton takes a position that runs counter to the preferences of many members of his party. The party isn't strong enough to carry the necessary votes, so Clinton must appeal to members of Congress who are closest to his position. Thus these switchers are both the moderate Republicans and moderate Democrats who are nearly indifferent to voting for or against NAFTA. So, although the partisan theory lacks predictive power in this switcher analysis, the preference-based theory indicates where to look for this type of switching behavior.

This type of cross-temporal analysis is not limited to the case of trade. Whenever similar bills are found in unified and divided governments, and the President takes a position not aligned with the preferences of his party, these types of tests can be constructed. For example, we previously carried out such a switcher analysis for the 1990 Bush budget deal compared to the 1993 Clinton reconciliation package (Brady and Volden 1998, 130–135). Both bills cut spending and raised taxes amounting to half a trillion dollars over five years. Both relied on filibuster-proof reconciliation rules. And, once again, the President (this time President Bush, who stood against his party) was found no better able to attract votes from his own party than from the opposition party.

As was the case with trade, the switchers on the budget can best be accounted for with a preference-based theory. Although those sticking with their pro- or anti-"Democratic budget deal" principles hold extreme preference positions, the switchers are much closer to the median pivot points. In the Senate, the mean ADA score for budget supporters (YYs) was 84.0, for budget detractors (NNs) 20.9, and for switchers 53.8.[15] Table 5.8 summarizes these preference scores for both the budget and trade votes.

TABLE 5.8   Preference Scores for Switching over Time

		Mean ADA Scores		
		Consistent Support	*Switching*	*Consistent Opposition*
Trade	Senate	41.0	60.1	72.5
	House	33.3	51.6	77.1
Budget	Senate	84.0	53.8	20.9
	House	80.1	53.3	17.6

In both of these cases of vote switching over a period of time, most members of Congress stuck to their original positions, not being swayed by a change in party stance. Those who did switch did not do so in a noticeably partisan fashion. Rather, they did so due to a change in preferences caused by their near indifference, changes in their constituents' leanings, off-issue bargaining, or other concerns. These switchers were those members near the relevant pivot points, the voters who have been found to be most crucial to determining the fate of all the legislation discussed in this book. The switcher analysis, combined with our discussions of particular bills, elaborates on our argument: (1) legislators switch their positions over time due to various incentives or changes in the bills; (2) this switching behavior is not due to partisan leanings, but rather to preferences and constraining institutions such as the veto or filibuster; (3) because the crucial members of Congress gain their power by their preferences and by these institutions, their positions of power do not change with a change in the party of the President; and (4) as a result, gridlock under divided government will continue under unified government, with the crucial voters now being those needed to invoke cloture rather than those needed to override a veto.

By studying the continuation of policy gridlock through the unified government period of the 103rd Congress, we find that the revolving gridlock theory of preferences and institutions influencing policy outcomes still holds. Those who claimed that divided government caused gridlock either explicitly or implicitly argued that giving one party control of government would lead to an end of gridlock—to nonincremental policy shifts. Our argument was that it is not parties that cause gridlock; rather, it is preferences of the members of the House and Senate in combination with supermajoritarian institutions like Senate Rule XXII that cause gridlock. A brief review of the major pieces of legislation proposed by President Clinton showed that in each case his proposals had to be acceptable to either the floor median voter or the filibuster pivot voter in order for the proposal to pass.

If the preferences of key members of Congress essentially drive policies, what further conclusions can we draw? The first is that the President's domestic policy-making powers are generally overrated by some scholars and the media, and that Congress ultimately determines policy results. Gridlock objectively means that neither conservative nor liberal Presidents can pull or push policy far away from where Congress wants it. Unified government gridlock simply means that policy change will be held back by the filibuster pivot Senators, rather than by the members needed to override a veto. In short, in order to get any kind of legislation from budgets to civil rights acts passed, Republican Presidents are forced to either place policies correctly or move their proposals to the left whereas Democratic Presidents must move theirs right. Second, since policy is maintained within a gridlock region controlled by the more moderate Democrats and Republicans, gridlock occurs under both unified and divided government. Third, the key to understanding what will happen to today's proposed policies is determining median floor preferences, filibuster preferences, and veto pivot preferences. If they are to pass, policy proposals must be modified to accommodate these key members.

The Rise of the Republican Congress

Those who mistakenly believed that the 1992 elections and the advent of unified government would bring an end to gridlock were further surprised by the 1994 elections, which showed that the public found the Clinton policy direction to be inappropriate. Democrats from conservative districts who voted for Clinton's policies were defeated (Brady, Cogan, Gaines, and Rivers 1995). In the words of V. O. Key (1964, 544), "The vocabulary of the voice of the people consists mainly of the words yes and no; and at times one cannot be certain which word is being uttered." Clearly the electorate seemed to say "No!" to President Clinton, but was there also a "Yes!" for Republican governance?

The press treated the 1994 election results with astonishment, referring to the Republican victories in terms traditionally reserved for natural disasters and acts of god—as a "tsunami," as the most dramatic congressional landslide in forty years or more. Walter Dean Burnham, the eminent scholar on realigning elections, wrote the piece "Realignment Lives: The 1994 Earthquake and Its Implications" (1995), asking, "What kind of event was the 1994 election? Very probably the most consequential off-year election in (exactly) one hundred years" (363). In the previous century, the 1894 election brought the Republicans to control in the Congress.[16] Two years later, the 1896 elections kicked off fourteen consecutive years of unified Republican government, ushering in policy changes in the areas commonly associated with turn-of-the-century capitalism—the gold standard, protective tariffs, and foreign expansionism.

Was the 1994 election a precursor to (or part of) another realignment? The major effect of the 1994 election from our perspective was that it shifted the Congress to the right. The newly elected Republican majority in the House had run on the strength of the "Contract with America," which promised major government reforms and substantive changes that would give America a balanced budget while cutting taxes. This agenda was clearly to the right of the status quo. There were now at least 218 House votes and 51 Senate votes that favored shifting public policy on average to the right. In short, the median voter in the House and Senate was (on most issues) a Republican who favored limited government. With the shift in congressional preferences to the right, the President's veto point on the left became a real and relevant constraint.

A liberal President willing to veto conservative legislation can either keep the policy at the status quo or induce the majority to shift proposals toward the left. After forwarding the argument that gridlock is not necessarily linked to divided government, it may seem surprising that we argue that gridlock would predominate under this again-divided government. But the new situation is simply a continuance of the same interplay of preferences and institutions. As Reagan and Bush did with the Democrats, Clinton would remind Republicans of the power of the supermajority institution known as the presidential veto.

The 104th Congress, especially the House of Representatives, came to Washington intent on shifting policy to the right. As Figure 5.4 indicates, they had good reason to believe that such shifts could be enacted, given that the released policies are on the left. President Clinton was now clearly left of the median voters in the House and the Senate. His veto threat defined the gridlock region on the left. The Republican agenda was set out in the Contract with America and it was clear that the new Speaker of the House (Newt Gingrich, GA) would have a majority for most of the agenda. In the more moderate Senate, the majority leader (Bob Dole, KS) faced a serious challenge in that he was running for the Republican nomination for President and would have to deliver the votes for the Contract agenda. His problems were that (1) the Senate was more moderate than was the House; (2) President Clinton's veto pen was ready and waiting; (3) proposals that the President found too politically costly to veto could be filibustered by moderate Democrats; and (4) failure to deliver on the Contract would generate intense criticism from more conservative Republican presidential candidates such as Phil Gramm (TX) and Pat Buchanan.

In one sense, President Clinton's life became much easier than it had been in the 103rd Congress. No longer would he be an agenda setter; rather, he would become responsible for moderating the Republican agenda. His congressional party may not have delivered majorities for him on his health care and campaign finance reform proposals, but they would stick with him on vetoing Republican

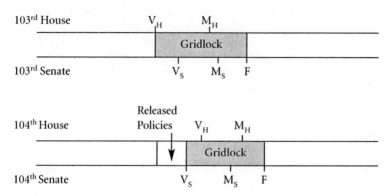

FIGURE 5.4   The 1994 Elections

legislation that was far from their preferences. In short, Clinton could now either take moderate positions and have the support of the moderates in his party or take liberal positions and count on enough Democrats to back him by sustaining a veto. He had gone from trying to build policy coalitions to acting with the automatic support of a blocking coalition. Note that this new situation hangs on the difference between the Republican proposals needing to focus on capturing Democratic members' support (at the veto pivot on the left), rather than on the President's proposed legislation needing to appeal to moderate Republicans (at the filibuster pivot on the right). Neither task is easy, especially when dealing with issues with severe budget consequences.

When Clinton was the agenda setter, he did not have the support to propose policies that would change the status quo by much; thus he was vulnerable to charges of ineffectual leadership and of forgoing his party's liberal principles. In the new scenario presented by the 104th Congress, the President could resist rightward shifts while his party and the media treated him as a principled leader standing foursquare for fair policies. Nothing changed except the position of the median voter in the Congress. The President's positions were the same and his personality was the same, yet political commentators and scholars began to talk and write about him in an entirely different fashion.[17]

A good share of the Contract with America involved governmental reform: a line-item veto, a balanced budget amendment, term limits, campaign finance reform, and internal congressional changes such as reduced staffs. Many of these items had been on the agenda of the Democratic freshman class of 1992, and they were popular with most segments of the American public. Under these conditions we would predict bipartisan support for some of the reforms. Those requiring a two-thirds majority (amendments to the Constitution) would have, naturally, a smaller chance of success. The real test for the Republicans would come when their substantive policies came to be incorporated in the budget.

We have argued that, since the 1970s, the budget has basically dominated congressional politics. Thus it is reasonable to expect that Republicans would have some successes early in the 104th Congress, especially on governmental reforms, but that the real test would occur over budget issues, and here the veto power of the President is crucial. In what follows we will (1) briefly review the results of the 1994 election; (2) describe the fate of various Republican proposals including government reforms and other items in the Contract with America; (3) show how the reconciliation budget was shaped and finalized, given the shift in preferences, by the threat and use of the presidential veto; and (4) evaluate Clinton's legislative successes given institutional constraints of revolving gridlock.

The 1994 Elections

When the 104th Congress convened in January 1995 it was the first Republican-controlled Congress in forty years. No Republican in the 104th House had ever been in the majority—none had ever been Chair of a committee or a subcommittee. The Republicans' majority status was a novelty to the members and a surprise to most analysts. We know of no well-known pollsters or pundits who had predicted a Republican victory in the House. Leading Democratic pollsters like Peter Hart and Republican pollsters like Bob Teeter were predicting a 20- to 25-seat Republican gain, about 20 seats short of what they would need to become the majority party. The conventional wisdom was that Republicans would gain some House seats but Democrats would remain in the majority as they had been for forty years. The results in the Senate were not as surprising because the Republicans did not need to gain many seats there to become the majority party, and they had recently been the majority, from 1980 through 1986. What accounted for the Republican victory, especially in the House?

Post-election analysis revealed that Republicans won control of the House by capturing 22 of 31 open-seat Democratic districts (the 31 districts in which a Democrat had retired after the 103rd Congress) and by defeating 34 of the 225 Democratic incumbents seeking reelection. This gain of 56 seats was only slightly offset by the Democratic capture of 4 open Republican districts, giving Republicans a net gain of 52 seats. Part of the reason for all of these Republican wins was that the contested districts were moderate or conservative to begin with. That is, Republican gains came in districts where neither Bill Clinton nor Michael Dukakis had done particularly well. If we take the percentage of the vote for Clinton in 1992 to represent the preferences of the voters, the results show that where Clinton was weak in 1992, Democrats stood a good chance of losing the seat in 1994. In the 31 previously Democratic open-seat districts, the Republicans won every seat where President Clinton had won less than 56 percent of the two-party vote and they lost every seat where Clinton had received more than 56 percent of the vote. The successful Republicans in these elections made Bill Clinton and his policies the issue.

The Republican victories over incumbent Democrats are more interesting because the famous "incumbency advantage" should have protected Democrats (Erikson 1976; Jacobson 1981; King and Gelman 1991; Alford and Brady 1993); yet thirty-four, including the Speaker of the House Tom Foley (WA), lost. We can account for the Republican takeover of the House by comparing district preferences with the candidates' support for President Clinton. Thus we expect that Republican wins over incumbent Democrats should come in moderate-to-conservative districts where the incumbent voted with Bill Clinton.

How important was support for the President's legislative agenda in contributing to the large loss of Democratic seats among House incumbents? Research on the 1994 elections shows that the President's policies affected election results differentially depending on district characteristics. The more moderate to conservative the district, the more a pro-Clinton voting record hurt.

This is the same pattern we note with regard to congressional elections during the Reagan–Bush years.[18] Members of Congress must be careful to represent their districts, even at the expense of their party, if they hope to be reelected (Canes-Wrone, Brady, and Cogan 2002). This finding is not new. Fenno (1978) emphasizes "reelection constituencies" to which members must appeal, and whose support they can maintain from one election to the next if they vote with their districts' preferences. Gilmour (1995) argues that actions that satisfy these constituencies often undermine the negotiations and compromise necessary to overcome political stalemate, leading to extreme proposals that have little chance of passing. Although we agree that district preferences and institutional structures lead to gridlock, we note that occasionally the desire to overcome gridlock puts members' seats at risk. In an attempt to please the party and the President, and to end gridlock, Democrats from conservative districts voted in ways that were considered too liberal at election time. This accounted for the Republican landslide in 1994.

In January 1995, the new Republican Congress (especially the House) came to Washington with the belief that they had received a clear mandate for change. Not only had their victories come over incumbent Democrats who had supported the President, but they had also signed a "Contract with America" promising a reduced and reformed government and a balanced budget.

The Republican House would now set the agenda for the 104th Congress, and a fundamental question became: How far to the right would their proposals be? On issues of governmental reform—a balanced budget, term limits, reduced congressional staffs, and the line-item veto—our view is that the new median member of the entire Congress was not far from the American public's preference, but that the median member of the Republican Party (and especially of the freshman class) was too conservative for the American people. If the Republicans held together as a party and made proposals to dramatically cut expenditures, especially entitlements, the political outcome would be clear. A substantial Republican agenda too far to the right of the public would put President Clinton in the position of being able to veto such legislation in the name of moderation, placing him in a favorable light and leaving the Republican Congress in the unenviable position the President had been in a year earlier—too far away from the center. In the discussion that follows we argue that this is exactly what happened. Republicans were largely successful in passing governmental reforms (indeed often with Democratic support). However, when it came time to vote for entitlement cuts to balance the budget, the President was able to position himself as the moderate. This is not to say that on certain issues, such as aid to farmers and environmental legislation, some moderate Republicans did not intervene to shift policy proposals back to the left. Rather, we argue that in general a unified Republican majority proposed and passed a budget that was "perceived" as being harsh (that is, right of center), thus giving President Clinton the middle ground between the liberals in his own party and the Republican majority.

The Republican Agenda

The Republicans in the 104th Congress were committed to political reform. They sought to reduce congressional staffs by one-third, restructure the committee system, eliminate the use of proxy votes in committees and subcommittees, restrict the number of terms a member could chair a committee, and limit the number of terms Speakers could serve. They also sought (1) a balanced budget amendment, (2) an amendment limiting the number of terms Representatives and Senators could serve in Congress, (3) a line-item veto for the President on budget issues, (4) an end to unfunded mandates, and (5) campaign finance reform. Of these reforms, all were majority-vote items in the House (if they received presidential support), except the two Constitutional amendments regarding a balanced budget and term limits. With regard to these, both the House and the Senate would have to deliver two-thirds of their membership in order to start the amendment process. Thus on both these items Republicans needed Democratic support in order to gain the necessary votes. All the other reform proposals would only require a simple majority in the House; however, in the Senate the Democrats could use the filibuster to move policy in their direction, and the presidential veto could provide an even greater constraint. Such were the constraints on other Republican proposals as well, including ending unfunded mandates and turning welfare programs over to the states. Table 5.9 shows the major proposals of the 104th Congress and their resolution. The following pages illustrate the politics behind many of these proposals.

Whether the battles were framed by the need for two-thirds support to propose a Constitutional amendment, an identical supermajority to override a presidential veto, or three-fifths support to overcome possible filibusters, the constraint would be in the more-moderate Senate. The Republican revolution may have captured the House by storm, but the battle lines would be drawn in the Senate.

Proposed Constitutional Amendments

The balanced budget amendment preferred by House Republicans would, upon ratification, require a three-fifths majority of both bodies in order to raise taxes to balance the budget. This was not surprising given that Republicans generally prefer a smaller government, resulting from reduced taxes and spending. Liberal Democrats, of course, would not support such an amendment; thus, in order to garner the two-thirds vote necessary to propose the amendment, attention focused on moderate, conservative, and southern Democrats like Charles Stenholm of Texas. The Conservative Democratic Caucus favored a balanced budget amendment that did not include the three-fifths tax requirement. Without these Democratic votes it was clear that the amendment would not pass the House. What was unclear was whether, if conservative Democrats' only choice was to vote for a balanced budget amendment that included the three-fifths tax requirement, they would vote for it over the status quo of no amendment. If the Republican leaders could be certain that these Democrats would vote for their amendment over the status quo, they could have the Rules Committee report out a rule requiring an up-or-down vote on only the Republican amendment. Stenholm was the primary spokesman for the

TABLE 5.9 Major Legislation in the 104th Congress

Type of Legislation	Bill	Initial House Proposal	Provisions	Changes	Pivotal Members
Constitutional Amendments	Balanced budget	Right of median	1. 3/5ths vote on tax increases 2. Balance by 2002	1. Stripped 2. Still lost in Senate	Bingaman (D, NM) Daschle (D, SD) Dorgan (D, ND)
	Term limits	Right of median	1. Three two-year terms	1. Six two-year terms 2. Still defeated	Senior Democrats and Republicans
Supermajority Legislation	Line-item veto	About median	1. Enhanced rescissions	1. Weakened slightly 2. Dole pressure	Breaux (D, LA) Heflin (D, AL)
	Unfunded mandates	Right of median	1. 3/5ths point-of-order override 2. $50 million on private business	1. Stripped 2. $100 million on private business	Conservative Democrats
	Budget	Right of median	1. Cut $894 billion in spending 2. Reduce increases in entitlements, e.g., Medicare, Medicaid 3. Reduce taxes $245 billion 4. Balance by 2002	1. Smaller cuts 2. Abandoned 3. Abandoned 4. Abandoned	Multiple coalitions attempted and abandoned
	Welfare	Right of median	1. $82 billion in savings (six years) 2. AFDC to states 3. Medicaid to states 4. School lunches, food stamps options to states	1. $54 billion in savings 2. Retained 3. Abandoned 4. Abandoned	Moderate Democrats up for reelection

conservative Democrats, and he went to great pains to say that the Caucus (about seventy votes) would not vote for the Republican amendment, thus ensuring its defeat. Stenholm, on the other hand, felt sure that the Republicans, if faced with a majority-rule amendment or no amendment, would vote for his alternate balanced budget amendment, which did not include the three-fifths tax condition. This was a case in which uncertainty about members' preferences would act in favor of the status quo.

The problem was resolved when the Rules Committee issued a "Queen of the Prom" amendment that allowed each alternative to be voted on against the status quo.[19] The first vote was to be on the Republican amendment and, if it passed, it would be the new status quo against which the Stenholm amendment would be pitted. If the Republican amendment collected two-thirds of the vote, then the Stenholm amendment would fail because Republicans would vote against it. If it failed to get these necessary votes, then the Republicans would have to choose between the status quo (no amendment) and the Stenholm amendment. The conservative Democrats were betting that the Republicans would vote with them on this latter vote. In the first vote on the Republican amendment the conservative Democrats voted no, thus killing the three-fifths tax clause amendment. The vote on the Stenholm amendment forced the Republicans to choose between either a failure to get any amendment or a balanced budget amendment that was not as strong on taxes as they preferred. In the end, the Republicans voted for the Stenholm amendment, as did more than seventy Democrats, which yielded the necessary two-thirds majority. Clearly, the supermajority Constitutional requirement forced a change in policy from what the majority preferred, and the policy had to be shifted left toward conservative and moderate Democrats in order to pass.

The Senate presented a different story. Because the Senate was more moderate than the House and Senators had not endorsed the Contract with America, the likelihood of passage was smaller. The chance that the Senate would pass an amendment with a three-fifths tax requirement was nonexistent, and thus they would clearly be voting on the Stenholm amendment. Furthermore, the Republican majority faced a worthy adversary in Senator Robert Byrd (WV), a former majority leader and a master of Senate rules, who led the battle against the amendment. As in the House, the crucial votes necessary for passage of the two-thirds majority were southern and moderate-to-conservative Democrats. Media accounts of key voters featured the names of moderate Democratic Senators like Nunn (GA), Ford (KY), Hollings (SC), and Bingaman (NM). These Senators were presented as moderate Democrats on the various preference rating scales discussed earlier in this chapter. Nunn and Ford were classified as median members on more rankings than any other Senators (Table 5.1). Bingaman is only slightly more liberal, positioned at about the veto pivot in the 104th Congress, given the shift to the right in the 1994 elections.

The Senate had voted on balanced budget amendments in 1986 and 1994, and in each case the amendment had failed. The sweeping nature of the Republican victory in 1994 gave the amendment's backers their best shot at victory. For five weeks the Senate debated the amendment, which called for a balanced budget every year starting in 2002, unless three-fifths of both Houses voted to suspend the requirement. It was clear that the amendment was supported by a majority in the Senate and in the country as a whole. Opponents of the amendment needed cover, and they found it in Social Security. As the Senate vote neared, opponents argued "that Social Security was somehow threatened, on the basis that the surplus revenue from the payroll tax used to pay for the program is being used to mask the size of the deficit" (1995 *Congressional Quarterly Weekly Report*, 673).[20] Several swing Democrats said that they would vote for the amendment if Social Security were exempted (which would mean that the unified budget that includes Social Security would no longer be the standard accounting mechanism). In the final vote, fourteen Democrats voted with fifty-one Republicans for the amendment, for a total of sixty-five votes.[21] Of these fourteen Democrats, seven were up for reelection in 1996, and three, Baucus (MT), Biden (DE), and Harkin (IA), changed their votes from 1994. Of the thirty-five Democrats voting against the amendment, six changed their 1994 "yes" votes to "no"—Bingaman, Daschle (SD), Dorgan (ND), Feinstein (CA), Ford, and Hollings—and none of them was up for reelection in 1996. Thus, once again, a balanced budget amendment had failed and the key was that moderate Democrats who were not up for reelection chose to vote against the amendment.

Because limiting the terms served by House and Senate members would necessitate a constitutional amendment, this reform also requires a two-thirds vote. The odds for passing it in the Senate were low given the Senate's more moderate nature, and passage of the amendment in the House was problematic because key Republicans like Bill Archer (TX; Chair, Ways and Means) and Henry Hyde (IL; Chair, Judiciary) were opposed to term limits. A majority of the congressional Democrats were also opposed, and the combination of Democrats and senior Republicans opposing the amendment was formidable. The freshman Republicans were adamant, however, and insisted that the House at least vote on the issue. The Judiciary Committee held hearings and reported out a bill limiting House members to six two-year terms (twelve years total) and Senators to two six-year terms. The only bargaining point was how many terms members should be limited to, with some freshman Republicans advocating three two-year terms. It was obvious that the greater the number of terms allowed, the greater the chance of passage, and thus the Judiciary Committee's bill was offered as a less-constraining alternative to freshmen desires. The hearings and the debate did little to change preferences. In the vote, the combination of senior Republicans and Democrats was enough to keep the amendment from receiving the necessary two-thirds supermajority. The final vote tallied 40 Republicans and 187 Democrats opposing— enough to defeat the Amendment. The correlation between seniority and the vote was high (over 0.7), indicating that recently elected House members were in favor of term limits whereas senior members were inclined to oppose. In fact, 30 of the 40 Republicans voting against the amendment chaired a committee or subcommittee. The issue was not likely to have much of an electoral effect because seniors like Archer and Hyde would be reelected in spite of their "no" votes, while freshmen who had campaigned for term limits could use this to their advantage in their reelection bids.

As can be seen, constitutional amendments fit well into the revolving gridlock model, along with statutory lawmaking. Proposed amendments that have too conservative a flavor must be tempered to gain votes. But the two-thirds voting restriction is very constraining, and thus most proposed amendments (even after moderation) will fail against the formidable status quo position of the unamended U.S. Constitution.

Reforms under Less-Restrictive Rules

Governmental reforms needing only a simple majority vote (or facing only filibuster possibilities) fared better. On January 4 and 5 the House passed a rules revision and a congressional accountability act. Congressional staffs were cut by one-third, committees were rearranged, Chairs' terms were limited (as was the Speaker's), proxy voting was ended, and House members were no longer exempt from federal laws. On January 11 the Senate passed the congressional accountability law. In these internal reform measures, majorities of House Democrats supported Republican rule changes; for example, term limits for the Speaker and committee Chairs passed 355 to 74. Pat Williams (D, MT) summed up many Democrats' feelings when he said: "A lot of what the Republicans are doing is good. Democrats should have done this if we could have, but we couldn't. . . . We had a stake in continuing the status quo" (1995 *Congressional Quarterly Weekly Report*, 13).

By March 7 the House and Senate had passed a paperwork reduction bill, the main feature of the bill being the reduction of paperwork requirements on business. The legislation authorized an annual 10 percent across-the-board decrease in paperwork and reauthorized the Office of Information and Regulatory Affairs (OIRA) in OMB to oversee the reductions. The vote in the House was 418 to 0 and the Senate passed the bill 99 to 0.

Line-Item Veto. The President's line-item veto for budget matters was more controversial, especially because the President was a Democrat. Nevertheless, by the end of March 1995, both the House and Senate had passed a line-item veto. Technically the bills passed were not line-item vetoes, because such a bill would require amending the Constitution (and even the bill that passed was later declared unconstitutional). Rather, the House and Senate bills increased the President's authority to propose spending cuts. The House bill extended the President's "enhanced rescissions" power to cut spending out of appropriations bills that had become law and allowed the President to target tax breaks going to fewer than one hundred individuals. As it was, the President could request rescinding expenditures but Congress was free to and did ignore such rescissions. The new "line-item veto" required that when the President proposed rescissions they take effect unless Congress were to block them via a complicated process requiring a two-thirds vote. The essential idea behind the veto was to curb the congressional tendency to slip "pork barrel" projects into appropriation bills that the President has to sign (in toto) or veto (in toto).

Critics argued that the bill tipped power too much toward the President, and that aggressive Presidents could rewrite appropriations bills wholesale to punish opponents and reward supporters. In voting for this bill, the House rejected a Stenholm "expedited rescission" bill that had passed in 1994. In addition, they rejected other Democratic amendments such as a proposal to allow the President to "veto" any tax bill benefiting the top 10 percent of taxpayers. The Republican bill passed 294 to 134, with 71 Democrats voting in favor. Note the difference between this bill and the balanced budget amendment. When the Republicans needed a two-thirds majority, they ended up supporting the Stenholm amendment that weakened their preferred proposal. Here, however, they rejected the Stenholm plan and passed their preferred plan; this was possible because they needed only a simple majority, 218 votes, to win. Democrats who favored "enhanced rescission" were forced to choose between the status quo (no veto) and the Republican plan, and most of these Democrats voted for the Republican plan—reversing the votes cast in the balanced budget amendment that included the three-fifths tax clause.

In late March 1996, a year after the initial proposals had been adopted, an agreement was reached in conference. Bob Dole had captured enough support in the primaries to be confident of his nomination as the Republican Party's candidate for President. He now turned his attention to passing some major legislation in the Senate. As such, he put pressure on Senate Republicans to support the stronger rescission provisions of the House's line-item veto proposal. Although the bill was weakened somewhat for the less-conservative tastes of the Senate, much of the language of the House bill was retained by the conference committee. In the end, it all came down to "whatever Bob Dole wants to do," as Thad Cochran (R, MS) put it (1996 *Congressional Quarterly Weekly Report*, 780). Dole was able to gain the support of fifty Republican Senators, with nineteen Democrats joining in passing the conference report, on March 27. The following day, the House followed suit by a vote of 232 to 177. The line-item veto was used sparingly by President Clinton and was later declared unconstitutional.

Unfunded Mandates Limitations.   The unfunded mandates bill passed the Senate on January 27, 1995. This bill was designed to curb the imposition of costly new requirements on state and local governments. Any federal legislation that would impose costs of more than $50 million on state and local governments would be subject to a "point of order." Once a point of order had been moved, majorities in each chamber would have to vote to waive it; if waived, the legislation would be sent to the floor. Bills relating to civil rights, national security, and disaster relief were exempt from this legislation. The idea behind the bill was that by forcing representatives to vote on mandates, there would be fewer mandates. Previously such unfunded mandates were routinely buried in bills, and members were not held accountable for them.

In Chapter 3 we showed how, given budget constraints, the Congress and the President had instead relied upon off-budget legislation, which pushed costs onto state and local governments, businesses, and consumers. The Americans with Disabilities Act is a case in point. That legislation requires governments, businesses, local schools, and other bodies to, among other things, provide special access to disabled persons. These kinds of renovations obviously cost money, and they are not funded by the federal government that required them in the first place. The increase in such off-budget items generated opposition from state and local government officials, who favored the unfunded mandates legislation.

Passage of the bill in the Senate was not easy. There were fifty-nine hours of debate on the bill and forty-four roll call votes before it finally passed, 89 to 10, with all dissenting votes coming from Democrats. The final arrangement was a compromise because Senator Gramm's amendment to require a three-fifths majority to override a point of order was withdrawn due to lack of support and a threatened filibuster. Democratic opponents failed in their attempts to amend the bill by exempting mandates that involved the health of children, pregnant women, and the elderly; public health and welfare; radioactive substances; and so on.

The House passed its version of the unfunded mandates bill on February 1, 1995. The House version, like the Senate bill, required a point of order on any mandate costing over $50 million. The same issues—civil rights, national security, and disaster relief—were exempted. The House bill differed in that it exposed federal agencies to lawsuits if the agencies fail to perform cost–benefit analyses or do not consult local officials. The House bill also required a point of order on unfunded mandates of over $50 million on private business, whereas the Senate version set the limit on businesses at $250 million. The conference committee faced some difficulties resolving these differences, which mirrored, of course, the difference between a more conservative House and a more moderate Senate. It is important to note that in the debates on unfunded mandates, the Americans with Disabilities Act and the Clean Air Act amendments of 1990 were most frequently mentioned as those acts that the new legislation was trying to correct. Democratic Senators were especially worried that, because federal agencies were still formulating the rules for enforcing the Clean Air Act (PL 101–549), the unfunded mandates bill might be used to restrict the Clean Air Act. An amendment to include revisions of previous mandates in the unfunded mandates bill was voted down as being too conservative even for the House.

Passage of the act in the House was not easy, with well over a hundred amendments proposed on the floor tying up the bill for two weeks. The opponents' strategy was to add public health, environmental, and labor laws to the exempted requirements. On average, about eighty Democrats joined Republicans in voting down these amendments. The eighty were conservative and moderate Democrats from southern, border, and midwestern states. The conference committee compromised on the House–Senate differences by setting a $100 million cost limit on private sector mandates and by requiring federal agencies to consult with local officials before passing mandates. Conservatives such as Phil Gramm felt that the bill was not strong enough, whereas liberals felt that it went too far. President Clinton signed the bill on March 22.

Other Reforms.   The Republican agenda had also called for passage of crime legislation, civil litigation overhaul, changes in product liability legislation, and welfare reform. Moreover, the Contract with America had proclaimed that this legislation would be passed in the House within the first one hundred days, and to a large extent the House succeeded. Between February 7 and 14 the House passed six new crime bills; by February 24 they had passed a moratorium on federal regulations; and by March 10 they had passed a civil litigation bill and a product liability act. Within a week the House had passed a welfare overhaul bill. Scholars "[were] amazed by the House Republicans' ability to keep the Contract with America on its steady 100-day time table" (1995 *Congressional Quarterly Weekly Report*, 909). The agenda setter was clearly the Republican House, not the President. One scholar, David Mayhew, went so far as to say: "Not only is the President not taking a major part, he is largely on the other side" (1995 *Congressional Quarterly Weekly Report*, 911). Other scholars compared these hundred days to the 1867 period when the Radical Republicans set the agenda and neutralized President Andrew Johnson by impeaching him and overriding his vetoes a record fifteen times. Professor James Thurber felt that the Republicans were "cutting back the scope of government rather than defining problems and finding solutions" (1995 *Congressional Quarterly Weekly Report*, 912). Regardless of their views about the desirability of the policies, they agreed that there were few precedents for the achievements of the 104th Congress.

In spite of the House's apparent achievements, by the end of the first session, exactly two of the Contract's ten provisions had been signed into law. One was the requirement that the Congress end its own exempt status from eleven workplace laws. The other was the above-mentioned unfunded mandates bill and a bill to reduce federal paperwork. Still unfinished were a major telecommunications bill, a final version of the line-item veto, an intelligence authorization bill, a defense authorization bill, the product liability bill, a significant banking reorganization act, some nonreconciliation farm matters, the Superfund toxic cleanup act, and the regulatory overhaul bill, among others. What accounts for the end-of-session malaise on substantive legislation despite the House's success after one hundred days?

The primary explanation is that the Senate had refused to pass the House legislation, as in the case of the balanced budget amendment; to pass the same version, as in the case of the line-item veto; or to act on the legislation at all. Considering just the items in the Contract, as of mid-December 1995 the Senate still had in committee House crime legislation including required restitution to victims (H.R. 665), modification of the exclusionary rule (H.R. 666), and block grants to give communities control over funds (H.R. 728). The national security legislation passed by the House (H.R. 7) had not been reported out of committee. The parts of the Contract covering civil law and product liability (H.R. 988) had not passed out of committee, and the Senate had not yet considered term limits (S.J. Res. 21). On those Contract items where the Senate had acted, they had passed or were about to pass legislation that differed from the House versions. As a result, legislation involving the line-item veto, welfare (H.R. 4 and H.R. 2491), tax credits, Social Security benefits, capital gains cuts, and frivolous lawsuits against companies were all in conference.

The major reasons for the Senate's inaction were as follows: (1) Senate rules allow individual Senators more influence, which leads to delays; (2) the possibility of a filibuster by the Democratic minority or of a presidential veto increases uncertainty over what will pass; and (3) the median Senator was clearly left of the median House Republican. In order for Senator Dole to win even a majority vote he had to have the votes of his party's moderates: Chafee (RI), Cohen, Specter, Kassebaum (KS), Jeffords, Campbell (CO), and others. In order to beat a filibuster he had to have all these votes plus the votes of moderate Democrats like Heflin, Nunn, Breaux, and Johnson (LA). And to override a presidential veto—well, that didn't seem likely at all. Thus getting major policy shifts passed was a delicate task given that the Senate was more liberal and that the rules prohibited speedy expedition of legislation.

Passing major policy shifts that downsized government would have been difficult under any conditions, but the actions of House Republicans, especially the freshmen, exacerbated the problem. In their fervor to "keep faith with America," the freshmen, who were unaccustomed to the give-and-take of politics, tried to push the Senate into action by attaching riders to bills they had passed.[22] For example, House Republicans attached to the appropriations bill for housing and other domestic programs a set of provisions that stripped the Environmental Protection Agency (EPA) of its power to regulate and enforce major sections of the air and water pollution laws. In another bill they attached a rider allowing exploratory drilling in the Alaska National Wildlife Refuge. These environmental riders went to the Senate Environment and Public Works Committee chaired by Senator Chafee, who refused to consider the House legislation, saying: "The so-called clean water bill they sent over went way beyond what was acceptable to me and way beyond what was acceptable in the Senate as a whole" (1995 *Congressional Quarterly Weekly Report*, 3712–3713).

The Republicans in the House had held together remarkably well throughout the first year. Overall, although there were some splits, the congressional Republican Party remained largely unified. The seventy-three first-term Republicans generally pulled the party to the right across a whole set of issues. They believed that they had been elected to transform American politics by downsizing the role of government as regulator, provider of entitlements, and tax collector. All year the Republican leadership had tried to carefully shift the status quo across a set of policies without moving so far that they would not be able to achieve their policy objectives. Internally they were divided over how far to go, with some arguing that being timid put them at greater risk with voters than did boldness. Freshman Republican Senator James Inhofe (OK) summed up this position when he said: "The old way of negotiating [splitting differences] and giving in is not what we want" (1995 *Congressional Quarterly Weekly Report*, 3709).

A summary of Republican legislative action in the 104th Congress typically boils down to a single question, as suggested by the revolving gridlock theory: How great of a supermajority constraint is institutionally imposed on the passage of particular pieces of legislation? The 1994 elections were indeed remarkable—the Contract with America attests to numerous policy areas where new majorities for change were established in the Congress. Yet, with the need for sixty votes in the Senate to overcome possible filibusters, much of the House legislation was held up or toned down. More significantly, where two-thirds supermajorities were needed—for the constitutional amendments balancing the budget and imposing term limits, and for vetoed legislation like the Republican budget and welfare plans—the proposals were stopped dead. The newly Republican Congress would not move policy to the left, and movements to the right that did not meet Clinton's approval resulted in sustained vetoes. The gridlock region in these cases truly resulted in gridlock, and in contentious politics between conservatives and liberals, between Congress and the President. Nowhere did this conflict provide better public drama than in the 1995–1996 debates over the budget.

The 1995–1996 Budget Battle

As noted above, the House Republicans believed that they had been elected to transform American politics by downsizing the role of government as regulator, provider of entitlements, and tax collector. President Clinton and the congressional Democrats believed Republican proposals went too far, and this conflict played out with considerable drama in the 1995–1996 budget battle. The newly elected Republican majorities had promised Americans that they would both reduce taxes and balance the budget by shrinking the size of the government. The vehicle for accomplishing this was the standard reconciliation budget.

The reductions in federal revenue that would result from the Republicans' proposed tax cut meant they would have to make large cuts in popular entitlement programs. One of the Republicans' earliest positions was to take Social Security off the table, so the largest entitlement program could not be touched. To achieve a balanced budget over seven years, the Republicans instead proposed reductions in Medicare and Medicaid, but these were the programs for which President Clinton and congressional Democrats were seeking increases, not decreases. The Republican congressional majorities thus had three possible strategies with regard to the budget package. They could (1) forge a budget deal that the President would sign; (2) attempt the unprecedented (and highly unlikely) maneuver of gaining the two-thirds necessary to override a veto of a budget bill; or (3) score some political points by proposing a major budget bill and having the President veto it, despite being unable to override the veto.

Given the fundamental differences in the preferences and rules between the House and Senate, and given the fact that a Democratic President could veto legislation, the reconciliation process ran behind schedule—though this is hardly unusual. In the past, continuing resolutions were easily passed before the end of the government's fiscal year to allow government spending to continue (at the previous year's level). In conjunction with this, the government would ordinarily seek an increase in the debt limit in order to borrow money to pay off the federal deficit. In 1995, the continuing resolution questions, the extension of the debt ceiling, and the final reconciliation budget all needed to be addressed simultaneously in early November.

The reconciliation budget passed by Republicans in Congress included $894 billion in cuts to projected federal spending by 2002, producing a $4 billion surplus. The bill proposed reducing welfare funding by $82 billion, Medicare by $270 billion, Medicaid by $163 billion, and proposed paring back agricultural subsidies with the ultimate goal of eliminating them. In addition, the reconciliation bill reduced taxes by $245 billion over seven years. Meanwhile, the President promised to veto any "bill that requires crippling cuts in Medicare, weakens the environment, reduces educational opportunity or raises taxes on working families" (1995 *Congressional Quarterly Weekly Report*, 3505). President Clinton had vetoed earlier temporary budget measures, signaling his willingness to use the veto to force Republicans to compromise on their reconciliation package.

Difficulties formulating the proposal meant that it was not sent to the President by the start of the new fiscal year. Republicans hoped to use this delay to their advantage, as the timing denied the President a chance to veto the reconciliation bill and the spending bills without simultaneously shutting down the government. But the President would not give in so easily. On November 13, 1995, President Clinton vetoed the measures. On November 14, more than 14,800,000 non-essential federal employees were sent home, and a public battle in the media began. House Republicans, led by Speaker Gingrich, blamed the President for the shutdown. Clinton said that he would not sign any bill with cuts too large, even if it takes "90 days, 120 days, or 180 days" (*CBS Evening News*, November 15, 1995). Given negative public reaction to the shutdown, and given the Republicans' inability to override the President's veto, both sides agreed to continuing resolutions to keep the government running until mid-December.

As a compromise gesture, Clinton agreed to a balanced budget by 2002 as scored by the Congressional Budget Office (CBO); in exchange, Republicans agreed to have the CBO re-estimate the effects of their budget given the stronger-than-expected growth in the U.S. economy in 1995 (thus fewer cuts would be necessary). The rough CBO estimates yielded about $130 billion more than the original estimates. By December, both sides began renegotiating the tax cuts and expenditures of the budget on an "oranges-to-oranges" basis.

Consensus budget politics, however, had died decades earlier, and was not to be resurrected. President Clinton successfully rallied public opinion on his side. His strategy of criticizing the Republican budget as too harsh and thus "against our [American] values" was being reflected in the polls. President Clinton's approval ratings climbed over 50 percent for the first time in more than a year. Moreover, the President and the Democrats had a 23 percent margin over Republicans in public opinion polls asking who could better handle the deficit—a major reversal from the early days of the 104th Congress. The December 15 deadline for a continuing resolution passed with no agreement, so parts of the government closed down once again. The President and Democratic legislators argued that it was the ideological freshman class of 1994 who were responsible for shutting down the government. Republicans insisted that the President was not to be trusted because he had not yet presented his own balanced budget proposal.

On January 6, 1996, the ball began to roll again. The Republican Congress passed and the President signed a series of continuing resolutions to keep parts of the government operating through September and all of it through at least January 26. The President submitted a budget (using CBO scoring) that would balance the budget by 2002 with cuts in Medicare, Medicaid, and welfare that were about one-half the size of those proposed by Republicans. The Clinton budget included tax cuts in the form of a $500 child credit and a small capital gains cut, while closing tax loopholes that would in effect increase taxes on corporations. And President Clinton refused to cut agricultural programs and student loans. Though Clinton's plan projected an increase of $97 billion more in savings than his December proposal, the Republicans were still proposing substantially more cuts than Clinton, including $99 billion more in Medicare, $65 billion more in Medicaid, $88 billion more in discretionary spending, $37 billion more in welfare, combined with a whopping $154 billion more in tax cuts. Despite attempts at new coalitions, there was still no politically viable solution to budgetary gridlock.[23]

The budget battle was still raging in the public relations arena. The initial Republican reaction was to try to portray the Clinton budget as more tax-and-spend liberalism. Clinton, on the other hand, portrayed his budget as a responsible plan that put the burden of payment where it belonged, while preserving the social safety net. And, again, Clinton won on the public relations battle, undoubtedly giving him more bargaining leverage (the veto threat seemed more credible if the public supported Clinton's views). Congressional Republicans made an attempt to negotiate with conservative and moderate Democrats in order to offer a bipartisan bill (still closer to their original bill) to try to force the President to move right. But, with the near impossibility that Congress could override a veto, the pivotal voter was a liberal who would never support such a bill. With the additional leverage and support received from the public relations boost, the legislation moved more dramatically toward Clinton's preferences, and toward the status quo established in his 1993 budget deal.

The President seemed to have won the day. The government shutdown was blamed on the Republican Congress, especially Speaker Gingrich. Prior to the government shutdowns (early 1995), the *Wall Street Journal/National Broadcasting Company* (WSJ/NBC) poll put Speaker Gingrich's job approval rating at plus 11 (46% approval, 35% disapproval). The first government shutdown occurred on November 14, 1995—on November 19, Speaker Gingrich's public approval rating was minus 33 (27% approval; 60% disapproval). Throughout the budget battle, his approval ratings never rebounded. In contrast, the President's approval ratings shot up. From January 1995—shortly after the Republican sweep in November—through April, the President averaged an approval rating of plus 4. For a President presiding over a relatively strong economy, these numbers were historic lows. From June through October in two WSJ/NBC polls, the President was plus 3 and plus 4. Five days after the first shutdown (November 19, 1995), the President increased to an approval rating of plus 7; by the first week in December, he was up to plus 11. Clinton ultimately fell back to a plus 3 approval rating by mid-January, but that was still 31 points higher than Speaker Gingrich—a reversal of over 40 points within a period of six to seven months.

In January through March of 1996, Congress sent the President individual appropriations bills dealing with parts of the budget. Clinton had forced substantial concessions, and thus felt comfortable signing many of the bills. On April 25, Congress passed an omnibus appropriations bill that rolled together all that remained of the thirteen appropriation bills. Though the bill covered only about 16 percent of the federal budget, these domestic appropriations represented the funding for all of the federal bureaucracy and nearly everything the government does other than defense and cash transfers. Republicans sought policies and budget numbers to the right of the President, who vetoed bills he did not like, believing that he could win the public opinion battle. Thus, the policies and the numbers moved left, back toward the President. The President was able to protect education, job training, and the environment. The original Republican proposals for cuts in Medicare, Medicaid, and other entitlement programs were left stranded because the President's veto could not be overridden. The final budget contained a 9.1-percent reduction (from previous baselines) in domestic appropriations over the 1995–1996 period (a $22 billion cut in expenditures), but the programs that Clinton deemed important were left relatively untouched.

In sum, on the budget (as with other reforms) an eager Republican Congress proposed significant policy changes. And the supermajority constraint of the presidential veto became real and relevant. Policy proposals that were modified significantly to the left passed; those that did not either died or were vetoed. The same politics played out on welfare reform, once it was decoupled from the budget bill.[24] Overall, the only policies to move out of the gridlock region were the ones that could be moved far enough toward President Clinton's preferences such that he was willing to sign them. As was theorized in Figure 5.4 and shown in Table 5.9, all major proposals in the 104th Congress had to appeal to the Senators near the veto pivot. In short, a liberal-to-moderate President willing to veto legislation he viewed as too conservative had an excellent chance to persevere if the newly elected Republicans pushed policies too far to the right. His party may not have gone with him on health care, fuel taxes, campaign finance, and a series of other policies in the 103rd Congress, but they would vote to sustain his vetoes on policies that they also viewed as too conservative. The revolving gridlock model shows that the historic Republican congressional victory in the 1994 election therefore was not a guarantee of major policy shifts to the right.

Clinton's Second Term

By vetoing legislation that he (and public polls) viewed as too conservative in the 104th Congress, Clinton boosted his own electoral fortunes and reduced the Republicans' chances to head a unified government after the 1996 elections. By Clinton's second term, it appeared that both he and the Republicans had come to terms with the fact that majority party control of Congress is not a sufficient condition for major policy change. As the revolving gridlock model predicts, and as we have illustrated throughout the 104th Congress, policy change is limited by supermajority institutional constraints and the preferences of individual legislators. Thus, Clinton's policy successes should be evaluated from this perspective. We now turn to a brief description of the preference structure of the 105th and 106th Congresses and then offer a preliminary assessment of Clinton's presidency within this context.

Preferences of the 105th and 106th Congresses: Political Familiarity

In the 105th Congress, the Senate median legislators remained moderate Republicans like Snowe (ME), Chafee (RI) and conservative Democrats like Breaux (LA). The filibuster on the right included Republicans such as Hatch (UT), Bond (MO), and Roberts (KS). In the House, the median included the usual set of characters: Lipinski (IL), Stenholm (TX), Skelton (MO), and the like. The veto pivots in both chambers were safely in the heart of the Democratic Party.

The midterm (1998) elections yielded a gain for the President's party for only the second time in the twentieth century, but still left him with a Republican-controlled Congress. The 106th Congress held preferences quite similar to the 105th with the exception that the Democratic filibuster pivot moved even further to the left—making it almost impossible for policy to shift in a conservative direction with or without a presidential veto. In the House, the median moved slightly left, but still left members like Taylor (D, MS), Kelly (D, NY), and T. Campbell (R, CA) near the center.

Policies of the 105th and 106th Congresses

Clinton's win in 1996 and the Republican loss of seats in 1998 (along with Newt Gingrich's resignation of the Speakership) meant that bipartisan compromise was essential for any policy changes. This seemed to largely be recognized by both the President and legislators, who were resigned to continued gridlock on many of their priorities. After the lessons of the 104th Congress, Republican legislators realized that they did not have the support to beat the filibuster in the Senate or to override a presidential veto. The only policies that could be moved out of the gridlock regions in the 105th Congress were characterized by bipartisan support—policies such as tax credits (for higher education, families with children), a balanced budget agreement given the robust economy, and a Clinton proposal to improve education. Likewise, the only notable policy changes in the 106th Congress were Clinton-supported proposals—extending permanent normal trade relations to China, and a bill expanding Medicaid and Medicare so that people with disabilities continue to receive health insurance coverage if they go to work. In general, the 105th and 106th Congresses did not produce an overwhelming number of policy outputs; they spent much of their time and energy on Clinton investigations and impeachment hearings. In fact, as was shown in Table 3.4, the 106th Congress produced the fewest major pieces of legislation of any Congress in the past forty years.

Realizing that major change was not forthcoming, the Republican Congress looked to score political points by passing some bills that they knew would never be signed into law. As one journalist noted, Congress "seemed to be almost as much about positioning for the elections as about making law" (*New York Times*, December 17, 2000, A48). The Republican Congress was again constrained by Clinton's veto pen in the 105th—a late-term abortion ban and school vouchers are notable examples. Republicans knew that these bills ultimately would not succeed, but passing the bills at least satisfied the conservative faction of the Republican Party. Similarly, in the 106th Congress Republicans passed repeals of the "marriage penalty" and estate taxes, which were successfully vetoed by Clinton.

Once again, much of the policy wrangling was over the budget. And, as in the 104th Congress, Clinton typically came out on top. President Clinton was able to achieve his most important goals—from eliminating several "anti-environment" riders to new money for schoolteachers, the International Monetary Fund, and distressed farmers. One journalist provides a telling assessment of Clinton's role in the 106th budget negotiations: "In some cases, Mr. Clinton has refused to accept legislation because it was missing something he very much wanted. . . . But most energy has been spent beating back last-minute riders he does not like. . . . The Republicans believe that they will profit from these confrontations. But Mr. Clinton has won these standoffs in the past, and there is no reason why he cannot do so now" (*New York Times*, November 1, 2000, A34).

Evaluating President Clinton

We have made the case that in the 103rd Congress, President Clinton could not have moved policy too far left due to supermajority institutions and the distribution of legislative preferences. Similarly, in the following Congress, the Republicans could not shift policy too far right for the same reasons. In the next two Congresses, both sides seemed to have adjusted their view of what was possible and the few substantive policy proposals that passed were more centrist. So what did this mean for Clinton's overall policy record? Although the President did not move American public policy in bold new directions, it is quite clear that Clinton was able to work within the institutional constraints created by a Republican-controlled Congresses and nonetheless champion his pet policies over the 104th through 106th Congresses.

As Table 5.10 illustrates, many of Clinton's favored programs actually had budget increases under the Republican-controlled Congress. Relative to inflation, spending increased in numerous areas, especially special education, Head Start, education technology, and dislocated worker assistance. However, that Clinton's favorite programs found increased financial support is not evidence in and of itself that Clinton had a successful policy record. After all, the strong economic times during Clinton's presidency may have led the Republicans to increase domestic spending across the board. And, in fact, the domestic budget as a whole did grow between 1993 and 2000 by roughly 14 percent. Yet the budget outlays on Clinton's preferred programs increased an average of 56 percent, a statistically and substantively significant difference. The expansion of Clinton's programs above inflation far eclipses the average increase in spending over all programs.

Clinton also enjoyed some success in creating and maintaining new programs, perhaps even more success than Republicans had at killing existing programs. Scholars have long noted the difficulty of both initiating and extinguishing government programs and agencies—though some antiquated programs like the Bureau of Mines and the Travel and Tourism Administration were actually shut down on the Republicans' watch. However, Clinton was not only able to be a moderator of Republican attempts to cut programs, but he also was able to propose and pass new programs. Figure 5.5 shows a few of the new programs (and their budgets during Clinton's presidency) that a Republican-controlled Congress still funded. Of these, only the Community Policing program had been scaled back substantially by 2000.

One explanation for these policy successes was that Clinton proposed policies that he knew he could win. In other words, Clinton was aware of the institutional constraints and proposed policies accordingly. And this largely seemed to be the case with regard to new policymaking following the lessons of the 103rd Congress. After the 1994 elections, Clinton picked his new policy proposals wisely. Compromises, like on welfare reform, succeeded, whereas holding fast to his liberal health care reform proposal had failed. Throughout his presidency, Clinton was faced with the harsh realities of the revolving gridlock theory. Members of Congress have preferences over policy outcomes and they form coalitions within institutional structures requiring supermajorities. Compromises struck through budgetary concessions were not possible given the nature of deficit politics and PAYGO rules that made budget tradeoffs explicit.

Given these constraints how did the President fare? In the 103rd Congress he did pass a budget further left than Republicans desired, but the failure of his health care legislation, the stimulus package, and a series of other issues such as gays in the military led to the first fully Republican Congress since 1954. The President's use of the veto and his management of public opinion in the 104th Congress thwarted the Republicans' euphoria of late 1994 through early 1995. Clinton

TABLE 5.10   Budget Increases in Clinton's Favorite Programs

Program	1993 Outlays (1993 dollars)	1993 Outlays (2000 dollars)	2000 Outlays Actual	Percentage Change above Inflation
Adult Education	$305	$345	$470	36%
Bilingual and Immigrant Education	237	268	406	52%
Education Research Programs	162	183	319	74%
Special Education	2,966	3,352	6,036	80%
Head Start	2,776	3,137	5,267	68%
Education Technology	23	26	769	2859%
Federal Work Study	617	697	934	34%
Dislocated Worker Assistance	517	584	1,589	172%
Job Corps	966	1,092	1,358	24%
Lands Legacy Initiative	380	429	727	69%
Mass Transit	3,774	4,265	5,785	36%
Solar and Renewable Energy	249	281	315	12%
Energy Conservation and Efficiency	592	669	745	11%
U.S. Global Change Research	1,323	1,495	1,701	14%
Water/Wastewater Grants and Loans	508	574	631	10%

Notes: Outlays are in millions of dollars adjusted to 2000 dollars. *Source:* Brady and Hillygus (2005).

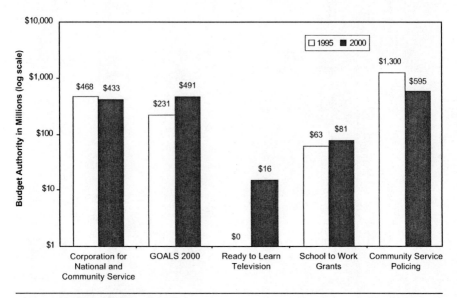

Source: Brady and Hillygus (2005).

FIGURE 5.5   Preservation of Clinton-Initiated Policies

turned what looked like a sure-fire Carter-like one-term presidency into a land-slide victory over Senate majority leader Bob Dole—making Clinton the first Democrat reelected since FDR. His personal victory, however, did not transfer to the Congress, as Republicans maintained majorities, albeit decreasing majorities in the 105th and 106th Congresses.

Whether under the unified government of 1993–1994 or divided government thereafter, the logic of the revolving gridlock model holds. Policy change toward the President under either scenario will typically be checked by filibusters in the Senate. Change away from the President will typically face presidential vetoes. Proposals will therefore need to be made to build supermajority coalitions. Clinton's more liberal proposals in the 103rd Congress and the Republican House's more conservative proposals in the 104th were doomed to end in gridlock unless sufficiently modified. Time after time, the politics described in this chapter tell the same story.

It is important to note that we have not claimed that this process yields good (or bad) policy. We have simply claimed that policy results can best be explained by looking at members' preferences and constraining institutions rather than at purely partisan variables. Ultimately the important questions are: What is the degree of agreement between key members' policy preferences and the public's preferences? and, Does the congressional system of representation of local and regional interests rather than national interests yield viable long-term policies?

Notes

1. The ratings used were AAUW, ACLU, ACU, ADA, ASC, BIPAC, CCUS, CFA, COPE, LCV, NAM, NCSC, NEA, NFIB, NFU, PCCW, TEAM, and UAW.

2. The rankings were based on votes in the 102nd and previous Congresses. Therefore, new members are not listed in Tables 5.1, 5.2, and 5.3. The point is that we want to analyze the Congress in a predictive fashion, as though it were new. Thus by taking returning members' scores and looking at their replacements (by party), we can guess whether congressional preferences shifted. This assumption is nonheroic in that a rich literature shows that members vote fairly consistently across time. Members who are liberal in their first Congress will be liberal in their tenth. See Kingdon (1973); Poole and Rosenthal (1991a), (1991b), (1997); and Groseclose, Levitt, and Snyder (1999).

3. See Anderson, Brady, and Cogan (2004) for an exploration of polling in specific policy areas.

4. Our findings are in line with those of Burden, Caldeira, and Groseclose (2000) who show significant similarities across multiple measures of Senators' ideology.

5. As mentioned previously, our notion of parties is not incompatible with either Cox and McCubbins's theory of parties (1993) or the theories of Rohde (1991) and Aldrich (1995). In Cox and McCubbins's view, the party leadership focuses on shaping committee appointments early in members' careers, and the connection between policy results and elections is loose. Our view allows for some party influence over member preferences, but brings district responsiveness and electoral success to the fore.

6. Note that we are clearly not saying that members of Congress have no concern for their party or for the public's perception of them via their party. It is in this sense that we are not making any argument against the "parties matter" camp. Clearly concern for the party does have an influence on an individual's preferences, but what matters in the end are district preferences and reelection, not just the party.

7. For the broader interest group politics on this issue, see Wright (1996, chap. 3).

8. Although some might claim that the Democrats as a party could not pass legislation against a strong filibustering Republican Party, it should be noted that even Democrats defected from the President's position. Additionally, the other examples show that appealing to the filibuster pivots, whether Democrats or Republicans, can get these key members to change their votes.

9. Part of this section is drawn from Brady and Buckley (1995).

10. That the status quo was to the right of the filibuster point was in question as of 1994. It seemed that nothing could pass, and yet, in the 104th Congress, the Kennedy-Kassebaum bill succeeded.

11. Clinton's national service program also fits this pattern, as it was cut in half to guarantee passage (Brady and Volden 1998, 119–120).

12. For "switching" behavior in the context of bill copartisanship, see Krehbiel (1995).

13. We used Roll Call because it allowed us to use all 100 Senators, while ADA and other scores had not yet been updated by the time of our first writing of this chapter. Analysis of switchers using ADA scores mirrors these results, showing three times as many switchers to the right of the median as to the left.

14. For the House, these figures were 33.3, 77.1, and 51.6, respectively, again with the switchers falling right in the middle. There is an additional separation between switchers toward Clinton and those away from him, with the switchers moving against the President (YNs) having a lower mean ADA score, but we do not speculate on this distinction here.

15. In the House, these figures were 80.1, 17.6, and 53.3, respectively. Again, there was a further distinction between YNs and NYs.

16. Mayhew (2002) offers a critique of the realignment literature, raising a series of objections and questions, many of which can be addressed through the lens of the revolving gridlock theory.

17. This argument is consistent with Nicholson, Segura, and Woods's (2002) evidence that divided government boosts presidential approval ratings.

18. For an analysis of this finding with regard to elections over the past forty years, see Brady and Cogan (1998).

19. For more detailed analysis of congressional procedures in choosing open and closed rules, as well as other procedures, see Oleszek (1989, 2004) and Bach and Smith (1988).

20. The standard unified budget has been used to assess the deficit by both parties for over three decades. In this standard budget, Social Security and other trust funds are included on the revenue side. Budgets not including Social Security and other trust funds show even higher deficits.

21. The actual numbers totaled sixty-six, one shy of the necessary two-thirds. In the final vote, however, Bob Dole voted against the amendment in a tactic that would allow him to raise the amendment again if an additional vote could be found.

22. Such early attempts to dramatically modify policy in 1995 are consistent with evidence from Peterson et al. (2003) that congressional politicians initially act as if their perceived mandate were to come to fruition, only to later return to reality.

23. The lack of middle ground on this and other issues is evident from the polarization seen in Figure A.6 in the Appendix.

24. See Brady and Volden (1998, 169–170).

6

George W. Bush and the Continuation of Gridlock

The 2000 presidential elections were similar to late nineteenth-century elections in that the results were very close and the Electoral College vote produced a different result than the popular vote. In addition, like the presidential election of 1876, the state of Florida electoral vote count was disputed until a judicial body (in this case the Supreme Court) ultimately determined the winner. Given the circumstances of the election and the fact that Bush was portraying himself as a "compassionate conservative," many observers felt that he should duplicate President Kennedy's policy decisions of 1960. At that time, Kennedy, also the winner by a razor-thin margin, decided to pursue a very moderate, non-innovative policy agenda. He and his advisors thought that the narrow winning margin signaled that the country was not ready for any major changes in policy; therefore, the President should not pursue his campaign agenda when he assumed the presidency. Pundits, observers, and others who had admonished President Elect Bush not to deviate from the Kennedy strategy were soon disappointed. President George W. Bush acted as though he had won an electoral mandate for his ambitious policy agenda.

In this final substantive chapter we first present the contextual background of the 2000 election. We then analyze the domestic agenda within the 107th and 108th Congresses, demonstrating how its successes and failures support the model of policymaking that we present in this book. We then turn briefly to an analysis of how recent foreign policy choices are characterized by the revolving gridlock theory. Finally, we examine the election of 2004 and the agenda in the current 109th Congress to offer our predictions on its trajectory.

The 2000 Elections

George W. Bush campaigned for the office of President on the platform of "compassionate conservatism." His campaign team made this decision for several reasons, the most important of which was history. They felt that the two losses to Clinton had been partially caused by the extremely controversial side of the Republican Party that had been in the forefront of both the 1992 and the 1996 National Conventions. First, in 1992, the anti-gay, seemingly intolerant forces of Pat Buchanan and the religious right, combined with the slumping economy, turned the American public against incumbent President George H. Bush. That the 1996 Republican Convention was again dominated by the same forces partially explains Bob Dole's loss to Clinton.[1]

In contrast, in 1998 George W. Bush won reelection as the governor of Texas with the magic numbers of 69, 59, and 49. Sixty-nine was the percentage of the popular vote that he won, 59 was the percentage of the women's vote won, and 49 was the percentage of the Hispanic vote won. These numbers impressed those in the Republican Party who wanted to recapture the presidency, and by early 2000 Governor Bush was the decided front runner for the Republican nomination. In the cross-voting primaries Governor Bush faltered some against Senator McCain (R, AZ) but once the primary season rotated toward Republican-only voting, Governor Bush easily won his party's nomination.[2]

After earning the support of the Republican Party, Governor Bush's road to the presidency was significantly more difficult. All of the major academic models used to predict presidential election outcomes asserted a Democratic victory in 2000.[3] Most of the accurate models to evaluate elections are retrospective, assuming that voters are evaluating the performance of the current presidential party. They feature the state of the U.S. economy as the major variable in explaining electoral outcomes. Thus, when the economy is in good shape—as it was in 2000—the candidate of the incumbent President's party wins the election. In 2000, the Dow Jones was over 11,000, the NASDAQ over 5,000, real income was up, more Americans owned their own home than at any previous point in history, and for the first time in over 50 years the government had back-to-back surpluses. The circumstances of the 2000 election were eerily like the 1988 election in which the Vice President George H. Bush had won his party's nomination. The U.S. economy was very strong, and Vice President Bush had promised to maintain the economic prosperity. And, of course, in 1988 Vice President Bush defeated Michael Dukakis to be elected the 41st President of the United States. This recent historical example and the combination of a strong economy and the apparently stable foreign relations throughout the world implied an incumbent party victory. Most sources predicted a Democratic victory in 2000, with margins up to 58 percent to 42 percent in favor of Vice President Albert Gore.[4]

Content of the Campaign

Although there were many components of Governor Bush's campaign, such as market environmentalism, private accounts for Social Security, and Medicare reform, it was his education policy and the promise of tax cuts that exemplified the two faces of the "compassionate conservatism" campaign—one for conservatives and one for moderates. Tax cuts are the one policy idea that both the religious and secular parts of the Republican Party endorse. Thus it was clear that any Republican presidential candidate would promise to return more of the American people's money to those who generated the income.

To counter the appeal of the prospering economy for the moderates, Governor Bush used his education policy of No Child Left Behind. Predictably, given his political leanings and experiences in Texas, this plan promised higher standards in schools and concern for all students, especially on the basics of reading, writing, and arithmetic. The unique aspect of the policy was that concern over meeting standards was tied to penalties for schools that did not meet the standards.

These two components of the campaign, in addition to the overall theme of compassionate conservatism, were successful in dispelling the Republican Party's 1992–1996 exclusionary image. This tactical move assured that the 2000 election would be closer than the 1996 election. Despite the updated version of the Republican Party, the Texas Governor would likely have lost the election were it not for several mistakes of the Gore team. In an insightful piece, Fiorina, Abrams, and Pope (2003) argue that if Gore had run a centrist campaign in which he promised four more years of economic growth without the Clinton melodrama, he would have easily won. Instead, Gore ran a campaign that featured changes that would have moved the county to the left: increased coverage in health care, more environmental regulation, and redistribution from the wealthy to the poor. This platform, in addition to Bush's campaign theme of compassionate conservatism, made the election closer than it should have been.

The Congress elected with the President was slightly more liberal than the 106th Congress in that the Republican House majority was reduced and the Senate was now an even 50–50 split. Near the House median was a set of fairly conservative members like Kolbe (R, AZ), Kirk (R, IL) and Bass (R, NH). As Table 6.1 shows, the Senators near the median were the moderate Breaux (D, LA) and the most liberal Republican Chafee (RI). In practice, this meant that the median House voter would vote for all of the tax reductions Bush would propose, would support vouchers for school choice and drilling in the Arctic National Wildlife Refuge (ANWR), but would not support domestic partner benefits in health care plans. In contrast, Senator Chafee would vote against vouchers, for a patient's bill of rights, and against much of the President's tax proposal. The filibuster pivotal members on the Democratic side were likely to be from the group of Senators with an ADA score of 85—quite a bit more liberal than Chafee and thus even less amenable to significant parts of the Bush policy agenda. In sum, the 2000 elections had not enhanced the President's chances of passing his platform.

Plans for the Presidency

George W. Bush, the 43rd President of the United States, was sworn into office on January 20, 2001. The inaugural address was largely written by the *New Yorker*'s Hendrich Hertzberg, who helped write President Carter's inaugural address, the

TABLE 6.1   Ideological Rankings of the 107th Senate (2001 ADA scores)*

Left of Median			Right of Median	
Biden	100		*McCain*	40
Graham	100		*Snowe*	40
Bayh	100		*Jeffords*	40
Harkin	100		*Specter*	40
Kennedy	100		**Miller**	35
Levin	100		*Collins*	35
Stabenow	100		*Smith (OR)*	25
Dayton	100		*DeWine*	25
Wellstone	100		*Hagel*	25
Reed	100		*Stevens*	20
Reid	100		*Ensign*	20
Corzine	100		*Warner*	20
Daschle	100		*Thompson*	20
Leahy	100		*Allen*	15
Cantwell	100		*Voinovich*	15
Rockefeller	100		*Cochran*	15
Boxer	95		*Fitzgerald*	15
Dodd	95		*Lugar*	15
Lieberman	95		*Campbell*	15
Nelson (FL)	95		*Hutchinson*	10
Akaka	95		*Hutchison*	10
Durbin	95		*Crapo*	10
Mikulski	95		*Bond*	10
Sarbanes	95		*Burns*	10
Kerry	95		*Domenici*	10
Clinton	95		*Inhofe*	10
Schumer	95		*Nickles*	10
Edwards	95		*Santorum*	10
Wyden	95		*Frist*	10
Feingold	95		*Enzi*	10
Carper	90		*Thomas*	5
Inouye	90		*Hatch*	5
Torricelli	90		*Bennett*	5
Bingaman	90		*Gramm*	5
Hollings	90		*Thurmond*	5
Kohl	90		*Smith (NH)*	5
Lincoln	85		*McConnell*	5
Feinstein	85		*Grassley*	5
Cleland	85		*Allard*	5
Landrieu	85	←About 2/5th pivot	*Kyl*	5
Carnahan	85		*Shelby*	5
Conrad	85		*Sessions*	5
Dorgan	85		*Murkowski*	0
Johnson	85		*Craig*	0
Murray	85		*Brownback*	0
Byrd	85		*Roberts*	0
Baucus	80		*Bunning*	0
Nelson (NE)	70		*Lott*	0
Chafee	65		*Gregg*	0
Breaux	55		*Helms*	0

* Republicans in italics, Democrats in bold.

best address of the last 40 years. It replicated the structure of the Bush campaign by stressing tax cuts and No Child Left Behind. Bush also reinforced another point he had made in his campaign—that he wanted to change the quality of discourse in Washington, meaning both that he would not behave like Bill Clinton, and that he wanted Washington to work in a bipartisan, less invective-driven fashion.

The newly elected President consciously chose not to emulate Kennedy in promoting a paced, moderate policy agenda. Instead he chose to advance boldly on two fronts—one moderately liberal and one conservative. The liberal policy choice was to substantially increase the federal government's financial contribution to K–12 education. Although No Child Left Behind had several conservative aspects such as vouchers and standardized testing of schools nation-wide, these components were offset by the amount of money the administration was prepared to pay in order to attain the goals of leaving no child behind.

Per usual, the conservative proposal was a tax cut. The general feeling in Washington was that it would be hard for the President to achieve the tax cut given the congressional climate. The Republican majority in the House was thin and the Senate was split 50–50 between the Democrats and Republicans, meaning that Vice President Cheney was the deciding vote. There were eight-to-ten moderate Republicans like Chafee (RI), Specter (PA), Jeffords (VT), Snowe (ME), and Collins (ME), who would likely not vote with the President on the issue of tax cuts without concessions toward a moderation of his proposals. Furthermore, Democrats in the House and Senate were attempting to increase taxes on the rich, the ideological opposite of Bush's proposal.

Although it was not clear that Bush could win the issue under normal circumstances, most thought it would be especially hard given the nature of his victory—that he won the electoral vote and not the popular vote. "Bush does not have a prayer of getting his touted $1.3 trillion tax cut through the next Congress, of course," Robert Reich declared (*Washington Post*, December 27, 2000). However, events began to benefit the President. First, the economy slowed, and as it slowed, Federal Reserve Chair Alan Greenspan and others moved toward supporting the 2001 tax cut.

The attacks on the U.S. on 9/11 caused further damage to the economy and helped pass two new pieces of tax legislation in 2002 and 2003. Together, these tax packages represented a significant movement to the right on budgetary policy, as discussed in the following section. Clearly, the terrorist attacks also changed American foreign policy in fundamental ways. There were two pivotal legislative issues involved in this foreign policy shift: the votes to authorize the President to go to war in Afghanistan and then in Iraq. These will be examined after an analysis of the domestic issues.

Tax Policy

In 2001, the President originally proposed a $1.6 trillion tax cut that made several promises: to reduce tax rates, to reduce and then repeal estate taxes, and to create tax breaks for savings, education, children, and married people.[5] The parameters changed in 2002, after the 9/11 attacks, when the tax cuts featured reduced tax burdens on business investments. There was a shift in tax policy again with the Republican win in the 2002 off-year elections, such that the 2003 tax cuts reduced taxes on dividends and capital gains and accelerated the timeline of the 2001 tax cuts. This section discusses how these bills came about, and what compromises were needed to secure their passage.

In combination, the three tax cuts reduced income taxes for the highest bracket of tax payers from 39.6 to 35 percent, while those who previously faced rates of 36, 31, and 28 percent each benefited from a 3 percent reduction. Under the Tax Relief Reconciliation Act of 2001 the fall in rates was gradual—with a small decrease effective on July 1, 2001, another in January 2002, and so on. An important component of the 2001 act mandated that all rates be effective until 2010, when they would revert to the 2000 levels. This ten-year lifetime of the tax cuts was, as we show later, a limitation imposed because of the President's inability to pass his policy with more than a bare majority of Senate supporters. The Jobs and Growth Tax Relief Reconciliation Act of 2003 accelerated the reductions schedule planned for 2004 and 2006 to January of 2003, but could not overcome the obstacles to make the tax cuts permanent.

These tax bills also reduced estate taxes over time to zero, although this tax was also due to revert to its 2000 level in 2010. The 2001 Act reduced the 15 percent income tax rate to 10 percent and eliminated the "marriage penalty" (the additional taxes that a married couple pays over what they would have paid if they had remained single and paid separate taxes). In addition, this act increased minimum levels at which taxpayers would have to pay the Alternative Minimum Tax (AMT) by $2,000 for singles and $4,000 for married couples. Despite this change, the number of taxpayers whose itemized deductions were limited by AMT was consistently increasing. The 2003 Act reduced capital gains taxes by 5 percent over both the 10 and 20 percent categories and allowed taxes on dividends to be counted under capital gains rules. Again, all these reductions had "sunset provisions," and after ten years would revert to their previous 2000 levels.

Any casual reading of the *Wall Street Journal* or *New York Times* would demonstrate that these tax cuts were viewed from different perspectives. The original 2001 tax proposal from the President occurred when there was a projected 5.6 trillion dollar surplus for the decade and a slight economic downturn. Bush strategically presented the 2001 tax bill as simply returning the previous decade of over-taxation to the citizens who generated the wealth originally. This theory was upheld by the observation that the cuts left more money after taxes for spending or investment by families, small businesses, and married couples. The Democratic counter-argument was that the tax cuts disproportionately benefited the highest bracket of taxpayers and only marginally benefited the middle class. Proponents of this belief felt that there should be a smaller tax cut for the wealthy and that the rest of the surplus should be placed in a "lock box" and then used to reduce the national debt or to make Social Security inviolable. A more alarmist theory put forward by some was that the Bush strategy behind the tax cuts was to create a deficit and then increase it to starve the "beast of government."

Since tax interests are established and organized in D.C., the different perspectives were all heard on Capitol Hill, and most Washington commentators in 2001 thought Bush would not be able to achieve his $1.6 trillion tax bill. Most thought $700–800 billion, an amount closer to what Vice President Gore had proposed in his 2000 campaign, was a more appropriate goal. Despite the circulation of these defeatist opinions, Bush and the Republican Party achieved more sizable tax cuts by successfully utilizing the political process in both chambers of Congress to gain the necessary votes. They then capitalized on the increasing numbers of congressional Republicans after 2002 in order to make the tax policies incrementally more conservative. Such changes were wholly consistent with expectations from the revolving gridlock theory. The rightward shift in policy expected following the 1994 Republican revolution had been denied through Clinton vetoes. With a supportive President, such changes were now possible, although securing the needed coalitions in Congress would shape the parameters of the policy changes.

Compromises of the 2001 Tax Cuts

The strategy for passing the tax cuts relied on exploiting House-Senate differences, specifically assuming that the more conservative House was more likely to pass legislation closer to the President's proposed cut, and that therefore it should be the first chamber to consider it. The situation was similar to that of the first Gingrich Congress, elected in 1994. At that time, the House passed eight of ten items in the Contract with America, while the Republican-controlled Senate was unable to act on the Contract items. The situation in 2001 was similar, and Senate differences favored Democrats. The Senate was split exactly 50–50 and the Senate committees did not have pro-Republican conservative majorities. Thus, the President wanted the House to act first to pressure the Senate to vote for a larger tax cut. However, in the House the Republicans had the majority by only six votes, making any defections crucial and the bargaining difficult.

The Democratic leadership in Congress opposed the Bush tax cut because of its magnitude both in terms of money spent and breadth of taxes cut. The leaders were unwilling, however, to let the President label them as taxers and spenders. Thus, they initially proposed a $300 billion tax cut that did not decrease rates in the highest bracket, making the distributional consequences more focused on the middle class than in the President's proposal.

The Republicans in the House, led by Bill Thomas (R, CA), chairman of the Ways and Means Committee, split the bill into parts to amend it. They first addressed the largest portion—income tax cuts worth $950 billion over ten years. With the economy's slowing over the first two months of the Bush administration and the President's promotion of his plan across the country, the Democratic leadership switched their policy to favor tax cuts of just over $700 billion (both income and other taxes included). Within the House, the Ways and Means Committee passed the income tax portion of the President's bill out of committee via strict party votes. Finally, on March 8, 2001, the House voted 230–198 to pass the tax cuts with every Republican House member voting affirmatively.

Following passage of the income tax portion of the Bush tax cuts, the House took up the marriage penalty and child tax credit provisions. House Republicans modified the presidential proposal by increasing the earned income tax credit, which benefited lower wage earners, and reducing the disparities resulting from the marriage penalty. This part of the tax cut package was estimated at about $400 to 450 billion. In late March, the House passed the cuts by a margin of 284 to 144. Once again, all Republicans voted yes and, for this portion of the legislation, 64 Democrats joined them. Democratic Party votes increased because this policy was more favorable to the left in redistributing more tax cuts toward blue collar and middle-income earners.

On the same day that the marriage and child credit cuts passed, the Ways and Means Committee passed the elimination of the estate tax (approximately $200 billion over ten years) on essentially a party line vote. In the first week of April the House voted 274 to 154 to pass the estate tax bill. This bill differed from the President's request in that the phasing in of the tax provisions was slower, lowering the short-term costs of the legislation. Thus, within the first three months of his presidency Bush succeeded in achieving House tax cuts that were much closer to his original proposal than those the Democratic leadership had proposed and than most pundits believed were possible.

In the Senate, however, the tax plans that had passed the House did not survive intact. In Chapter 2, we discussed the need for 60 Senate votes on most issues to overcome a filibuster. In Chapter 3, however, we noted that on major budgetary issues reconciliation rules could be used, which only require a simple majority in the Senate. On the Bush tax cuts, 60 votes were nowhere to be found. Thus the reconciliation rules would be needed, and thus the tax cuts would be limited to a 10-year period instead of being permanent. Even then, getting 50 votes was difficult. Only one Democrat, Zell Miller (GA), supported the House policies, and several moderate Republicans such as the two Senators from Maine (Snowe and Collins) pledged to vote against the House bill. Senators Grassley (R, IA) and Baucus (D, MT) of the Finance Committee began to draft a compromise tax plan that would move the President's (House) plan to the left in order to get 50 votes for passage. The main elements of the compromise were a reduction in the amount of the tax cuts, a slight move toward redistribution to the middle class and, most importantly, a phase-in over ten years—slower that that proposed by the President. The result was a tax policy in which the President got about 80 percent of the amount and direction of the tax cuts he originally proposed but sacrificed the speed and permanence of the cuts.

In the midst of these deliberations, rumors flew that Senator Jeffords (R, VT) would switch from a Republican to an Independent, thus putting the Democrats into majority status (50 Democrats, 49 Republicans, and 1 Independent). Some Democrats saw this as an opportunity to stop the progress of the tax cuts and to redraft the bill closer to the original Democratic proposal. In general, the press viewed this switch as detrimental for the President's agenda. The theory put forward in this book is that in terms of voting on the floor of the Senate the Jeffords switch does not matter because Jeffords's position on tax cuts is induced by his constituency or his ideology, not his party affiliation. Jeffords would vote for the Baucus-Grassley alternative because that is where his preferences lie irrespective of party. Incidentally, he would vote for a form of the President's No Child Left Behind Act for the same reason. The proof of our view is that on May 22, 2001, Senator Jeffords met with Vice President Cheney to let him know that he would switch parties, and later that day President Bush met with Jeffords and asked him to delay the date of the switch until after the tax bill had passed. Waiting to switch assured that the Republicans in the Senate would control the committee and floor procedures thus helping passage of the bill the President badly wanted and needed. Had party mattered more than our theory suggests, Jeffords could have earned considerable credit from Democratic leaders by switching parties earlier, thus allowing Democrats to try to move the tax bill further to the left. Instead, Jeffords secured the policy outcome most in line with his preferences by delaying his switch and voting for the $1.3 billion tax cut.

The revolving gridlock theory does not assert that the Jeffords switch would not have had an effect on the progress of the tax cuts through Congress. Indeed, party and committee control may have an influence on setting the political agenda. Democratic control of the Senate would have meant that the new committee chairs could push their agenda items in the press, in committee hearings, and so on. But, were a proposal to reach the floor, the same pivotal members would have decided the key parameters of the tax cuts. Imagine Jeffords had switched before the 107th Congress, making Democrats the bare majority party. Committee chairs would have switched, the rhetoric would have been more openly opposed to the Bush plan, and the President's redistribution scheme would have been heavily criticized for benefiting the rich. Yet, the policy result would have still been approximately the $1.3 billion cut. This is similar to the Reagan tax cut when the Democrats controlled the House but lost many conservative Democrats to the Reagan plan, and it is also similar to President Clinton's victory over the Gingrich-led Republicans shown in the last chapter. Clinton, without party control of either branch of Congress, cleverly used the veto, its threat, and the votes of moderate Republicans to attain his ends instead of Gingrich's.

Tax Cuts of 2002 and 2003

The story of the 2002 tax changes is quite simple and we will not spend much time analyzing it. The terrorist attacks of 9/11 exacerbated the slowing of the economy, which caused business interests to become risk-averse. With little acrimony, the President and Congress agreed to broaden deductions in order to encourage businesses to invest and grow. The President wanted a new large tax cut, but the limited time until the 2002 congressional elections and difficulties in passing the bill to establish the Department of Homeland Security left little opportunity for a major change. The outcome of the 2002 midterm elections would be crucial to further tax cuts. The history of midterm elections portended bad results for the President. In only one election since the Civil War (1861–1865) had a President in his first term gained seats in the Congress—FDR in 1934. Given this historical record and the economy, the signs were not pointing toward a Republican victory.

President Bush decided to contribute to the 2002 congressional election in a serious way and his effort was unprecedented. He campaigned in about 25 House races, 16 Senate races, and a number of gubernatorial races. In addition he attended numerous fundraisers that raised about $150 million for Republican campaigns. This effort varied by state and district but typically focused on the Homeland Security Act and the President's efforts to stimulate the economy. He also emphasized a large increase in agricultural subsidies since so many midwestern Senate seats were up for reelection.

Contrary to historical and press expectations, the President's efforts paid off. Republicans regained control of the Senate, gaining two seats and making the new distribution 51 Republicans, 48 Democrats, and Jeffords. In the House, the Republicans gained six seats, moving from 221 to 227–208, and more than doubling their margin. Moreover, Republicans gained governorships and greatly increased their seats in state legislatures. In sum, the President's risky strategy of getting involved in the election was rewarded by the electorate.[6]

The Congress that met in 2003 was immediately presented with a bold tax cut and stimulus plan valued at approximately $730 billion over a decade. The President's plan accelerated the phasing-in of the tax cuts passed in the 2001 act. Also included in the policy was the elimination of the double taxation of corporate dividends and accelerated child tax credits. There were many, including some of the President's advisors and some prominent Republican House and Senate members, who thought the $730 billion proposal was too large given the budget deficit and the approaching war in Iraq. The explicit strategy was the same as that used in 2001; have the House pass a conservative bill and use the House bill and reconciliation rules to move the Senate closer to the Bush position. True to form, the House narrowly passed a tax bill that was close to what the President wanted. However, passage was harder than was the case in 2001 and the Republican leadership in the House had to go to great lengths to pass the bill. It was easier to pass the bill in 2001 because there was a budget surplus and because Republican members of Congress felt that voting for cuts larger than those ultimately passed by the Senate would not hurt them with their supporters back home. In contrast, the 2003 cuts occurred when there was a deficit and funds were needed from the taxpayers to pay for the war in Iraq. Thus the selling of the program in 2003 was indeed harder. Moreover, the cuts of 2003 were on top of those already secured in 2001, thus moving policy even further to the right.

The revolving gridlock theory predicts that on majority-based reconciliation bills legislative outcomes will result in the policy favored by the median Senate or House voter rather than the party median. Table 6.1 above showed the distribution of Senators in the 107th Congress, using Americans for Democratic Action (ADA) scores. The results showed that the Senators at or around the median were moderate Republicans like Snowe (ME) or moderate Democrats like Breaux (LA). Given this distribution and limited change in 2002, we could predict that the 2003 tax cuts would be where Senators like Snowe and Breaux wanted them, not where the House tax cut was located nor what the President desired. Nor would the cuts be those preferred by the Senate Republican median. Senators Snowe and Voinovich (R, OH) signed a pledge to oppose any tax cut greater than $350 billion. The combination of moderate Republicans opposed to any cut over $350 billion and Democrats opposed to any tax cut at all prevailed in the vote and the Senate limit on the cut was $350 billion. Realizing that further cuts were not achievable in the Senate, negotiators settled on this amount for the budget resolution that ultimately passed in the 108th Congress.

In sum, the thesis of this book seems to be perfectly exemplified in the case of the tax policy of President Bush in his first term. Proposals at about the House median but too conservative for the Senate median are brought into line by moving them left toward the Senate median voter. The 2001 Bush plan given the surplus was not cut much because moderate Republicans like Snowe and Collins could vote for it, whereas given changed economic conditions in 2003 they could not and significantly moved the President's proposal to the center. In previous chapters we have demonstrated this point by showing that Representatives and Senators who shift positions on issues are more moderate than those who vote consistently. We duplicated this analysis for the full set of the 2001, 2002, and 2003 Bush tax cuts. The results show how, over a set of roll calls, those who switch their votes are moderates relative to the House and Senate members who vote consistently either for or against all tax cuts. Such moderates are the pivotal members in the revolving gridlock theory. On majoritarian legislation, they are the members near the floor median. Again, the idea is that Snowe or Specter will not vote for a $730 billion tax cut. Conservatives will vote for both tax cuts while liberals will vote against both tax cuts.

House voting patterns reveal that there were 221 Republican stalwarts voting positively on the 2001–2003 tax cuts, with a mean ADA score of 7.5. In contrast, the 206 Democratic stalwarts had an average ADA score of 88. The switchers were in the middle with the nine Republican switchers having an average ADA score of 22 while the 14 Democratic switchers had an average ADA score of 44. Table 6.2 shows these numbers for the House and Senate. These results are consistent with those found for previous Houses—as the policy moves to the center, moderates switch their votes. The major difference is that from 1993 through today the number of moderate switchers has declined dramatically as the parties have sorted on a left–right dimension in the House post–1994. Nevertheless, those who switch votes are still the moderates.

A similar pattern emerges in the Senate. Again, compared to previous Senates, the number of stalwarts is up, while the switchers are down due to the sorting effect of the 1994 election. In sum, the policy moved to the left due to median Senate

TABLE 6.2   Preference Scores for Switching on 2001–2003 Tax Cuts

	Mean ADA Scores		
Consistent Support (Republicans)	Switching Republicans	Switching Democrats	Consistent Opposition (Democrats)
House	7.5	22.0	44.0	88.0
Senate	12.0	52.0	72.5	89.0

voters such as Breaux. The same phenomenon is present across the Bush tax cuts, with the stalwarts in the Republican Party numbering 49 and representing an average ADA score of 12. Their Democratic counterparts numbered 46 and had an average ADA of 89. The switchers, like those in the House, are down in number from 1993 but have centrist scores of 52 for the Republicans and 72.5 for the Democrats. At least two lessons can be drawn from these results as we move forward. First, the pivotal members even under unified Republican government are near the center of the Congress, rather than the center of the Republican Party. And, second, very few members changed their positions between 2001 and 2003 despite the 9/11 terrorist attacks and talk immediately thereafter of a more united country and Congress.

Non-Budgetary Domestic Policy

Beyond the tax cuts, the Bush administration confronted a variety of other domestic policy areas in its first term, but was ultimately defined by the war on terrorism. Outside of tax policy and terrorism, George W. Bush's largest policy successes were arguably education and Medicare reforms and his largest failure was on energy policy. In the next several subsections, we explore these three policy areas in detail. We also briefly summarize other domestic policy initiatives of the 107th and 108th Congresses, showing how they collectively support the revolving gridlock theory. We then tackle foreign policy and the collective response of Congress and the Bush administration to terrorism, to gauge how well the theory explains policymaking during foreign policy crises.

Education Policy

The 2001 Bush education plan differed significantly from the tax policy strategy and from most past conservative policy proposals. It increased domestic spending, thus deviating from a traditional conservative approach of lower taxes and lower spending. The basic No Child Left Behind education policy would increase the amount of money sent from the federal government to the states and would allow the states to use this money flexibly. However, states were to institute tests, and both states and the schools within them would be monitored on progress. The plan also originally included educational vouchers that promoted school choice as part of the consequences of failure to meet achievement goals. That is, if a school under-performed for a number of years, federal funds would be given to the parents so that they could pay for their children to attend other schools. The increased spending for education appealed to Democrats like George Miller (CA). Mandating accountability through sanctions and the voucher payments appealed to conservatives. But could these two elements be put together in a fashion that would guarantee a sufficient coalition for passage in both the House and the Senate?

Given the disparate ideologies involved in the legislation, the presidential strategy was to begin not with a "bill" but with a 30-page legislative blueprint. The blueprint featured: a broad block-grant program with flexible spending, consolidated categorical grants, the annual testing of students in grades three through eight, and the release of the results by ethnic and economic groups. In addition states would be required to participate in the National Assessment of Educational Progress each year. No specific corrective action was specified, but public school choice and "exit vouchers" were included. Liberals liked the increased spending and the concern for minorities but did not like school choice and vouchers, and had questions about the nature of the "tests" and the accountability standards.

The 30-page blueprint allowed the President to set out the grand overview and left the relevant legislators to iron out the details and arrange the necessary trade-offs for a majority vote (or for a supermajority if there were to be a filibuster). It also helped the President that he was placing his policy under the auspices of reauthorizing the 1965 Elementary and Secondary Education Act (ESEA) passed in the 89th Congress (1965–1966) and signed by President Johnson. The 106th Congress had not been able to agree on a reform and had simply reauthorized the ESEA at the previous year's budget rate. The approach for obtaining votes was an atypical (but not unheard-of) middle-out strategy, in which the bill is initially written to appeal to the center of the spectrum and then modified as needed to hold or increase the size of the majority. Realizing that conservatives could be lost based on too much spending and liberals could be lost on school choice, this strategy required careful maneuvering by the President and congressional leaders.

Early meetings with the President featured Democrats like Tim Roemer (IN) and Evan Bayh (IN) and Republicans like Jeffords (VT)—moderate centrist legislators from both parties. Early in the game the President signaled that vouchers were not a deal breaker—that is, if vouchers were not included he could still sign a bill. Senator Kennedy (D, MA) came into the picture by agreeing that parts of the Bush plan were acceptable to him. The coalition in favor of the bill at this point was fairly broad. It included: conservatives because state-controlled testing and accountability were proposed; moderate Democrats because, as Senator Lieberman (D, CT) said, the President had built upon the centrist Democratic plan from the 1998 Democratic Leadership Council (DLC) meeting; and liberals like Kennedy because it increased federal aid to education. There were, however, serious stumbling blocks to overcome before final passage. Would the bill move toward Kennedy, who favored more funding and less choice, or toward House conservatives?

The crucial tests for passage would be over testing and funding. The testing provisions were viewed as too harsh by the governors and education officials in the various states. Their view was that the standards were too high and they did not like reporting the test results by race. Mainly they did not wish to face a yearly report showing that their states were failing to adequately educate too high a portion of their states' youth. Bush and Republican leaders compromised in this case by setting the standard for adequate improvement at 1 percent a year per group, with progress judged over a three-year period, and improvement standards weighted to favor lower achieving students. In regard to money the compromise upped the spending increase to $181 billion over a decade and boosted compensatory spending by $132 billion over ten years. In short, the compromise needed to maintain liberal support in the Senate moved the policy to the left and away from the conservatives. Vouchers were kept intact and accountability was weakened.

The bill reported out of committee in the House stripped vouchers to please liberals further and shifted spending to include not just states but individual districts. The committee vote was bipartisan 41–7 with House opposition coming from both the far left and right. The left sought more funding and even weaker standardized testing while the right wanted vouchers and more state and local control over student testing. The conservatives sought and won the right to vote on vouchers but these votes failed and the House bill passed roughly as it came out of committee. The "extremes" coalition opposing the bill was led by Representative Frank (D, MA) and Representative Hoekstra (R, MI).

After passage in the House the bill then moved to Conference Committee to resolve the many differences between the House and Senate versions. Liberal Senators had a strong hand because they could always threaten to remove support for the President's bill and kill it with a filibuster. It is not surprising, therefore, that one significant House–Senate difference was that the Senate funding levels were higher than the House authorizations. Yet moving too far in the liberal direction risked losing the support of conservative Republicans in the House. In the final compromise, Senate spending levels were reduced toward House levels, but the Senate standards for accountability were preferred and there would be no punishment for states with low scores. In the words of Andrew Rudalevige (2003), the final bill was adopted "with opposition again limited to an odd amalgam of discontented far left and far right. The process, said Roemer, had 'brought the middle together, and held it!'"

Over the course of the legislative process there were numerous votes on amendments trying to, among other things: increase or decrease spending amounts, include or exclude vouchers, and weaken testing and reporting requirements. As in previous chapters we analyze the patterns of switching to show that policy moves toward the centrist House and Senate voters. In the case of the education bill, which was a middle-out coalition, the assumption is that centrists in both parties will vote no on conservative proposals like vouchers and on liberal proposals like funding that is too high, but then ultimately vote for centrist final passage proposals. The far left and far right will be fairly consistent. Vouchers will be supported by conservatives and opposed by liberals while more funding will receive the reverse effect. As in previous chapters, the switching analysis will show that centrists switch their votes across proposals until something near the median is reached.

The analysis of votes on amendments over vouchers in the House shows that, as was the case regarding taxes, party stalwarts were at the extremes of the distribution, with Republicans at 4.5 and with Democrats at 86.5 average ADA scores. Switchers who voted against the bulk of their party, as expected, had more centrist ADA scores—Democratic switchers were at 29.3 while Republicans in this category were at 16. These figures are shown along with the Senate in Table 6.3. The major difference between tax legislation and education is that a center-out coalition will have larger numbers of switchers; more members in a bimodal distribution will have cause to vote against some amendment to the legislation while ultimately voting for final passage. Thus, there were three times as many switchers in the education area than there were over tax legislation.

TABLE 6.3   Preference Scores for Party Voting on Vouchers (107th Congress)

	Mean ADA Scores			
	Supporting Party (Republicans)	*Against Party (Republicans)*	*Against Party (Democrats)*	*Supporting Party (Democrats)*
House	4.5	16.0	29.3	86.5
Senate	10.0	25.0	90.0	91.3

The Senate shows a similar pattern with stalwart Democrats and Republicans being at the extremes of the distribution with ADA scores of 91.3 and 10 respectively. Switchers for Democrats had average ADA scores of 90 while their Republican counterparts had an average ADA average of 25. There are almost four times as many Republican switchers (11) as Democrats (4) because Republican centrists were pulled away from the bill on amendments from the right in their own party. On center-out legislation the number of switchers will almost always exceed the number of switchers on right–left legislation because centrists can be pulled in both directions on amendments, and this occurred on the No Child Left Behind Act.

When a Republican President advances a policy proposal that may be seen as more in line with the Democratic Party than the Republican Party, it should not be surprising that an odd coalition would form. We have seen such politics before, when Ronald Reagan or George H. Bush needed to get behind tax increases or when Bill Clinton called for support of NAFTA. Despite the odd shape of such coalitions, most of the lessons of the revolving gridlock theory remain valuable. The policy change of No Child Left Behind illustrates how individual preferences and institutional rules affect the building of substantial coalitions. When putting together a proposal that appealed to centrists of both parties, party leaders were tempted to move the legislation too far in a conservative or liberal direction. The threats of centrist members, who were willing to desert their parties and switch their votes when necessary, however, kept such proposals at bay and allowed this legislation to pass.

Energy Policy

During the 2000 campaign, Governor Bush did not focus extensively on energy issues, although he did promise to explore new sources of energy during his presidency. However, when the California energy crisis hit, energy policy came to the fore. The President's plan sought to expand exploration for oil and natural gas, including drilling in the Arctic National Wildlife Refuge (ANWR), and to limit increases in the 1977 Corporate Average Fuel Economy Act (CAFE) standards. These policies generated opposition from environmentalists, who instead advocated less drilling on federal lands and higher average miles per gallon across all cars and trucks. In short, on a dimension where one could choose to conserve energy or to create incentives to expand production, the President heavily favored expanding production. In ideological terms, this places the President's proposal on the conservative side, to the right of the median Senator and further right of the liberal filibuster pivot.

As would be expected under these circumstances, the Senate was the chamber most resistant to the President's energy policy. Since Senate Rule XXII encompasses energy legislation, Bush needed 60 votes to beat a filibuster and pass his expansionary program. Fulfilling this quota seemed unlikely for several reasons. First, all the Democratic Senators, except those from oil and gas states like Louisiana, favored the conservation end of the spectrum. Furthermore, Republican moderates were indicating that they were against increased drilling on federal lands, especially ANWR. Finally, a majority of Senators had voted to increase CAFE standards on several occasions. Although Senator Jeffords's switch to Independent did not change floor voting outcomes, it did enable the Democrats to chair the relevant committees that structured the agenda. In sum, the circumstances of the Senate gave the Democrats a policy advantage. Even the prospect of obtaining a majority vote for the President's expansionist legislation seemed unlikely.

The political dynamics were different in the House, where Republicans had a majority and there are no supermajority requirements. House leaders quickly moved to pass a bill close to the President's proposal of enhancing production of energy supplies. Representative DeLay of Texas was a major player in this legislation, leading the built-in majority that favored energy production expansion. This majority included almost all of the Republicans, as well as Democrats from oil and gas states such as Texas, Oklahoma, and Louisiana. In the House these fairly populous states are well represented, while in the Senate they receive no more representation than any other state. The majority group then began to rally the lobbying forces of trade unions and Teamsters who would benefit from increased exploration for and production of energy. After these union groups pledged their support, the coalition was sufficiently large enough to block amendments that attempted to weaken the bill by increasing CAFE standards and prohibiting drilling in ANWR. The final passage vote in the House was 240 in favor of the President's proposal and 189 opposed.

After the House passed a version of the President's energy bill, the Republicans were able to go into the 2002 elections without facing the charge that they had not delivered a bill. The party's leadership agreed that the Democratic Senate was to blame for gridlock, so they were encouraged when the results of the 2002 elections increased Republican seats in Congress. However, the new Senate majority just barely shifted control of the Senate to the Republicans by a margin of 51–48 with Jeffords an Independent, and it was fairly clear that the preferences of the Senate had not dramatically moved. Although they gained seats, they lost a pro-expansion vote in Arkansas when Senator Huchinson was defeated by former Senator Pryor's son. Of the three formerly Democratic seats they overtook, in Missouri (Talent the winner) and Georgia (Chambliss) they specifically gained on the energy expansion issue. In Minnesota, former Republican Governor Coleman won the Senate seat, although on the energy issue he would favor the environmental–conservation end of the spectrum. In short, while the Republicans were again in the majority, they certainly did not have 60 votes to override Democratic filibusters, and it was still unlikely that they would achieve even a bare majority for an energy bill that included the components of Bush's policy. This proved to be the case over the next two years, as the Senate failed to move an energy bill that complemented the House pro-energy expansion bill.

The 2004 elections once again increased the Republican majority in the House and brought a gain of four seats to the Senate Republicans, making the 109th Senate 55 Republicans to 44 Democrats to 1 Independent. This congressional election increased the number of Senators favoring expansionist energy policy to the extent that there is now a majority for a House-like bill, but there are certainly not 60 votes for such a bill. In Colorado and Illinois the Republicans lost seats, and in both cases the pro-conservation forces were enhanced. Republicans gained seats in Florida, Georgia, North and South Carolina, and South Dakota, and these moved the median voter toward the President's end of the energy spectrum. The party also gained a seat in Louisiana, but the switch from Breaux (D) to Vitter (R) did not change the energy preferences, as Breaux supported an expansionist energy policy.

The changes in congressional dynamics resulting from the 2004 election plus the recent surge in world oil prices to over $55 a barrel increased the chances that during the 109th Congress a pro-expansion energy bill will be passed in the Senate. This was exemplified by the budget resolution passed on March 16, 2005, which included a provision that would open up the Arctic National Wildlife Refuge to drilling. Because it was a budget resolution, it could not be filibustered, and its passage by a narrow vote of 51 to 49 demonstrated that there is majority support in the Senate for expanding exploration. The arguments on both sides were typical, with liberals pro-conservation and conservatives pro-expansion. Senator Kerry (D, MA) argued that creating a policy to conserve energy would save more resources and would not destroy the environment. Senator Domenici (R, NM) countered by saying that it was better to both produce and conserve given the price of oil. He claimed that drilling technology was sufficiently advanced to minimize destruction of the environment. Seven moderate Republicans—Chafee (RI), Coleman (MN), Collins (ME), DeWine (OH), McCain (AZ), Smith (OR), and Snowe (ME)—voted to strip the provision from the budget resolution while three Democrats—Akaka and Inouye (HI) and Landrieu (LA)—voted to keep the provision.

The 51-to-49 Senate vote approving drilling in ANWR was a victory for the President but the battle is far from over. First, there will be parliamentary objections to placing the provision in a budget bill where it cannot be filibustered. Next, this budget bill still has to be passed, which will present challenges given the ensuing disagreements over Medicaid, Social Security, and tax cuts. Surely the ANWR provision will be one of the bargaining chips in the forthcoming debate. However, the important changes in the Senate regarding the placement of the median voter on the dimension of energy policy, the price of oil at nearly $60 a barrel, and the altered requirement of 50 votes instead of 60 may yield pro-expansion legislation in the next few years.

Medicare Reform

The Medicare Prescription Drug Improvement and Modernization Act of 2003 was arguably the most significant bill of the 108th Congress. The rising costs of health care and prescription drugs in addition to the aging population of baby boomers (people born between 1946 and 1960) presented a set of circumstances that politicians could not resist—a problem and a large population of voters who wanted it to be addressed. Liberals favored command-and-control solutions reminiscent of Clinton proposals, ranging from a single-payer plan to increased benefits. Conservatives preferred competitive market solutions that would allow insurance companies, health maintenance organizations (HMOs), hospitals, and pharmaceutical companies to deal with cost problems through incentives and limited governmental expenditures. There were thus important ideological differences over how to deal with the problem of rising health care costs.

In addition to the ideological differences there was a serious political problem for Republicans. When the Clintons attempted to overhaul the health care system in 1993 they were unsuccessful. Then, President Clinton proposed expanding Medicare to include a prescription drug benefit in 1999. He and the supporters of the bill claimed that the original 1965 Act that established Medicare had not needed to cover drug treatments for elderly patients who were not in hospitals because there were few drug treatments available to seniors in outpatient form. They felt that the advancements in efficient drug treatments required a change in Medicare to include this coverage. Republicans in Congress were opposed to this proposal because they thought it would create yet another new entitlement program.

Between the Clinton proposal's defeat and the Bush election in 2000, health care was addressed incrementally, with health insurance portability legislation to cover adults between jobs and the Children's Health Insurance Program offering grants to the states. Yet none of these types of provisions effectively addressed soaring health care costs, especially for prescription drugs. Democratic control of the Senate following the Jeffords's switch meant that perceived responsibility for addressing health care problems was spread across the parties. After the 2002 elections, which returned the majority to the Republicans in both chambers, however, the Republicans became tacitly responsible for the health care problem. That is, if they did not present a bill dealing with some of the major health care issues, they knew the Democratic members of the House and Senate would claim that the inaction was indicative of the uncaring mentality of the Republican Party. Attempting to pass a complicated act with unknown effects was defendable during the 2004 campaigns, whereas not doing anything was inexcusable. The President and the unified government he headed knew they had to have some kind of bill.

In his 2003 State of the Union Address, President Bush highlighted a Medicare revision that featured guaranteed drug coverage at affordable prices, with costs varying by patients' ability to pay and with competition among insurance companies, pharmaceutical companies, HMOs, and preferred provider organizations (PPOs). The original House plan also required Medicare to compete with private health care insurers for benefits covered under Medicare A (dealing with hospitals) and Medicare B (dealing with physicians). The projected costs of the program varied widely because it was hard to predict what choices seniors would make, given the number of options available to them. For example, Health and Human Services estimated the 2004–2013 total costs to be $395 billion higher than the estimates of the Congressional Budget Office.

Liberals thought that Medicare should provide one standard benefit and advocated for higher funding and for a fallback mechanism in the event that private plans chose not to provide Medicare benefits. In contrast, conservatives advocated for the involvement of private companies in combination with premium support from the government, enabling Medicare A and B to compete with private plans on price. As usual, the Democrats and Republicans focused their efforts on the Senate and House, respectively, and most of these ideological differences showed up in the bills passed by the two chambers. In the House, H.R. 1 was introduced on June 25, 2003, and on June 27, 2003 at 2:32 in the morning the House passed the bill by a vote of 216–215. There were 207 Republicans and nine Democrats voting yes with 19 Republicans and 195 Democrats voting no.

The Senate received H.R. 1 on July 7 and struck all but the enacting clause. They replaced it with their bill, S1, a compromise between Democrats and Republicans that had been framed by moderate Republicans like Snowe (ME), Collins (ME), Chafee (RI), and Specter (PA), and Democrats like Breaux (LA) and Baucus (MT). The Senate support for the bill was 40 Republicans and 35 Democrats voting yea with 11 Democrats and 10 Republicans and Jeffords voting nay. Like the education bill in the 107th Congress, this center-out coalition was opposed by extreme conservatives and liberals in the Senate. As with the education bill, such a center-out coalition could be expected with the President and Republican leadership supporting increased domestic spending, thus risking the loss of their most conservative members for whom larger government was a move in exactly the wrong direction. Some Democrats were needed for this legislation to gain the 60 votes necessary to overcome filibuster threats. Upon losing the most conservative Republicans, even more Democrats were needed in the coalition, and those likely to join this effort would be the more moderate members—thus producing the center-out coalition. Democrats supporting the bill had ADA scores of about 80 while Democrats that opposed it had ADA scores of over 90. The Republicans opposing the bill had ADA scores lower than 10, with Senator McCain of Arizona as the only exception to this trend. The median ADA score of the 108th Senate was 45. Of the Senators anywhere near that point, all except McCain supported the bill.

The conference committee would prove to be crucial given that the House bill was to the right of the Senate bill. House conservatives tried to influence the conference committee members by binding them to a conservative bill that featured competition for Medicare A and Medicare B. In turn, conferees tried to placate conservatives by agreeing to create health savings accounts and certain tax free accounts for employers. At one point, Chairman Thomas (R, CA) barred all Democratic members of the conference committee, save Breaux (LA) and Baucus (MT), from discussion on the grounds that they were too liberal and would not compromise. Slowly, the movement in committee was toward adopting characteristics of the Senate bill, in terms of dollars committed and competition for Medicare, although competition was given experimental status and was implemented in only six metropolitan areas.

Since the House was more conservative than the Senate, most felt that the Conference Report would not be well received in this chamber. Although Speaker Hastert positively stated, "We're very upbeat," House conservatives were anything but. Representative Flake (R, AZ) said, "The enormous cost of this proposal will only hasten Medicare's insolvency" (*New York Times*, Nov. 18, 2003). Other House conservatives had been against the bill for quite a while, arguing the bill would be the biggest expansion of the federal government since the Great Society of the 1960s. On November 21, the House received the Conference Report. The Rules Committee limited the debate to one hour. On November 22, at 2:39 A.M., the House rejected a motion to recommit the bill with instructions. Shortly after that, the final vote came to the floor.

House leaders left the vote open for almost three hours before they eked out a 220–215 victory. Normally, members have only 15 minutes to vote electronically on legislation, but after the first 15 minutes the yes vote was trailing by 24 votes—a major defeat for the President and the Speaker of the House. Republican leaders kept the vote open and Speaker Hastert and majority leader DeLay began calling members, telling them how important this bill was to the Republican Party. They had some success, and by 4 A.M. the vote was 216 yes and 218 no. Then, President Bush and Secretary Thompson (Health and Human Services) began calling members and the Secretary came to the floor to jawbone members. Seven Republican no voters were all pushed very hard and finally two, Otter of Idaho and Franks of Arizona, agreed to switch their votes, bringing the vote tally to 218 yeas against 216 nays. Then, in a slight flurry of vote switching, the final vote became 220 in favor to 215 opposed.

The party breakdown was 204 Republican yes votes with 25 no votes, while Democrats voted 16 yes and 189 no. The sole independent, Sanders (VT), voted no. The Republicans who voted no were toward the conservative side of the party, with an average ADA score of about 12. The 16 Democrats voting yes averaged about 65 on the ADA index. Thus, the victory on the House side was hard, costly, and narrowly won. The Speaker, the President and the HHS Secretary were credited with turning the tide at the last possible moment. The bill was a bitter pill for many House conservatives. Some who voted yes agreed with one member who said, "We voted for the next election not for the next generation."

Given the ideological placement of the Conference Report and previous coalition building we would expect the bill to pass more easily in the Senate. There were two crucial votes before final passage; the first, a vote to end Senator Kennedy's filibuster, and the second, a vote on Senator Daschle's (D, SD) motion that the bill was not consistent with the budget resolution. The vote to end Senator Kennedy's filibuster was 70 to 29, and 26 of the nay votes were from Democrats. The no votes were overwhelmingly from the liberal wing of the party, with the Democratic senators supporting Kennedy representing an average ADA of about 93. Those Democratic Senators who voted against Kennedy had an average ADA of 73. The other vote was on majority leader Daschle's motion to kill the bill because he thought it was more costly than allowed by the budget resolution agreement. This motion failed on a 61-to-39 vote, with 36 Democrats joining with Daschle to attempt to defeat the bill on the grounds that it violated frugality—a vote easier to defend at home than had been a potentially perceived obstructionist filibuster. Final passage was by a 54-to-44 vote, with 7 conservative Republicans voting against the final bill on grounds that it had been stripped of conservative content. Eleven Democrats joined 42 Republicans and Jeffords of Vermont to create the final margin. That Jeffords supported this bill despite having left the Republican Party should be no surprise, given his moderate preferences.

Clearly, in the Senate, the bill had been a compromise between Republicans and moderate Democrats led by Breaux (LA) and Baucus (MT), opposed by conservatives in the Republican Party and liberals in the Democratic Party. Senator Breaux summed up the story when he said, "This is a great victory for a coalition built from the center out. People on the far left and the far right were not necessarily part of the team" (*New York Times*, Nov. 26, 2003). There were three policy consequences of the legislation that were offensive to conservatives. First, the bill mandated more spending than they wanted. Then, the bill limited competition over Medicare, and finally, it benefited organizations like the American Association of Retired Persons (AARP) more than conservatives wanted. On the other hand, the bill spent less than liberal members of Congress wanted to spend, and utilized market forces and benefited pharmaceuticals more than they preferred. The final legislation was roughly where the median members of the Senate preferred policy, and was supported by Republican leaders and the President to take a likely losing issue off the table before the 2004 election campaigns.

Other Domestic Policies: Faith-Based Initiative Program

Another Bush policy item proposed in his first term was the faith-based initiative program. On January 29, 2001, President Bush announced the establishment of the White House Office of Faith-Based and Community Initiatives and the corresponding Center for Faith-Based and Community Initiatives in each of five departments. The President envisioned a "faith-friendly public service square where faith-based organizations can compete equally with other groups to provide government or privately funded services." This was couched as an expansion of the 1996 Welfare Reform Act, but it generated strong objections. For example, Americans United for the Separation of Church and State opposed giving federal funding to churches and religious groups at all.

After the January announcement the Bush administration developed legislative proposals regarding the role of faith-based organizations in the delivery of services. The House acted quickly and had passed the Community Solutions Act of 2001 by July. This piece of legislation established tax incentives for charitable gifts from both individuals and businesses, expanded the "charitable choice" provision of the 1996 Welfare Reform Act, and provided a specific and controversial way in which churches and governments might partner to provide services. The Senate version of the House bill was called the Charity Aid Recovery and Empowerment Act of 2002 (CARE). Given supermajority rules and the more centrist preferences of the Senate, our theory predicts that the faith-based initiative of the President would face more intense opposition in that chamber, and indeed it did. Despite attempts at compromise by moderates, there simply were not enough votes to move the legislation forward in 2002. A further attempt in 2003 passed the Senate by wide margins, but only through extensive watering down of the legislation. Ultimately, the distance between the House and Senate bills was too great to generate a fruitful conference committee.

In September of 2004 the President chose to pursue the faith-based initiative through administrative means instead of depending on congressional legislation. The administration therefore has been attempting to lower the requirements for religious organizations to participate in the federal funding process by utilizing "executive actions," which can be used to reinterpret (and thus change) federal regulations. Such an approach is consistent with our analysis from Chapter 2 of how Presidents cope with legislative gridlock.[7] President Clinton used a similar tactic in the post-Gingrich era of Congress with success. In sum, we have once again seen how a presidential proposal has faced difficulty in Congress because it was too far right of the median or filibuster pivot Senators. In this case, the President used executive orders and actions that were protected from congressional action to move toward his goals. The point, however, is that the President was unable to achieve his desired policy result through the legislative process and had to turn elsewhere.

Campaign Finance

Although the President did not view campaign finance reform as a pivotal issue, his chief rival in the 2000 primaries, John McCain (R, AZ), pushed hard to keep this issue at the fore. It had been before Congress for some time in the form of the McCain-Feingold bill, a piece of legislation favored by many Democrats and some Republicans. The collapse of Enron and the various other business debacles in 2001 led to the perception that the federal government was too cozy with big business, and brought additional pressure on Congress to reform its campaign finance procedures. While the President did not favor the McCain-Feingold bill, he saw that opposition would be costly. He therefore adopted a hands-off approach, stating that he would not veto any campaign finance act brought to him for a presidential signature. This strategy implied that House and Senate Republicans would have to defeat the bill without the threat of a presidential veto, a tougher task and one that would be too politically costly. When Congress passed a form of McCain-Feingold the President kept his promise and signed the bill. Opponents would look to the courts and the Federal Election Commission to weaken the law's provisions.

Summary of Domestic Affairs

Table 6.4 summarizes the most significant components of the domestic Bush legislative record through the 108th Congress. Three main points are worth noting. First, on majoritarian taxation proposals, the pivotal members were near the median in the Senate, and Bush proposals had to be modified toward their ideal points. Second, on supermajority legislation, broader coalitions were needed. These were impossible to construct in the Senate on policy movements solely to the right, such as on energy proposals. But on education and on Medicare prescription drugs, larger coalitions could be generated through increased domestic spending in traditionally Democratic areas. Because of budget surpluses and public inattention to renewed deficits, such coalitions were achievable in 2001 and 2003. The most conservative Republicans balked at such increased spending, meaning additional Democrats were needed to fill out the coalition. And it was these moderate members who determined the parameters of the final legislation. Given the polarized parties in Congress, this legislative history shows the limits on rightward movement even under the current unified Republican government. Outside of the use of budget reconciliation procedures, conservatives are unable

TABLE 6.4 Summary of Major Legislative Changes in the 107th and 108th Congresses

Type of Legislation	Bills	Presidential Proposal	Key Provisions	Changes	Pivotal Members
Majority Only	2001 Budget Act	Right of Senate median	1. $1.6 trillion in reduced rates 2. Five-year plan	1. $1.3 trillion 2. Ten-year sunset	Breaux Jeffords
	2003 Budget Act	Right of Senate median	1. $730 billion tax cuts	1. $350 billion	Snowe
Supermajority	Education, 2001	Right of Senate median Left of House median	1. Increased federal aid 2. Testing and accountability 3. Vouchers	1. Greater increase 2. Weakened testing 3. Dropped	Kennedy Chafee Jeffords
	Energy, 2001	Right of Senate median	1. Pro-development 2. Drilling in ANWR	Did not pass in Senate	Chafee Collins
	Energy, 2003	Right of Senate median	1. Pro-development 2. Drilling in ANWR	Did not pass in Senate	Chafee Collins
	Medicare Prescription Drugs, 2003	Right of Senate median Left of House median	1. Prescription drug benefits 2. Competition	1. More money 2. Trial basis	Breaux Baucus Thomas

to achieve their goals due to the threat of a filibuster in the Senate. Supermajorities are only obtained then when the President and congressional leaders take more liberal spending positions. When the public takes note of the mounting budget deficits, even this option will be off the table, and gridlock will return as strong as ever.

The third point to note is that we have discussed legislation between 2001 and 2004 as if the terrorist attacks of September 11, 2001, had never occurred. This may have come as a surprise to those who thought that Bush's success in the 108th Congress was the result of more general cross-partisan agreement. It is true that the terrorist attacks of 9/11 brought about a period of bipartisanship not seen in the nation's capital since the Eisenhower administration or perhaps more accurately since the first months after the beginning of WWII. Along with the bipartisanship, the terrorist attacks brought about unprecedented approval rankings for President Bush. However, this "rally round the flag" effect was not long lived. Even the Homeland Security Act ran into legislative trouble late in 2002 when the President and conservatives in Congress objected to making airport security personnel union workers. In contrast, liberals in the House and Senate favored unionization and thus bipartisanship was over fairly quickly. The war in Iraq and the subsequent military activity amplified the differences between the parties and, in combination with the 2002 elections, made the Senate and the President even more at odds.

Our point is that post–9/11 one might assume that the President, because of his high marks from the public and the bipartisan rally-round-the-flag effect, could have his way. The analysis in this chapter shows that both pre– and post–9/11 policy outputs in the legislative process moved to the pivotal Senators' preference points. The President's $730 billion tax cut proposal in 2003 was cut by more than 50 percent when pivotal Republican Senators Snowe and Voinovich said they would not support a tax cut over $350 billion. The Congress approved a $350 billion cut— the Senate median ideal point. On energy policy and on faith-based legislation the President failed to get either bill enacted—pre- or post–9/11. The education act was as shown above a center-out coalition but even here the President had to give up vouchers, weaken penalties for schools not meeting standards, and soften the report card measurements in order to keep the bill's centrist coalition together. Even in the supposedly united period after 9/11, members of Congress did not automatically or even eventually accede to the President's policy issues.

Foreign Affairs

The terrorist attacks of 9/11 brought about a period of bipartisanship that lasted far less than a year in the Congress. It is not surprising that an act of war that kills nearly 3,000 people in America's major city would bring about a period of national unity. Citizens' focus on domestic policies takes a back seat to international issues. The decision by the government to go after the Taliban rulers of Afghanistan was a popular and essentially non-controversial choice. The decision to go to war with Iraq without an explicit United Nations authorizing resolution was another matter. A significant minority of Americans and a majority of our European allies were opposed to military action in Iraq until and unless there was a U.N. resolution agreeing to the combat. Given the opposition to the war in Iraq, why, in this case, did the President get his way in the Congress relatively easily? Why, in spite of the fact that a majority of Americans feel that the war is going badly, does the President get what he asks for in appropriations? Why doesn't he face votes in Congress forcefully expressing displeasure with the situation in Iraq? In domestic politics Bush was thwarted on energy and got less than he wanted on taxes, education, and Medicare reform, yet on Iraq he faces only verbal criticism and not legislative defeat. In this section we address why foreign policymaking differs from domestic policymaking, but still can be understood in the context of the revolving gridlock theory.

Our model of policymaking uses traditional variables like members' preferences, the location of the current policy, and the median voter in the legislature to explain why policies pass or fail. Our contributions to the literature are that we also include in the model the supermajoritarian institution of Senate Rule XXII (filibuster) and the presidential veto, and we explain the role of budget circumstances in overcoming or adding to gridlock. Using the location of current policy (the status quo) relative to the median voters (House and Senate) and supermajority pivots we define the gridlock region as the area between the relevant pivots. Policy can be altered when there are election results or other exogenous shocks placing the status quo outside of that gridlock region. Although we allow for some uncertainty in all policy areas, our model of domestic policy assumes that members of Congress can fairly accurately calibrate how shifts in policy will affect their political careers. In the example using minimum wage law, the assumption is that, by the time of her vote, a congresswoman knows pretty well how she and members in her district will be affected by a dollar increase in the minimum wage.

Put simply, with few exceptions, there is not much uncertainty in domestic policy, relative to that in foreign policy. If the minimum wage rises, and a member represents a district with lots of small businesses using part-time teenage labor to run their operations, the member undoubtedly knows how the owners, teenagers, and their parents feel, and can vote accordingly. Washington, D.C., is a city of information, set up to let members know how thousands of interest groups and millions of citizens feel across almost all areas of domestic legislation. In the 109th Congress, within a couple months of President Bush's State of the Union Address, every member of Congress had a good idea about how hundreds of interest groups felt about the President's plan to privatize some Social Security funds.

In addition to all of the interest group information that members receive on domestic legislation, there are literally hundreds of polls taken by and for members showing how Americans, including those in their state or district, feel about any given domestic issue. Thus members can calibrate interest group information against public opinion polls, focus groups, and district meetings to determine how legislation will affect their long- and short-term career ambitions.

Herein lies an important difference between foreign and domestic policy. In foreign policy there is relatively more uncertainty surrounding policy alternatives.[8] There are far fewer interest groups in this arena and public opinion is less predetermined, which allows the President as commander in chief and head of state to take the lead on policy formation. His goal is clear—keep America and Americans safe—but the means of keeping us safe are controversial. Some view international institutions as the proper means for ensuring peace while others counter that we should have a strong military ready to harm our enemies if need be.[9] Still others believe that a combination of international institutions and force works best. Additionally in foreign policy much of the available crucial information is of a highly secure nature and is thus attached to the executive office. All of which is to say that in foreign policy there is great uncertainty about how policy—say toward the Arab world—will affect a member of Congress at reelection time. Is the presence of U.S. troops in Iraq, Kuwait, Saudi Arabia, and Afghanistan really increasing the number of terrorists ready to attack us? Do the elections in Iraq and Palestine mean democracy has a future in the troubled Middle East? Should the U.S. try to strengthen the United Nations, or leave it as it is, or weaken it further? These are difficult questions where real information is often not present or in very small supply.

Given that members wish to be reelected and that their constituents do not expect them to resolve the Iraq situation or the Israeli–Palestinian problem, members can decide not to act. In a previous chapter, we noted the role of uncertainty in the downfall of the Clinton health care plan. There, if the bill passed and cost too much, Democrats would have been held responsible and Republicans would field good candidates to run against them on that issue and others. If the Clinton bill passed and over the next several years a supporting member's constituents discover they can't choose the doctor they want, the member will likely face an opponent who mobilizes that discontentment into votes. Deciding not to report out a bill due to high uncertainty surely makes electoral sense, especially when the status quo is not seen as too problematic.

After the 9/11 attacks, sticking with the status quo was no longer an option, but there was immense uncertainty about the world, and members of Congress generally preferred the President to act first, act quickly, and act decisively. Indeed, much of the country looked to the President for leadership and offered him their support. The President experienced the well-known rally-around-the-flag effect.[10] In late August of 2001, CNN, Gallup, and Pew Research identified the President's job approval rating at a little over 50 percent; on September 11 and 12, the *New York Times* had his approval at 76 percent. During action in Afghanistan the President was never under 83 percent approval and was often right at 90 percent approval. The initial reaction of the Congress toward U.S. policy in Afghanistan reflected the public's positive views of the President. There were several votes on Afghanistan. The most significant one, occurring on September 14, authorized the use of armed forces against those responsible for the 9/11 attacks. In the Senate the vote was 98–0 and in the House 420–1 with Berkeley representative Barbara Lee (CA) being the sole no vote. Supplemental appropriations for the Afghanistan action also passed with bipartisan ease. The victory over the Taliban put the President by his 2002 State of the Union speech at an 89 percent approval rating according to CBS News.

The steady march toward war with Iraq began to put some members under pressure to speak up about the role of Congress in the foreign policy process. By mid-July of 2002, some members of the President's own party were pushing for a greater decision-making role. Senators Specter (PA) and Hagel (NE) warned that there had to be a national dialogue on the issue to avoid some of the mistakes of Vietnam. Some House and Senate Democrats were trying to use the Appropriations Committees as means to affect Iraq policy. While some congressional noise about Iraq policy was present, it was evident to most members that they should vote with the President since that vote was easy to defend. There was a great deal of uncertainty over Iraq's intentions and weapons, and, unlike on domestic issues, neither Congress nor the President controlled the status quo policy. That is, even without congressional passage of personal accounts for Social Security or of Clinton's health care, there are still Social Security and health care programs. However, on foreign policy the U.N. Security Council, the Arab world, and al Qaeda were all going to move and change the status quo, irrespective of the Congress.

Members of Congress thus faced great uncertainty over the present and future status quo. Voting to let the President do as he preferred would be the safest strategy for House members and Senators who feared electoral retribution. Members from safe (liberal in this case) seats could afford to object to the war in Iraq without affecting their electoral careers, while those from mixed or moderate states and districts could not afford such a vote. Rather their strategy would be "wait and see how things go"—if it goes well "I voted with the President," and if it doesn't go well, "I can object to the direction he's taken and still be reelected." Given this reasoning it is clear why the President would go to Congress for a resolution authorizing force against Iraq, since risk-averse members would give him a victory there.

The House voted on October 10, 2002, to authorize the use of force against Iraq. The first vote was to recommit the bill with instructions and that failed 325 to 101 with 100 of these losing votes coming from liberals, while 106 Democrats joined 219 Republicans to beat the recommital.[11] After the recommital failed the final vote came to the floor and passed 296 to 133. This time only 81 Democrats joined 215 Republicans to pass the act. In sum, the victory in the House had significant bipartisan support—far more than would have been needed for a simple majority. The Senate voted on the next day and, after several amendments and the defeat of a filibuster, the final vote on was 77 yeas and 23 nays. There were 22 Democratic opposition votes and their average ADA score was over 95. Moreover, of the 34 Senators up for reelection, 31 voted for the resolution. Democrats up for election and supporting the resolution included Kerry (MA), Lautenberg (NJ), and Rockefeller (WV), all of whom differed from their same-state same-party fellow Senator who voted no. In sum, uncertainty over outcomes coupled with electoral considerations to produce the vote for the war.

Our argument has been that foreign policy and especially national security issues fit within our model, with the major difference being that, relative to domestic politics, there is far more uncertainty. The uncertainty leads members, who cannot control the status quo, to turn to the President. The greater the uncertainty for a member the more likely a member is to take the safe route and cede power to the President. The Afghanistan action responded to a Taliban-sheltered al Qaeda attack that gave the President a very high job approval rating. Voting for a resolution to attack those who attacked us was not risky, and all such votes were very one-sided. The move to war in Iraq was different in that Iraq was not responsible for 9/11, the U.S. was acting without explicit U.N. backing, the exact nature of the Saddam Hussein threat was not certain, and the President's approval rating was down by 20 to 30 percentage points from its high of 90 percent. Liberals from safe districts were less uncertain about how a no vote would affect them. Yet those Democrats up for election voted with the President more frequently than those not up for election because it was an immediately safer bet.

Such consistent and theoretically sound behavior in the past makes predicting the future much easier. The 109th Senate will continue to vote in support of appropriations for the military and for the Iraq effort. There is still a great deal of uncertainty about America's Iraq and Middle East efforts. Will there be relative peace between Israelis and Palestinians? Will the newly elected Iraqi government bring stability and, if so, how soon? As long as answers to these questions and others like them are not clear, uncertainty prevails which helps the President to win votes for his foreign policy.

The 109th Congress and the Bush Agenda

With the passage of the Medicare prescription drug act, congressional Republicans went into the 2004 elections in good shape. The economy was performing reasonably well, there were no major issues over which Democrats could claim the 108th was a do-nothing Congress, and five Southern Democrats were retiring from the Senate: Hollings (SC), Graham (FL), Edwards (NC), Miller (GA), and Breaux (LA). The presidential race featured two Senators, John Kerry (MA) and John Edwards (NC), against Bush–Cheney. The war in Iraq was an important issue, as was terrorism. The war split along party lines, making Bush intensely disliked by many Democrats and beloved by Republicans. The campaigns were reasonably well run with the exception of Kerry's early statements on the war, including taking positions both for and against the war and its funding. The Kerry strategy was retrospective, claiming that Bush had not done well enough as President to be reelected, as evidenced by the state of the economy, the conduct of the war, and the country's preparation for future terrorist activity. This approach was most successful on domestic issues. For example, in May, Bush and Kerry were close on the economy, Social Security, health care, and education, but by October Kerry was ahead on all these issues. The Bush campaign strategy was to attack Kerry with the claim that he was not an acceptable alternative to the President given an unsafe world; and this strategy was successful enough to ultimately win the election. Republicans were most effective in painting Kerry as not tough enough on terrorism—on this and on character issues Bush led Kerry throughout the campaign. Turnout in the election was very high with Republicans doing a slightly better job at getting out their vote. Bush won with just over 62 million votes to Kerry's 59 million votes and with an Electoral College margin of 286 Bush to 252 Kerry.

While most of America's attention was devoted to the presidential election, it is ultimately the results of congressional elections that yield the pivot points that determine policy outputs. The 2004 election slightly improved conservative forces in the House. In the 108th House (elected in 2002) the Republicans held a 229–to–205 advantage over the Democrats (with one Independent) and after the 2004 election they held a 232–to–202 advantage over the Democrats. Incumbency was, as it has been throughout history, a real advantage, as only two Republican incumbents lost. Democratic incumbents fared slightly worse with five of them losing. Of the five, four were from Texas and had been redistricted by the Republican state legislature. In the 36 open-seat races (House seats without an incumbent running) almost all stayed with the party of the returning incumbent. In short, the 109th House looked much like the 108th House with the difference being a slight shift to the right as a few Democrats like Frost of Texas were replaced by conservatives like Republican Pete Sessions.

The 108th Senate was 51 Republicans to 48 Democrats and Jeffords of Vermont. The 2004 elections shifted the Republican majority to 55 with the Democrats at 44. The five open Southern Senate seats mentioned above elected Republicans to replace moderate Democrats and Oklahoma kept the seat Republican by electing former Congressmen Tom Coburn. Two open seats held by Republicans in the 108th Senate went to Democrats with Obama winning in Illinois and Salazar winning in Colorado. The only incumbent defeated was Tom Daschle (D, SD) who lost to former congressman John Thune. The four-seat gain resulted in a shift of the median to the right, away from Senators like Snowe and Collins of Maine with scores around 40 to 45 on the ADA measure to Senators like Specter of Pennsylvania and Smith of Oregon, closer to 20–25 on the ADA scale. Due to the limited number of centrists in the Senate, this is a relatively significant shift in preferences, despite the small shift in numbers. However, it should be noted that the filibuster pivot for the Democrats remains quite liberal, with forty-one members unlikely to vote with Smith and Specter on many issues at all.

The President seemed undeterred by the remaining filibuster threat, claiming a broad victory and enhanced political capital. He pushed several major policies in his State of the Union speech, many of which will not be acted on in the 109th Congress. The broad presidential agenda items getting the most consideration include: seeking to make permanent the tax cuts of 2001 and 2003; attempting to reform Social Security by privatizing some accounts; pushing for approval of more of his judicial nominees; and continuing on with present foreign policy objectives.

Given the thesis of this book, what are the chances the President will succeed in passing such legislation? Our answer is based on noting the gulf in preferences between the median and the filibuster pivot in the Senate. With some minor caveats, the President's positions will succeed with majority support, but will suffer when a supermajority is required. In particular, some aspects of tax policy can be altered under majority rules through reconciliation procedures but others cannot, Social Security reforms can be filibustered, and whether judicial nominees can be filibustered is presently open for debate.

Legislation for additional tax cuts remains popular in the House and the Senate. The House passed bigger cuts in 2003 than did the Senate, and with the 109th House slightly more conservative the expectation is that the House will vote to make many of the 2001 and 2003 tax cuts permanent. The 109th Senate has shifted toward the conservative end of the spectrum, and a majority will support making the cuts permanent. The key questions are: whether 60 votes are available to secure permanent tax cuts over a filibuster threat, whether a compromise will be struck to gain those key votes, or whether Republicans will once again rely on reconciliation rules to pass cuts with a bare majority. If a handful of the less liberal Senate Democrats up for reelection need tax cuts as a campaign issue, momentum from passage in the House might tip the support for permanent cuts over the top. These Democrats will be in a pivotal position to negotiate the depth of the cuts made permanent, and may strike a deal. If they are not willing to deal, Republican leaders in the Senate can instead attempt to formulate another budget reconciliation package, which could generate deeper, but still not permanent cuts.

The strategy for the President's Social Security privatization proposal has been based on several Bush tactics from past legislative successes. First, as with his 2001 tax cuts, the President is promoting his plan around the country. Second, as was the case for education reform, no specific bill was initially proposed, thus allowing the President to stay on the broad message and leave the details to others. However, unlike tax cuts, reforming Social Security comes with a cost (perhaps with lower benefits, an increased retirement age, or more taxes), making it less attractive to the public and to members of Congress. Also unlike the tax cuts, a supermajority would be required for change. And unlike education reform, the President does not seem to be moving sufficiently in a liberal direction (in terms of increased spending) to bring about a center-out coalition. These differences, coupled with the high degree of uncertainty surrounding private accounts, lead us to a skeptical view of Social Security reform in the 109th Congress (and especially for reforms including the President's personal accounts).

Liberals in the Congress will oppose any privatization of Social Security on the grounds that privatization is dangerous. Ted Kennedy suggested that the President's proposal is designed to destroy Social Security. Mike Thompson (D, CA) argued that the only crisis over Social Security was that caused by the President's plan. From prominent Democrats like Kennedy to less prominent new Democratic office holders, the anti-privatization preference is clear. Thus, in order to get legislation, the President has to have 218 (largely Republican) votes in the House and a supermajority in the Senate. House Republicans are afraid of acting first on this issue until a complete deal is secured, as they could be portrayed as working to end Social Security, a well-loved program. The worst outcome for them is to vote for the President's proposal without its ultimate passage in the Senate. Such a lesson was not learned by House Democrats surrounding Clinton's 1993 initial budget package (with energy taxes and the rest) until they lost dramatically in 1994. The current majority party is unlikely to repeat that mistake.

The Social Security issue has burned the Republican Party on several occasions in the past and so they will proceed with caution. Uncertainty will add to this hesitance. Members are realistically uncertain about how a pro-Bush vote on Social Security will affect present and future reelection chances. When there is substantial uncertainty and the status quo is unacceptable, members gather all the information they can and then act. But when uncertainty is high and the status quo is acceptable, members of Congress would prefer not to act. This explains why so much of the current debate centers around how much of a crisis the current Social Security system is in. To be successful, the President would have to convince the public of the crisis, resolve the uncertainty around his proposal, hold together the 55 Senate Republicans, and win a handful of Democrats. Each step is problematic, and collectively they may be insurmountable.

The average age of the U.S. Supreme Court, and especially Chief Justice William Rehnquist's health, have focused a good deal of attention on Supreme Court appointments, and judicial appointments more generally. The President mentioned in his 2005 State of the Union Address that his court nominees (lower courts up to this time) deserved to be voted on in the Senate, a clear reference to the filibusters that have kept several of his Appellate Court nominees from being confirmed. Even if it were to hold together, the present Republican majority of 55 is not enough to stop a filibuster on judicial nominations, and there are not five conservative Democrats left in the Senate. This means that liberal Senators can and have stopped certain nominees.

Recently members have been talking about what the press calls the "nuclear option" in regard to judicial nominees. Although Senate Rule XXII covers filibustering, and Senate rules can only be changed through a two-thirds vote, the nuclear option would end the filibustering of judges through a simple majority vote. Put simply, a Republican member could object to the filibuster of judicial nominees on constitutional grounds. The U.S. Constitution gives the Senate an advice and consent role over the President's judicial nominees, but does not specify the voting rule. Conservatives could claim that a proper interpretation of the Constitution is consent by a majority rather than a supermajority. Liberals would claim that the Constitution allows the Senate to formulate its own rules, which includes the filibustering of judicial nominees under Rule XXII. This debate would be resolved not by constitutional lawyers, but by a vote in the Senate. And the voting rule for such a procedural issue is a simple majority. Thus, if a majority of Senators wish to interpret the Constitution as disallowing supermajority votes for judicial nominees, they could do so.

Fearing this approach, Democratic leaders have promised to tie the Senate in knots if such a rule change passes. They could do so by continually objecting to the unanimous consent agreements that allow the Senate day-to-day operations to run fairly smoothly. Whether this would be "nuclear," ending all action in the Senate, or whether the public would demand the Senate go ahead with its business, remains an open question. For our present purposes, it is sufficient to wonder: do the pro-rule-change forces have 51 votes (or 50 with support of the Vice President)?

The passage of the "nuclear option" will hang on the votes of moderate Republican Senators. As of April 2005, Olympia Snowe (ME), Lincoln Chafee (RI), and John McCain (AZ) have already said they will not vote for the change in the filibuster rule. That leaves Senators Collins (ME), Smith (OR), Warner (VA), Murkowski (AK), Hagel (NE), and Specter (PA) as crucial players on this issue. All 44 Democrats and Jeffords of Vermont would likely vote no on the change along with the three Republicans noted above. Therefore, for a victory the Senate majority leader Bill Frist (R, TN) needs four of the six undeclared Republicans, leaving academics and pundits alike to wonder what will happen if such a vote is taken.

This cliffhanger is a fitting end to our chapter, because such press coverage and such a dire label as "the nuclear option" reinforces one of our main points. The difference between a majority rule in the Senate and a supermajority rule is important. What we hope to have established here is that it is important not only for judicial nominees, but also for the most significant aspects of domestic and foreign policy. Tax cuts that were passed under a majority rule could not be passed if filibustered or vetoed. Education and health care reforms require significant compromises across the political spectrum, compromises that came in 2001 and 2003 with a budgetary price tag. And movements in a liberal or conservative direction on any policy require broad support that is tough to find in today's Congress.

Notes

1. See the analyses by Polsby and Wildavsky (2000) and Abramson, Rohde, and Aldrich (1999).

2. See the assessment by Mayer (2000).

3. See Bartels and Zaller (2001) and surrounding articles in *PS: Political Science and Politics* for the debate these predictions caused.

4. See the analyses of Weisberg and Wilcox (2004).

5. For a liberal critique of these cuts, see Gale, Orszag, and Taylor (2005), and see Hubbard (2004) for a counter-view.

6. See Keele, Fogarty, and Stimson (2003) for an alternative view. Note, however, that even if the analysis shows no effect, Washington insiders and members of Congress believed that the President's campaigning mattered, which enabled him to push for further policy change.

7. The use of executive orders under these circumstances is what political scientists like Deering and Maltzman (1999) and Howell (2003) would expect.

8. Our argument here is tied to the "Two Presidencies" idea discussed in Chapter 2.

9. For some windows into this debate, see Kissinger (1957), Keohane (1993), and Mearsheimer (1994).

10. See Brody (1991) for an in-depth discussion.

11. Over 100 votes against authorization for war is high by historical standards— that is, compared to similar votes on the Gulf War or WWI—but the margin of victory on the floor was still quite high.

Conclusion

Over the past three chapters we have told the same story in different contexts. In each, we recounted the hopeful nature of those with policy proposals and the harsh reality of political processes in Congress. Whether in the 1980s or early 2000s, considerations arise that are remarkably similar to those of 1995. The freshman Republicans in the 104th Congress, like their counterparts in the 103rd Congress, came to Washington to "change" policy. Yet in both cases their hopes exceeded their achievements. Many of the Democratic freshmen elected to the 103rd House suffered the fate of Marjorie Margolies-Mezvinsky (PA) and were not reelected to the 104th House. Eleven members of the freshman Republican class of 1994 met the same end and were not reelected. As they returned to the towns, cities, and prairies of home, they faced an electorate that wanted to know what they had achieved. Why had they not achieved more or why had they achieved as much as they did? Both the Democrats in 1992 and the Republicans in 1994 had reason to believe when they first came to Washington that their victories were part of a larger whole, wherein their elections and votes would count for change. The Democrats in the 103rd were part of the first unified government in twelve years, led by a dynamic young President. The Republicans in the 104th Congress were members of the first Republican-controlled Congress in forty years. No wonder they felt that "change" was in the air.

Implicit in these members' notions of being a part of change was that their individual victories were part of a bigger, significant electoral shift, the first group to a unified government and the second to a Republican revolution. The premise is that elections matter and that certain elections move the elected representatives relatively uniformly toward policy changes. The literature on electoral politics backs up this notion. From V. O. Key's theories on "ballots not bullets" and critical elections to Popkin's theory (1991) of rational ignorance, the scholarly consensus is that some elections matter more than others. Certain elections, some argue, shift the majority party, which in turn changes policy; whereas others argue that elections don't predict policy shifts accurately but that electoral results can nevertheless account for policy (Mayhew 1974a). In short, elections create majorities that derive their power from the fact that the governed have consented to be governed and have put their imprimatur on these members via the electoral process.

The policy process in its most basic sense prescribes that the majority of those elected by the people are free to legislate at least until the next election. The American system of representation thus relies on the people's consent to be governed by a majority of those elected, and leads freshman members in Congresses like the 103rd and 104th to believe that rapid change is forthcoming. Both the freshman Democrats and Republicans in the 103rd House expected battles over important reforms. Minority leader Robert Michel (R, IL) said that forty of the forty-seven new Republicans were hard-liners, creating a GOP conference that was "the most conservative and antagonistic to the other side" that he had seen in his 40 years (1993 *Congressional Quarterly Weekly Report*, 810). The Democratic freshmen were just as optimistic going in, and many of those defeated for reelection to the 104th Congress attributed their defeat to the failure of the 103rd Congress to enact new legislation.

The revolving gridlock theory is about elections and policy outcomes. Members of Congress develop preferences over policies that reflect, among other things, the views of their districts and their desire to be reelected. These preferences translate into policy outcomes through the majority and supermajority institutions surrounding the policymaking process. The harsh reality that new members discover is that developing supermajority coalitions around complex issues is difficult. Policy gridlock is the result of not being able to build such coalitions without violating the trust of the folks back home.

Soon after the 1993 legislative session began, Speaker Tom Foley (D, WA) commented, "The euphoria of the inauguration has been tempered by the reality of the problems" (*National Journal*, March 13, 1993, 606). As the session moved along and gridlock set in, members' views grew darker. On the now-famous budget vote, Democrats from moderate districts were caught between party and constituency. Said one senior House Democrat:

> The day before the vote a few [Democrats] said they intended to vote no but if their votes were crucial they would vote for the budget. When it was tied a lot of us were arguing with Ray [Thornton, AR], Pat [Williams, MT], and Marjorie [Margolies-Mezvinsky], trying to get them to vote for it. Then Ray said he couldn't do it and walked away. So Pat and Marjorie voted for it. . . . Sure we were wondering why Ray [from a safe district] made Marjorie take the hit. He saw his state as conservative, and he didn't want to vote for a tax increase. Sure we were yelling, and we were pissed at him. But there was little we could do. (Matsui 1995, 28)

Congresswoman Margolies-Mezvinsky lost her seat in 1994.

There is nothing new about the fact that congressional freshmen are excited about changing things. John Kingdon (1973) and others have found this phenomenon to be long standing. The phenomenon is not limited to members of Congress; newly elected Presidents often overestimate their power and potential to bring about change. John Kennedy, in a famous interview at the end of his first two years, said that what surprised him most was "how hard it was to get things done around here." Lyndon Johnson went from being the greatest legislator in 1965 and 1966 to resigning from the presidency in 1968. Presidential honeymoons with the public, the Congress, and the bureaucracy are short lived. The enthusiasm to bring about change in policy and process exceeds the ability to actually effect change; this holds true for Presidents as well as members of Congress.

What happens between the November election with its euphoria and anticipation, and the reality of the first two years in office?

The newly elected Congress and President arrive in Washington, ready and willing to enact the people's wishes; yet, except under very rare circumstances, this does not occur. In this book we offered a partial explanation of why change is usually not forthcoming. First, members of Congress and the President are dealing with complex issues about which there is little consensus, especially when it comes to change. Everyone agrees the that United States cannot continue its entitlement programs at present levels without (1) increasing taxes, (2) decreasing benefits, or (3) increasing the deficit and thus the burden on future generations. But the issue is more complex than a simple multiple-choice test. Some favor increasing taxes; others favor decreasing expenditures; many favor a mixed strategy; but what generally happens is an increase in the national debt. Complex problems generate complex solutions, and both are grounded in the complex and varied preferences underlying policy choices. Thus building policy majorities is hard.

The second reason for gridlock is that supermajority institutions, particularly the President's veto and Rule XXII in the Senate authorizing the filibuster, exacerbate the problems of building a consensus for change. They enable actors far from the median to affect policy outcomes beyond their single vote. The sixtieth (filibuster pivot) or sixty-seventh (veto pivot) Senator can move policy their way or keep the status quo even though a majority favors change.

In addition, not only is there a lack of consensus in the Congress, there is a lack of consensus among the public about what should be done.[1] "The budget should be balanced while taxes are cut and expenses increased" is a classic example of the American public's contradictory views on policy. It is hard to determine whether voters are inherently unrealistic or whether they have been induced to be unrealistic. Consider the budget problem. The public (a majority of respondents in various surveys) believes that we can reduce taxes, increase expenditures (in different areas, depending on the respondent's particulars), and have a balanced budget all at the same time.[2] One view drawn from such results is that the public is uninformed, irrational, and/or unrealistic. A counter to this would be: What should we expect from a public that for decades has been told that solving the budget problem will be painless? From Jimmy Carter's characterization of the energy crisis as "the moral equivalent of war" to Walter Mondale's pledge to raise taxes to George H. Bush's breaking of his opposing pledge of "no new taxes," politicians who admitted that pain was involved in problem solving have not fared well on election day. Politicians from LBJ (with his Great Society) to Ronald Reagan (with his Morning in America) who focused on the positive have done much better at the polls.

In short, politicians often tell the public that problems can be solved without pain. Whether right or wrong from a policy standpoint, George W. Bush did not take the bait in 2004 when Democrats asked him to demand sacrifices from the American people during the war on terrorism and the war in Iraq. Emphases on tax cuts to encourage economic growth and on private accounts to save Social Security are seen more positively than rolling back tax cuts and making benefit cuts or tax increases as part of entitlement reforms. That's simply good electoral politics. And we should not be surprised that, after decades of being told that budget problems can be solved without cutting middle-class entitlements or raising middle-class taxes, the public may well have begun to believe it.

Yet making public policy differs from talking about it in an election. In the policy world, Presidents must propose the specifics of how they are going to reduce the deficit, enhance health care coverage, deal with terrorism and alliances in the world, and improve educational opportunities for American children. Such proposals entail tradeoffs that have real consequences for citizens and thus for their elected representatives. These hard choices make it difficult for the Congress and the President to actually shift policy. In short, the status quo is hard to change for a variety of legitimate reasons both within and outside the legislative arena, not the least of which is that most Americans own their own homes, have decent jobs with health insurance, and feel their children are being well educated.

Little Stories That Make Up the Big Picture

Despite all of this talk of big proposals and grand electoral strategy, ultimately congressional decisions are made by 435 Representatives and 100 Senators. Take the battle over deficits in the 104th Congress, for instance. The big story of the 1995 budget was, of course, President Clinton's veto of the Republican proposal. Because the veto point was to the left of the Republican reconciliation bill, the veto pulled the final budget outcome to the left. In addition to this big picture, there are hundreds of local stories at the district level that also demonstrate a pull toward the status quo and gridlock on the budget proposals; we cannot cover all of these stories or even any one in great detail. Funding for the Los Alamos laboratories in New Mexico was in part protected by Senator Domenici (R, NM) who in general favors smaller government. This is not an uncommon story. Barry Goldwater (the former Republican Senator from Arizona and Republican presidential nominee in 1964) was known as "Mr. Conservative," yet he favored funding the Central Arizona Water Project because, without the Colorado River water, Arizona's population growth was limited. In short, no matter how conservative and pro–balanced budget a congressional member might be, that member has a constituency that benefits from federal programs. Budget issues, especially when they involve real tradeoffs between programs and revenues, force members to choose what to do regarding programs that benefit their constituents. To the extent that they fight to preserve benefits, and win, they may be seen as either moving policy to the left or as making it hard to achieve balanced budgets.

Our point is that decisions on the budget (and thus on most legislation) are even more complex than any overarching theory can capture. Since we cannot deal with the hundreds of local issues that affect expenditure levels, we choose to give one example as an illustration of the process. Our example is the 1995 reconciliation budget's agricultural appropriations for dairy farmers. Agricultural politics is a good choice because much has been written on the subject. Grant McConnell (1953, 1966) and Theodore Lowi (1969) feature agricultural politics in their theories of interest group liberalism. Roughly, there exists in agricultural politics an iron triangle of interests that exchange goods, services, votes, and campaign contributions, which in combination formulate policy. Farmers want programs that benefit them—price supports, parity payments, favorable tax legislation, and so on—and in order to get these programs, they and their organizations (interest groups) support candidates who favor them. In turn, those elected representatives serve on committees (Agriculture and Appropriations) that prepare policies beneficial to their constituents. These benefits programs are administered by bureaucratic agencies (mainly in the Department of Agriculture) that make the payments—that deliver the services to the constituents. The bureaucrats benefit because, by administering the programs that the farm interests desire, they develop a clientele that supports their agency. In short, politicians exchange favorable policies for financial and electoral support; farmers and farm interests exchange votes for programs; and the agencies formulate and administer programs that farmers and representatives want, thus ensuring their careers and their agencies' continued existence.

Somewhat more recent work, especially Mark Hansen's *Gaining Access* (1991), has modified this picture somewhat by showing that elected representatives want information about how different policies will affect them politically, and that over time the interest groups with the best information win out. Nevertheless, the general picture is that, since the passage of the 1933 Agricultural Adjustment Act, the federal government has been subsidizing various crops and products. Nowhere have these subsidies been more noticeable than in the area of dairy products and especially *milk*. John Connelly, a former Secretary of the Treasury and Republican presidential hopeful, was brought to trial over his alleged link to increases in the subsidy for milk prices. Present policy bases price supports for milk on regions. Since 1937 the country has been divided into geographical regions and each region has milk marketing orders that determine how much the milk processors, like those who make cheese, dried milk, and ice cream, must pay farmers for raw milk. The regional price is based on a set of complicated factors such as how far a particular farmer lives from the nation's center of efficient milk production—Eau Claire, Wisconsin.

The intention of the legislation in 1937 was to take into account the costs of the factors of production, which vary by climate, soil fertility, and other conditions. For purely economic reasons the upper Midwest, particularly Wisconsin, is where milk can be produced most efficiently. More recently, however, sophisticated methods of refrigeration and fast transportation have made it economically efficient for the upper Midwest to produce a greater percentage of the nation's milk. Freeing the market from milk subsidies would save taxpayers money (in reduced subsidies) and lower the price to consumers; it would also, however, in all probability greatly reduce the number of dairy farmers, particularly in the eastern United States where milk can only be produced inefficiently.

The original House version of the 1995 reconciliation budget reduced aid to farmers who raise wheat, corn, rice, cotton, peanuts, and almost every other crop. This legislation dropped milk marketing orders entirely. Dropping the subsidy to milk producers was supported by dairy farmers in the Midwest and opposed by dairy farmers in the East. Enter Representative Gerald Solomon (R, NY), the Chair of the Rules Committee. Solomon represented the twenty-fourth district in New York, essentially the upper Hudson Valley including Saratoga Springs. In the safely Republican district, Solomon had averaged over 70 percent of the vote across his nine consecutive elections to the House. Representative Solomon's district was the twentieth largest milk-producing district in the country and although he served on the Rules Committee and not the Agriculture Committee, he had consistently voted for agriculture bills containing subsidies for his milk producers. Given his position as Rules Chair, Solomon led the way, along with Representative Dreier (R, CA), in configuring the special rules under which the Contract with America was voted through the House. In short, Representative Solomon had been a key player in the Republican leadership.

But how should Representative Solomon behave in regard to the cuts in milk subsidies? Should he go with the Speaker and do his share to cut the deficit or should he fight to retain the milk subsidies for his constituents? If he wins concessions for his constituents, then he keeps expenditures higher than they would be if he were to go with the cuts. Obviously, Solomon chose to fight the subsidy reduction. On December 6, 1995, the *New York Times* reported that Representative Solomon had told the House leadership—while the bill was in a House–Senate conference committee—that unless they restored the milk subsidies he would lead the entire New York Republican delegation in a vote against the entire reconciliation budget. Solomon said, "Never in my life have I ever joined a rump group, but I did it because it's a matter of life or death." The Republican leadership could not afford to lose the New York delegation votes, so they stripped the bill of the anti-milk subsidy provisions, thus ensuring the continuance of regional subsidies. In short, this action pushed expenditures to the left by keeping the milk subsidies, and moved the deficit higher.

In some sense budget decisions represent a hodgepodge of little arrangements like the milk subsidy settlement. Of course, not all members chair the Rules Committee and some members occasionally give ground on issues important to their constituents. Nevertheless, the Solomon story is not unrepresentative, as congressional members worry much less about benefits that do not affect their own constituents; and to the extent that members succeed in serving their constituents the budget is harder to balance. Programs like Social Security that have significant numbers of beneficiaries in every district are particularly hard to change. Even programs like inefficient milk subsidies are, as we have seen, hard to cut.

Representative Solomon's case shows the power of individuals even in the strongly partisan Republican House. Despite talk of party cohesion, individual Republicans and groups of Republicans often act on their own against the wishes of their leadership. Again the story comes down to the individual preferences and positions of members of Congress. And again the preferences along with institutional rules explain the lack of policy change.

Gridlock Continues

Although we have reached a conclusion—the continuation of gridlock—similar to that reached by others, we believe that the revolving gridlock theory provides an explanation of policymaking strikingly different from those found elsewhere. For example, by the late 1990s, everyone had reached the conclusion that health care reform in 1994 was plagued by the disease of gridlock. Hacker (1997) focuses on the Clinton plan as trying to appear moderate to moderates and liberal to liberals. Skocpol (1996) argues that Clinton lost labor support due to his position on NAFTA. Broder and Johnson (1996) believe that no policy change was possible. Although they capture the details of the health care reform attempts, they show how the big picture can be missed by politicians, scholars, and journalists alike. Our argument is that a shift to the left, such as Clinton's reform proposal, must appeal to those at the median and to the right of the median (here the filibuster pivot). The exclusion of and inability to address the concerns of these pivotal members—conservative Democrats such as Mike Andrews (TX) and liberal-to-moderate Republicans—meant one of two things. Either the proposals were focused on the wrong members or the status quo policy was already inside the gridlock region. In order to understand policy outcomes, we must pay greater attention to those pivotal members necessary in forming the requisite majorities and supermajorities. This is an important lesson not only for those of us observing the process, but also for those attempting to bring about policy change. Where this lesson has not been learned, gridlock becomes even more likely.

When President Bush made a proposal early in 2005 to reform Social Security, media coverage focused on the size of the crisis, the nature of personal accounts, and the costs of reform. Cable news shows featured conservative Republicans arguing against liberal Democrats. Yet, the theory presented here suggests that such stories were attracting attention to the wrong areas of concern. Change in a conservative direction in the 109th Congress depends on satisfying the filibuster pivot. Thus any political analysis of proposals like Social Security reform must ask two questions. First, who are the five Democratic Senators interested in joining the fifty-five Republicans for change over a possible filibuster? And, second, should we even expect the fifty-five Republicans to hold together, given different preferences across their diverse states? If no moderate Democrats can be found and there are Republican defectors, then the proposed policy change is a non-starter.

But, if gridlock results from differences in preferences even under unified government, the public may be confused about how their votes translate into policy outcomes. Voters will continue to perceive the President and the Congress as muddling through at best—struggling to find consensus and appearing to be out of touch with regard to where Americans expect them to be. Public dissatisfaction with Congress, as Hibbing and Theiss-Morse (1995) have shown, in part results because the public does not like the give-and-take of politics—the debate and subsequent compromise. In part, as pointed out earlier, the public perceives that policy solutions are easier to achieve than in fact they are. In one sense, supermajority institutions have added to the dissatisfaction, making politics more cumbersome and perhaps more heated. Jones (1994) reminds us of the complexity of policy-making given the separation of powers, yet he does not call for a simplification of the system. On the other hand, Binder and Smith (1996) argue that the gridlock resulting from the filibuster gives reason enough to abandon this supermajority institution. We do not take such a normative stand here. We believe, rather, that an inability to override vetoes or end filibusters is a further testimony to the lack of policy consensus in the United States.

This is not to say that we are not troubled by policy gridlock. If the median member of Congress is representative of the median in the country as a whole, then it follows that policy change preferred by a majority in Congress is preferred by a majority of U.S. citizens.[3] The revolving gridlock theory predicts that often the majority view is tempered by the need to secure supermajorities, and by the complexity of the issues. Where the will of the majority is continually thwarted by diverse preferences and supermajority institutions, the public may turn to elections to align politicians' preferences. But when politicians are already representing diverse district preferences, gridlock continues. Gridlock thus represents a lack of policy consensus regarding the difficult decisions we ask our representatives to make. Whether caused by complex issues or supermajority institutions, the political wrangling and subsequent inability to break gridlock leaves the public feeling dissatisfied.

The predicament of contemporary politics in America could be relieved by lowering public expectations about what the government is able to achieve, given the diversity of views held by Americans and the complexity of the problems with which the country is faced. Some commentators point to political reform— campaign finance reform, balanced budgets, and electoral reforms—as ways to improve the overall situation.[4] In general, we do not believe that political reforms will solve these more fundamental problems. Democratic countries from Japan and Korea in the Far East to Europe and Canada all face the same problems—corporate downsizing, high wages in the face of competition from the third world, exorbitant entitlements, electorates unhappy with high tax rates, aging populations, and questions about foreign policy in an unsafe world. Forms of government in these countries range from strong parliamentary systems to decentralized American-style governments. None has the answer, and in fact one could argue that America has moved further toward solving these common problems than have other countries, perhaps due to the policy gridlock of the past, which resisted public preferences for policies that were unsustainable in the long run: dramatic increases in entitlements, changes in the tax codes, and increased government regulation.

We do not mean to claim that all political reforms are therefore hopeless; rather, our point is that such reforms as those mentioned above are not likely to resolve the dilemmas and policy problems faced by modern nations. No political reform will provide a consensus on the proper mix of taxes and entitlement spending. If political reform, then, is not the answer, what is? Our view is that the answer is patience, time, and struggle. In a democracy like the United States, policy is worked out through elections, debate about policy changes, further elections, and finally the passage of policy changes. When Bill Clinton and the Democrats pushed too hard to the left in 1993 and Newt Gingrich led Republicans down the primrose path when he shut the government down over Christmas, the American electorate brought them back to reality. Similar moves to the right currently will be checked if they exceed the wishes of the electorate. In the process, the public will be displeased—the debate will get heated and the result will probably anger both sides. Nevertheless, until the debate over the direction of the country (on one issue or many) is resolved by the public's voting into office a President and a Congress with a common vision, Americans shall continue to muddle through.

Notes

1. This lack of consensus may lead voters to place checks on politicians whom they believe would move policy too far in one direction or the other (Alesina and Rosenthal 1989, 1995), often leading to divided government (Fiorina 1991a, 1996).

2. Mark Hansen (1998) argues that these responses come from surveys offering the public a "free lunch." Anyone offered a tax cut, lower deficit, or more spending without other consequences would rightly take it. He reports results from surveys that explore the tradeoffs more fully, with many interesting findings.

3. While we both feel that Congress generally reflects public preferences, we are divided in opinion over just how representative it is. For example, some segments of the population may be less well-represented than others, the public may vote for politicians to "balance out" other politicians already in office, and the weighting of district and state preferences may skew representation. As such, it may not be the case that the congressional median and population median are identical. Evidence suggests that Congress is more polarized than is the electorate at large (Fiorina 2005). Nevertheless, we both feel that changes in the public view lead, through elections, to changes in membership and preferences in Congress. We are deeply concerned that political institutions (whether electoral, within Congress, or elsewhere) might not allow the will of the people to be carried out, and suggest that Americans therefore need to be vigilant.

4. See Sundquist (1993, 1995).

Appendix:
Distribution of ADA Scores

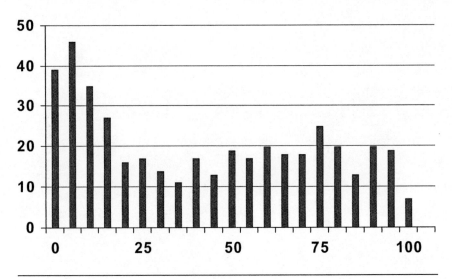

Source: Americans for Democratic Action website.

FIGURE A.1   1976 ADA Scores (94th House)

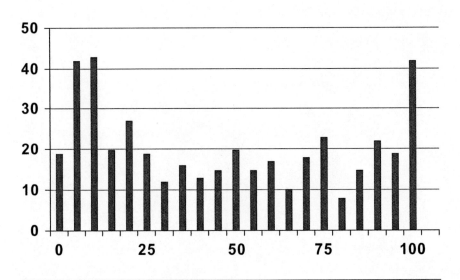

Source: Americans for Democratic Action website.

FIGURE A.2   1980 ADA Scores (96th House)

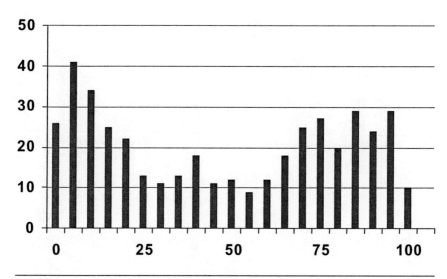

Source: Americans for Democratic Action website.

FIGURE A.3   1984 ADA Scores (98th House)

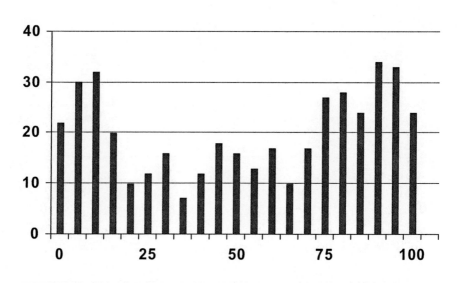

Source: Americans for Democratic Action website.

FIGURE A.4   1988 ADA Scores (100th House)

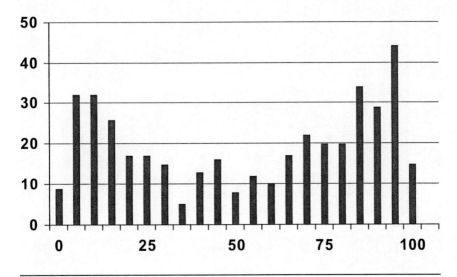

Source: Americans for Democratic Action website.

FIGURE A.5   1992 ADA Scores (102nd House)

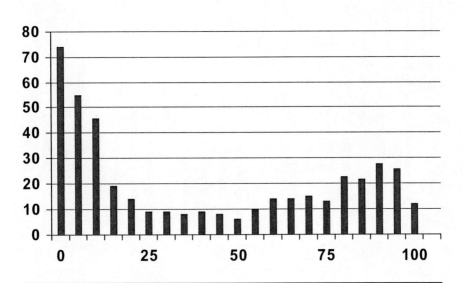

Source: Americans for Democratic Action website.

FIGURE A.6   1996 ADA Scores (104th House)

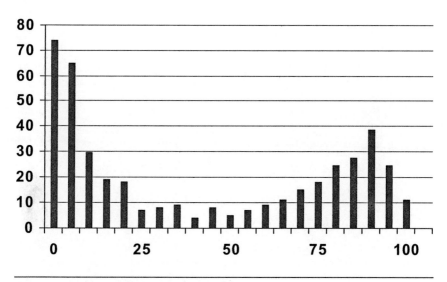

Source: Americans for Democratic Action website.

FIGURE A.7   2000 ADA Scores (106th House)

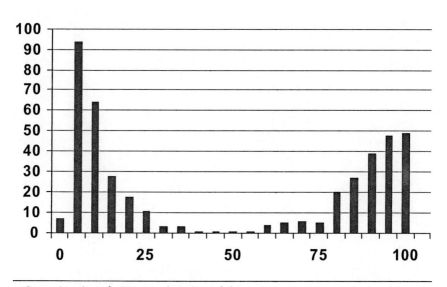

Source: Americans for Democratic Action website.

FIGURE A.8   2003 ADA Scores (108th House)

Bibliography

Aberbach, Joel. 1991. The President and the Executive Branch. In *The Bush Presidency: First Appraisals*, edited by Colin Campbell and Bert Rockman. Chatham, NJ: Chatham House Publishers.

Abramson, Paul R., David W. Rohde, and John H. Aldrich. 1999. *Change and Continuity in the 1996 and 1998 Elections*. Washington, DC: CQ Press.

Aldrich, John H. 1995. *Why Parties? The Origin and Transformation of Party Politics in America*. Chicago: University of Chicago Press.

Alesina, Alberto, and Geoffrey Carliner, eds. 1991. *Politics and Economics in the Eighties*. Chicago: University of Chicago Press.

Alesina, Alberto, and Howard Rosenthal. 1989. Partisan Cycles in Congressional Elections and the Macroeconomy. *American Political Science Review* 83(2):373–398.

———. 1995. *Partisan Politics, Divided Government, and the Economy*. Cambridge: Cambridge University Press.

Alford, John, and David Brady. 1993. Personal and Partisan Advantage in U.S. Congressional Elections, 1846–1990. In *Congress Reconsidered*. 5th ed., edited by Lawrence Dodd and Bruce I. Oppenheimer. Washington, DC: Congressional Quarterly Press.

Alt, James, and Robert Lowry. 1994. Divided Government, Fiscal Institutions, and Budget Deficits: Evidence from the States. *American Political Science Review* 88:811–828.

Alt, James, and Kenneth Shepsle, eds. 1990. *Perspectives on Positive Political Economy*. Cambridge: Cambridge University Press.

American Political Science Association. 1950. *Toward a More Responsible Two-Party System*. Washington, D.C.: American Political Science Association.

Anderson, Martin. 1990. *Revolution: The Reagan Legacy*. Stanford: Hoover Institution Press.

Anderson, Sarah, David Brady, and John Cogan. 2004. The Pivotal Politics of Appropriations. Paper presented at annual meeting, American Political Science Association, Chicago.

Ansolabehere, Steven, David Brady, and Morris Fiorina. 1992. The Vanishing Marginals and Electoral Responsiveness. *British Journal of Political Science* 22:21–38.

Arnold, R. Douglas. 1990. *The Logic of Congressional Action*. New Haven: Yale University Press.

Arrow, Kenneth Joseph. 1951. *Social Choice and Individual Values*. New York: John Wiley.

Bach, Stanley, and Steven Smith. 1988. *Managing Uncertainty in the House of Represen-tatives: Adaptation and Innovation in Special Rules.* Washington, DC: Brookings Institution.

Baron, David, and John Ferejohn. 1989. Bargaining in Legislatures. *American Political Science Review* 83(4):1181–1206.

Bartels, Larry M., and John Zaller. 2001. Presidential Vote Models: A Recount. *PS: Political Science and Politics* 34(1):9–20.

Beam, David R., Timothy Conlan, and Margaret Wrightson. 1990. Solving the Riddle of Tax Reform: Party Competition and the Politics of Ideas. *Political Science Quarterly* 105(2):193–217.

Binder, Sarah A. 1999. The Dynamics of Legislative Gridlock, 1947–96. *American Political Science Review* 93(3):519–533.

———. 2003. *Stalemate: Causes and Consequences of Legislative Gridlock.* Washington, DC: Brookings Institution Press.

Binder, Sarah A., and Steven S. Smith. 1996. *Politics or Principle? Filibustering in the United States Senate.* Washington, DC: Brookings Institution.

Birnbaum, Jeffrey H., and Alan S. Murray. 1987. *Showdown at Gucci Gulch.* New York: Random House.

Black, Duncan. 1958. *The Theory of Committees and Elections.* Cambridge: Cambridge University Press.

Black, Duncan, and R. A. Newing. 1951. *Committee Decisions with Complementary Valuation.* London: Hodge.

Brady, David W. 1988. *Critical Elections and Congressional Policy Making.* Stanford: Stanford University Press.

Brady, David W., and Kara M. Buckley. 1995. Health Care Reform in the 103rd Congress: A Predictable Failure. *The Journal of Health Politics, Policy, and Law* 2:447–457.

Brady, David W., and John F. Cogan. 1998. *Getting It Wrong: Liberal Democrats and Conservative Republicans in Elections, 1954–96.* Stanford: Stanford University Press.

Brady, David W., John F. Cogan, Brian J. Gaines, and Douglas Rivers. 1995. *How the Republicans Captured the House.* Stanford: Hoover Institution Press.

Brady, David W., and David Epstein. 1997. Intraparty Preferences, Heterogeneity, and the Origins of the Modern Congress: Progressive Reformers in the House and Senate, 1890–1920. *Journal of Law, Economics, and Organization* 13:26–49.

Brady, David W., and D. Sunshine Hillygus. 2005. Assessing the Clinton Presidency: The Political Constraints of Legislative Policy. In *Vantage Points: Perspectives on the Clinton Presidency,* edited by Todd Shields and Don Kelley. Fayetteville: University of Arkansas Press.

Brady, David W., Keith Krehbiel, and Craig Volden. 1994. Unified Gridlock. Paper presented at the American Institutions and Economic Performance Conference, Hoover Institution.

Brady, David W., and Craig Volden. 1998. *Revolving Gridlock: Politics and Policy from Carter to Clinton.* Boulder, CO: Westview Press.

Broder, David, and Haynes Johnson. 1996. *The System: The American Way of Politics at the Breaking Point.* Boston: Little, Brown.

Brody, Richard A. 1991. *Assessing the President: The Media, Elite Opinion, and Public Support.* Stanford, CA: Stanford University Press.

Burden, Barry C., Gregory A. Caldeira, and Tim Groseclose. 2000. Measuring the Ideologies of U.S. Senators: The Song Remains the Same. *Legislative Studies Quarterly* 25(2):237–258.

Burnham, Walter Dean. 1965. The Changing Shape of the American Political Universe. *American Political Science Review* 59(1):7–29.

_____. 1970. *Critical Elections and the Mainsprings of American Politics.* New York: W. W. Norton.

_____. 1995. Realignment Lives: The 1994 Earthquake and Its Implications. In *The Clinton Presidency: First Appraisals,* edited by Colin Campbell and Bert Rockman. Chatham, NJ: Chatham House Publishers.

Burns, James MacGregor. 1963. *The Deadlock of Democracy.* Englewood Cliffs, NJ: Prentice-Hall.

Cain, Bruce, John Ferejohn, and Morris Fiorina. 1987. *The Personal Vote: Constituency Service and Electoral Independence.* Cambridge: Harvard University Press.

Cameron, Charles M. 2000. *Veto Bargaining: Presidents and the Politics of Negative Power.* Cambridge: Cambridge University Press.

Campbell, Colin. 1991. The White House and Cabinet Under the "Let's Deal" Presidency. In *The Bush Presidency: First Appraisals,* edited by Colin Campbell and Bert Rockman. Chatham, NJ: Chatham House Publishers.

Campbell, Colin, and Bert Rockman, eds. 1991. *The Bush Presidency: First Appraisals.* Chatham, NJ: Chatham House Publishers.

_____. 1996. *The Clinton Presidency: First Appraisals.* Chatham, NJ: Chatham House Publishers.

Canes-Wrone, Brandice. 2001. The President's Legislative Influence from Public Appeals. *American Journal of Political Science* 45(2):313–329.

Canes-Wrone, Brandice, David W. Brady, and John F. Cogan. 2002. Out of Step, Out of Office: Electoral Accountability and House Members' Voting. *American Political Science Review* 96(1):127–140.

Canes-Wrone, Brandice, Julia Rabinovich, and Craig Volden. Forthcoming. Who Parties? Floor Voting, District Ideology, and Electoral Margins. In *Process, Party, and Policy Making: Further New Perspectives on the History of Congress,* edited by David Brady and Mathew McCubbins. Stanford: Stanford University Press.

Carmines, Edward G., and James A. Stimson. 1989. *Issue Evolution: Race and the Transformation of American Politics.* Princeton: Princeton University Press.

Chiou, Fang-Yi, and Lawrence S. Rothenberg. 2003. When Pivotal Politics Meets Partisan Politics. *American Journal of Political Science* 47(3):503–522.

Chubb, John E., and Paul Peterson, eds. 1985. *The New Directions in American Politics.* Washington, DC: Brookings Institution.

_____. 1989. *Can the Government Govern?* Washington, DC: Brookings Institution.

Cogan, John F. 1997. *The Federal Budget: A Consistent Historical Data Base.* Manuscript, Hoover Institution.

Cogan, John F., Timothy Muris, and Allen Schick. 1994. *The Budget Puzzle: Understanding Federal Spending.* Stanford: Stanford University Press.

Cohen, R. 1993. Leadership Test. *National Journal* (March 13):606.

Coleman, John J. 1997. The Decline and Resurgence of Congressional Party Conflict. *Journal of Politics* 59(1):165–184.

_____. 1999. Unified Government, Divided Government, and Party Responsiveness. *American Political Science Review* 93(4):821–835.

Collender, Stanley. 1991. *The Guide to the Federal Budget.* Washington, DC: Urban Institute Press.

Collier, Kenneth, and Terry Sullivan. 1995. New Evidence Undercutting the Linkage of Approval with Presidential Support and Influence. *Journal of Politics* 57(1):197–209.

Congressional Budget Office. 2005. *The Budget and Economic Outlook: Fiscal Years 2006 to 2015.* Washington, DC: Congressional Budget Office.

Cooper, Joseph, and Gary Young. 1997. Partisanship, Bipartisanship and Cross-partisanship Since the New Deal. In *Congress Reconsidered.* 6th ed., edited by Lawrence C. Dodd and Bruce I. Oppenheimer. Washington, DC: Congressional Quarterly Press.

Cox, Gary W., and Samuel Kernell, eds. 1991. *The Politics of Divided Government.* Boulder: Westview Press.

Cox, Gary W., and Mathew D. McCubbins. 1993. *Legislative Leviathan: Party Government in the House.* Berkeley: University of California Press.

Cronin, Thomas. 1977. *The Presidency Reappraised.* 2nd ed. New York: Praeger.

_____. 1982. *Rethinking the Presidency.* Boston: Little, Brown.

Cutler, Lloyd. 1987. The Cost of Divided Government. *New York Times,* November 22.

_____. 1988. Some Reflections About Divided Government. *Presidential Studies Quarterly* 17:490.

_____. 1989. Now Is the Time for All Good Men. *William and Mary Law Review* 30:387–402.

Davidson, Roger. 1985. Senate Leaders: Janitors for an Untidy Chamber? In *Congress Reconsidered.* 3rd ed., edited by Lawrence C. Dodd and Bruce I. Oppenheimer. Washington, DC: Congressional Quarterly Press.

Davidson, Roger, ed. 1992. *The Post-Reform Congress.* New York: St. Martin's Press.

Deering, Christopher J., and Forrest Maltzman. 1999. The Politics of Executive Orders: Legislative Constraints on Presidential Power. *Political Research Quarterly* 52(4):767–783.

Dodd, Lawrence C., and Bruce I. Oppenheimer, eds. 1985. *Congress Reconsidered.* 3rd ed. Washington, DC: Congressional Quarterly Press.

_____. 1993. *Congress Reconsidered.* 5th ed. Washington, DC: Congressional Quarterly Press.

Downs, Anthony. 1957. *An Economic Theory of Democracy.* New York: Harper and Row.

Edwards, George. 1989. *At the Margins.* New Haven: Yale University Press.

_____. 1991. George Bush and the Public Presidency: The Politics of Inclusion. In *The Bush Presidency: First Appraisals,* edited by Colin Campbell and Bert Rockman. Chatham, NJ: Chatham House Publishers.

Edwards, George C., III, Andrew Barrett, and Jeffrey Peake. 1997. The Legislative Impact of Divided Government. *American Journal of Political Science* 41(2):545–563.

Edwards, George, John Kessel, and Bert Rockman, eds. 1993. *Researching the Presidency: Vital Questions, New Approaches.* Pittsburgh: University of Pittsburgh Press.

Epstein, David, and Sharyn O'Halloran. 1996. Divided Government and the Design of Administrative Procedures: A Formal Model and Empirical Test. *Journal of Politics* 58(2):373–397.

Epstein, David, and Sharyn O'Halloran. 1999. *Delegating Powers: A Transaction Cost Politics Approach to Policy Making under Separate Powers.* Cambridge: Cambridge University Press.

Erikson, Robert S. 1976. Is There Such a Thing as a Safe Seat? *Polity* 8:623–632.

_____. 1988. The Puzzle of Midterm Loss. *Journal of Politics* 50(4):1011–1029.

_____. 1989. Why the Democrats Lose Presidential Elections: Toward a Theory of Optimal Loss. *Political Science and Politics* 22(1):30–35.

_____. 1990. Roll Calls, Reputation, and Representation in the U.S. Senate. *Legislative Studies Quarterly* 15:630.

Feldstein, Martin, ed. 1994. *American Economic Policy in the 1980s.* Chicago: University of Chicago Press.

Fenno, Richard F., Jr. 1973. *Congressmen in Committees.* Boston: Little, Brown.

_____. 1975. If, as Ralph Nader Says, Congress Is "The Broken Branch," How Come We Love Our Congressmen So Much? In *Congress in Change: Evolution and Reform,* edited by Norman J. Ornstein. New York: Praeger.

_____. 1978. *Homestyle: House Members in Their Districts.* Boston: Little, Brown.

Ferejohn, John. 1991. Changes in Welfare Policy in the 1980s. In *Politics and Economics in the Eighties,* edited by Alberto Alesina and Geoffrey Carliner. Chicago: University of Chicago Press.

Ferejohn, John, and Randall Calvert. 1984. Presidential Coattails in Historical Perspective. *American Journal of Political Science* 28(1):127–146.

Fiorina, Morris P. 1991a. Divided Government in the States. In *The Politics of Divided Government,* edited by Gary W. Cox and Samuel Kernell. Boulder: Westview Press.

_____. 1991b. Elections and the Economy in the 1980s: Short- and Long-Term Effects. In *Politics and Economics in the Eighties,* edited by Alberto Alesina and Geoffrey Carliner. Chicago: University of Chicago Press.

_____. 1996. *Divided Government.* 2nd ed. Boston: Allyn and Bacon.

_____. 2005. *Culture War? The Myth of a Polarized America.* New York: Pearson Longman.

Fiorina, Morris, Samuel Abrams, and Jeremy Pope. 2003. The 2000 U.S. Presidential Election: Can Retrospective Voting Be Saved? *British Journal of Political Science* 33(2):163–187.

Fiorina, Morris, and Timothy Prinz. 1992. Legislative Incumbency and Insulation. In *Encyclopedia of the American Legislative System,* edited by Joel Silbey. New York: Charles Scribner's Sons.

Fullerton, Don. 1993. *Who Bears the Lifetime Tax Burden?* Washington, DC: Brookings Institution.

_____. 1994. Tax Policy. In *American Economic Policy in the 1980s,* edited by Martin Feldstein. Chicago: University of Chicago Press.

Gale, William G., Peter R. Orszag, and Timothy T. Taylor. 2005. *Taxing the Future: Fiscal Policy in the Bush Administration*. Washington, DC: Brookings Institution Press.

Gilligan, Thomas W., and Keith Krehbiel. 1987. Collective Decision-Making and Standing Committees: An Informational Rationale for Restrictive Amendment Procedures. *Journal of Law, Economics, and Organization* 3:287–335.

———. 1990. Organization of Informative Committees by a Rational Legislature. *American Journal of Political Science* 34(2):531–564.

Gilmour, John B. 1995. *Strategic Disagreement: Stalemate in American Politics*. Pittsburgh: University of Pittsburgh Press.

Ginsburg, Benjamin, and Martin Shefter. 1990. *Politics by Other Means*. New York: Basic Books.

Glad, Paul. 1966. *The Trumpet Soundeth: William Jennings Bryan and His Democracy, 1896–1912*. Lincoln: University of Nebraska Press.

Greenstein, Fred I. 1982. *The Hidden-Hand Presidency: Eisenhower as Leader*. New York: Basic Books.

Groseclose, Timothy. 1995. An Examination of the Market for Favors and Votes in Congress. *Economic Inquiry* 30:320–340.

Groseclose, Tim, and Nolan McCarty. 2001. The Politics of Blame: Bargaining before an Audience. *American Journal of Political Science* 45(1):100–119.

Groseclose, Timothy, and James M. Snyder. 1996. Buying Supermajorities. *American Political Science Review* 90(2):303–315.

Groseclose, Timothy, Steve Levitt, and James M. Snyder. 1999. Comparing Interest Group Scores across Time and Chambers: Adjusted ADA Scores for the U.S. Congress. *American Political Science Review* 93(1):33–50.

Hacker, Jacob S. 1997. *The Road to Nowhere: The Genesis of President Clinton's Plan for Health Security*. Princeton: Princeton University Press.

Hall, Richard L. 1996. *Participation in Congress*. New Haven: Yale University Press.

Hansen, John Mark. 1991. *Gaining Access: Congress and the Farm Lobby, 1919–1981*. Chicago: University of Chicago Press.

———. 1998. Individuals, Institutions, and Public Preferences over Public Finance. *American Political Science Review* 92(3):513–531.

Heclo, Hugh. 1977. *A Government of Strangers*. Washington, DC: Brookings Institution.

Hetherington, Marc J. 1996. The Media's Role in Forming Voters' National Economic Evaluations in 1992. *American Journal of Political Science* 40(2):372–395.

Hibbing, John R. 1991. *Congressional Careers*. Chapel Hill: University of North Carolina Press.

Hibbing, John R., and Elizabeth Theiss-Morse. 1995. *Congress As Public Enemy*. Cambridge: Cambridge University Press.

Howell, William G. 2003. *Power without Persuasion: The Politics of Direct Presidential Action*. Princeton: Princeton University Press.

Howell, William, Scott Adler, Charles Cameron, and Charles Riemann. 2000. Divided Government and the Legislative Productivity of Congress, 1945–94. *Legislative Studies Quarterly* 25(2):285–312.

Hubbard, R. Glenn. 2004. Huh? A Surprising Success. *The International Economy* 18(3):28–33.

Jacobson, Gary C. 1981. Incumbents' Advantages in the 1978 United States Congressional Elections. *Legislative Studies Quarterly* 6(2):183–200.

_____. 1983. *Strategy and Choice in Congressional Elections*. 2nd ed. New Haven: Yale University Press.

_____. 1989. Strategic Politicians and the Dynamics of United States House Elections, 1946–86. *American Political Science Review* 83(3):773–793.

_____. 1990. *The Electoral Origins of Divided Government*. Boulder: Westview Press.

_____. 1991. The Persistence of Democratic House Majorities. In *The Politics of Divided Government*, edited by Gary W. Cox and Samuel Kernell. Boulder: Westview Press.

_____. 1993. Deficit-Cutting Politics and Congressional Elections. *Political Science Quarterly* 108(3):375–402.

Jacobson, Gary C., and Samuel Kernell. 1982. Strategy and Choice in the 1982 Congressional Elections. *Political Science and Politics* 15(3):423–430.

Jones, Charles. 1991. Meeting Low Expectations: Strategy and Prospects of the Bush Presidency. In *The Bush Presidency: First Appraisals*, edited by Colin Campbell and Bert Rockman. Chatham, N.J.: Chatham House Publishers.

_____. 1994. *The Presidency in a Separated System*. Washington, DC: Brookings Institution.

Jones, David R. 2001. Party Polarization and Legislative Gridlock. *Political Research Quarterly* 54(1):125–141.

Keele, Luke, Brian J. Fogarty, Brian and James A. Stimson. 2003. *Presidential Campaigning in the 2002 Congressional Elections*. Typescript, University of North Carolina.

Keohane, Robert O. 1993. Institutional Theory and the Realist Challenge after the Cold War. In *Neorealism and Neoliberalism: The Contemporary Debate*, edited by David A. Baldwin. New York: Columbia University Press, pp. 269–300.

Kernell, Samuel. 1993. *Going Public*. 2nd ed. Washington, DC: Congressional Quarterly Press.

Kettl, Donald F. 1992. *Deficit Politics: Public Budgeting in Its Institutional and Historical Context*. New York: Macmillan.

Key, V. O. 1955. Theory of Critical Elections. *Journal of Politics* 17(1):3–18.

_____. 1961. *Public Opinion and American Democracy*. New York: Alfred A. Knopf.

_____. 1964. *Politics, Parties, & Pressure Groups*. 5th ed. New York: Crowell.

_____. 1966. *The Responsible Electorate*. Cambridge: Harvard University Press, Belknap Press.

Kiewiet, D. Roderick, and Mathew D. McCubbins. 1988. Presidential Influence on Congressional Appropriations Decisions. *American Journal of Political Science* 32:713–736.

_____. 1991. *The Logic of Delegation: Congressional Parties and the Appropriations Process*. Chicago: University of Chicago Press.

King, Anthony, ed. 1990. *The New American Political System*. 2nd ed. Washington, DC: AEI Press.

King, Anthony, and Giles Alston. 1991. Good Government and the Politics of High Exposure. In *The Bush Presidency: First Appraisals*, edited by Colin Campbell and Bert Rockman. Chatham, NJ: Chatham House Publishers.

King, Gary, and Andrew Gelman. 1991. Systemic Consequences of Incumbency Advantage in U.S. House Elections. *American Journal of Political Science* 35:110–138.

Kingdon, John W. 1973. *Congressmen's Voting Decisions*. New York: Harper and Row.

Kissinger, Henry A. 1957. *A World Restored: Metternich, Castlereigh and the Problems of Peace, 1812–22*. Boston, MA: Houghton Mifflin.

Krehbiel, Keith. 1988. Spatial Models of Legislative Choice. *Legislative Studies Quarterly* 13(3):259–319.

_____. 1991. *Information and Legislative Organization*. Ann Arbor: University of Michigan Press.

_____. 1993. Where's the Party? *British Journal of Political Science* 23:235–266.

_____. 1995. Cosponsors and Wafflers from A to Z. *American Journal of Political Science* 39(4):906–923.

_____. 1996. Institutional and Partisan Sources of Gridlock: A Theory of Divided and Unified Government. *Journal of Theoretical Politics* 8(1):7–40.

_____. 1998. *Pivotal Politics: A Theory of U.S. Lawmaking*. Chicago: University of Chicago Press.

_____. 1999. Paradoxes of Parties in Congress. *Legislative Studies Quarterly* 24(1):31–64.

Krehbiel, Keith, and Douglas Rivers. 1988. The Analysis of Committee Power: An Application to Senate Voting on the Minimum Wage. *American Journal of Political Science* 32(4):1151–1174.

Krutz, Glen S. 2000. Getting around Gridlock: The Effect of Omnibus Utilization on Legislative Productivity. *Legislative Studies Quarterly* 25(4):533–549.

Light, Paul. 1983. *The President's Agenda*. Baltimore: Johns Hopkins University Press.

Lowi, Theodore. 1969. *The End of Liberalism: Ideology, Policy, and the Crisis of Public Authority*. New York: W. W. Norton.

Manley, John. 1970. *The Politics of Finance: The House Committee on Ways and Means*. Boston: Little, Brown.

Matsui, Brian. 1995. *The Politics of Reelection Versus Change*. Senior honors thesis, Stanford University.

Mayer, William G., ed. 2000. *In Pursuit of the White House 2000: How We Choose Our Presidential Nominees*. New York: Chatham House.

Mayhew, David R. 1974a. *Congress: The Electoral Connection*. New Haven: Yale University Press.

_____. 1974b. Congressional Elections: The Case of the Vanishing Marginals. *Polity* 6:295–317.

_____. 1991. *Divided We Govern*. New Haven: Yale University Press.

_____. 1997a. Clinton, the 103rd Congress, and Unified Party Control: What Are the Lessons? Working paper, Yale University.

_____. 1997b. Important Laws, 1995–96. Working paper, Yale University.

_____. 2002. *Electoral Realignments: A Critique of an American Genre*. Yale: Yale University Press.

_____. 2004. *Updates to Divided We Govern*. Typescript, Yale University.

McCarty, Nolan. 2000. Proposal Rights, Veto Rights, and Political Bargaining. *American Journal of Political Science* 44(3):506–522.

McCarty, Nolan, Keith T. Poole, and Howard Rosenthal. 2001. The Hunt for Party Discipline in Congress. *American Political Science Review* 95(3):673–687.

McConnell, Grant. 1953. *The Decline of Agrarian Democracy*. Berkeley: University of California Press.

———. 1966. *Private Power and American Democracy*. New York: Alfred A. Knopf.

McCubbins, Mathew D. 1991. Party Governance and U.S. Budget Deficits: Divided Government and Fiscal Stalemate. In *Politics and Economics in the Eighties*, edited by Alberto Alesina and Geoffrey Carliner. Chicago: University of Chicago Press.

McKelvey, Richard. 1976. Intransitivities in Multidimensional Voting Models and Some Implications for Agenda Control. *Journal of Economic Theory* 12:472–482.

McKenzie, Calvin, and Saranna Thornton. 1996. *Bucking the Deficit: Economic Policymaking in America*. Boulder: Westview Press.

Mearsheimer, John J. 1994. The False Promise of International Institutions. *International Security* 19(3):5–49.

Merrill, Peter R., Stanley E. Collender, and Eric W. Cook. 1990. Tax Legislation and the Budget in the 1980s. In *National Tax Association-Proceedings of the Eighty-Second Annual Conference, 1989, Atlanta, Georgia*. Columbus, OH: National Tax Association.

Mezey, Michael. 1991. *Legislatures in the Policy Process*. Cambridge: Cambridge University Press.

Moe, Terry. 1985. The Politicized Presidency. In *The New Directions in American Politics*, edited by John E. Chubb and Paul Peterson. Washington, D.C.: Brookings Institution.

———. 1993. Presidents, Institutions, and Theory. In *Researching the Presidency: Vital Questions, New Approaches*, edited by George Edwards, John Kessel, and Bert Rockman. Pittsburgh: University of Pittsburgh Press.

Moe, Terry M., and William G. Howell. 1999. The Presidential Power of Unilateral Action. *Journal of Law, Economics, and Organization* 15(1):132–179.

Neustadt, Richard Elliott. 1960. *Presidential Power*. New York: John Wiley.

Nicholson, Stephen P., Gary M. Segura, and Nathan D. Woods. 2002. Presidential Approval and the Mixed Blessing of Divided Government. *Journal of Politics* 64(3):701–720.

Oleszek, Walter. 1989. *Congressional Procedures and the Policy Process*. 3rd ed. Washington, DC: Congressional Quarterly Press.

———. 2004. *Congressional Procedures and the Policy Process*. 6th ed. Washington, DC: Congressional Quarterly Press.

Palazzolo, Daniel. 1992. *The Speaker and the Budget*. Pittsburgh: University of Pittsburgh Press.

Peterson, David A. M., Lawrence J. Grossback, James A. Stimson, and Amy Gangl. 2003. Congressional Response to Mandate Elections. *American Journal of Political Science* 47(3):411–426.

Petrocik, John R. 1991. Divided Government: Is It All in the Campaigns? In *The Politics of Divided Government*, edited by Gary W. Cox and Samuel Kernell. Boulder: Westview Press.

Plott, Charles. 1967. A Notion of Equilibrium and Its Possibility Under Majority Rule. *American Economic Review* 57:787–806.

Polsby, Nelson W., and Aaron Wildavsky. 2001. *Presidential Elections: Strategies and Structures of American Politics*. New York: Chatham House.

Poole, Keith, and Howard Rosenthal. 1991a. Patterns of Congressional Voting. *American Journal of Political Science* 35: 228–278.

———. 1991b. The Spatial Mapping of Minimum Wage Legislation. In *Politics and Economics in the Eighties*, edited by Alberto Alesina and Geoffrey Carliner. Chicago: University of Chicago Press.

———. 1997. *Congress: A Political-Economic History of Roll Call Voting*. Oxford: Oxford University Press.

Popkin, Samuel. 1991. *The Reasoning Voter: Communication and Persuasion in Presidential Campaigns*. Chicago: University of Chicago Press.

Quirk, Paul. 1991. Domestic Policy: Divided Government and Cooperative Presidential Leadership. In *The Bush Presidency: First Appraisals*, edited by Colin Campbell and Bert Rockman. Chatham, NJ: Chatham House Publishers.

Rivers, Douglas, and Nancy Rose. 1985. Passing the President's Program: Public Opinion and Presidential Influence in Congress. *American Journal of Political Science* 29(2):183–196.

Rockman, Bert. 1991. The Leadership Style of George Bush. In *The Bush Presidency: First Appraisals*, edited by Colin Campbell and Bert Rockman. Chatham, NJ: Chatham House Publishers.

Rohde, David W. 1991. *Parties and Leaders in the Postreform House*. Chicago: University of Chicago Press.

Romer, Thomas, and Howard Rosenthal. 1978. Political Resource Allocation, Controlled Agendas, and the Status Quo. *Public Choice* 33:27–43.

Romer, Thomas, and Barry Weingast. 1991. Political Foundations of the Thrift Debacle. In *Politics and Economics in the Eighties*, edited by Alberto Alesina and Geoffrey Carliner. Chicago: University of Chicago Press.

Rosenstone, Steven J. 1983. *Forecasting Presidential Elections*. New Haven: Yale University Press.

Rosenstone, Steven J., and John Mark Hansen. 1993. *Mobilization, Participation, and Democracy in America*. New York: Macmillan.

Rudalevige, Andrew. 2003. The Politics of No Child Left Behind. *Education Next* 3(4):62–69.

Schattschneider, E. E. 1942. *Party Government*. New York: Holt, Rinehart and Winston.

Schick, Allen. 1981. *Reconciliation and the Congressional Budget Process*. Washington, DC: AEI Press.

———. 1995. *The Federal Budget*. Washington, DC: Brookings Institution.

Shepsle, Kenneth. 1979. Institutional Arrangements and Equilibrium in Multidimensional Voting Models. *American Journal of Political Science* 23:27–60.

Shuman, Howard E. 1984. *Politics and the Budget*. Englewood Cliffs, NJ: Prentice-Hall.

Silbey, Joel, ed. 1992. *Encyclopedia of the American Legislative System*. New York: Charles Scribner's Sons.

Sinclair, Barbara. 1989. *The Transformation of the U.S. Senate.* Baltimore: Johns Hopkins University Press.

_____. 1991. Governing Unheroically (and Sometimes Unappetizingly): Bush and the 101ˢᵗ Congress. In *The Bush Presidency: First Appraisals,* edited by Colin Campbell and Bert Rockman. Chatham, NJ: Chatham House Publishers.

Skocpol, Theda. 1996. *Boomerang: Clinton's Health Security Effort and the Turn Against Government in U.S. Politics.* New York: W. W. Norton.

Skowronek, Stephen. 1993. *The Politics Presidents Make.* Cambridge: Harvard University Press, Belknap Press.

Snyder, James M. 1991. On Buying Legislatures. *Economics and Politics* 3:93–109.

Snyder, James M., and Tim Groseclose. 2000. Estimating Party Influence in Congressional Roll-Call Voting. *American Journal of Political Science* 44(2):193–211.

Sorauf, Frank. 1992. *Inside Campaign Finance.* New Haven: Yale University Press.

Steuerle, C. Eugene. 1992. *The Tax Decade.* Washington, DC: Urban Institute Press.

Stewart, Charles H., III. 1991. The Politics of Tax Reform in the 1980s. In *Politics and Economics in the Eighties,* edited by Alberto Alesina and Geoffrey Carliner. Chicago: University of Chicago Press.

Sundquist, James L. 1981. *The Decline and Resurgence of Congress.* Washington, DC: Brookings Institution.

_____. 1988. Needed: A Political Theory for the New Era of Coalition Government in the United States. *Political Science Quarterly* 103(4):613–635.

_____. 1993. *Beyond Gridlock?* Washington, DC: Brookings Institution.

_____. 1995. *Back to Gridlock?* Washington, DC: Brookings Institution.

Thurber, James A., ed. 1991. *Divided Democracy: Cooperation and Conflict Between the President and Congress.* Washington, DC: Congressional Quarterly Press.

Truman, David. 1959. *The Congressional Party.* New York: John Wiley.

Volden, Craig. 1998. Sophisticated Voting in Supermajoritarian Settings. *Journal of Politics* 60(1):149–173.

_____. 2002. A Formal Model of the Politics of Delegation in a Separation of Powers System. *American Journal of Political Science* 46(1):111–133.

Volden, Craig, and Elizabeth Bergman. Forthcoming. How Strong Should Our Party Be? Party Member Preferences over Party Strength. *Legislative Studies Quarterly.*

Weaver, R. Kent. 1986. The Politics of Blame Avoidance. *Journal of Public Policy* 6:371–398.

_____. 1988. *Automatic Government.* Washington, DC: Brookings Institution.

Weisberg, Herbert F., and Clyde Wilcox, eds. 2004. *Models of Voting in Presidential Elections: The 2000 U.S. Election.* Stanford, CA: Stanford University Press.

Wildavsky, Aaron B. 1966. The Two Presidencies. *Transaction* 4(December):7–14.

_____. 1988. *The New Politics of the Budgetary Process.* Glenview, IL: Scott, Foresman.

Wilkins, Vicky M., and Garry Young. 2002. The Influence of Governors on Veto Override Attempts: A Test of Pivotal Politics. *Legislative Studies Quarterly* 27(4):557–575.

Wright, John R. 1996. *Interest Groups and Congress: Lobbying, Contributions, and Influence.* Boston, MA: Allyn and Bacon.

Index

229